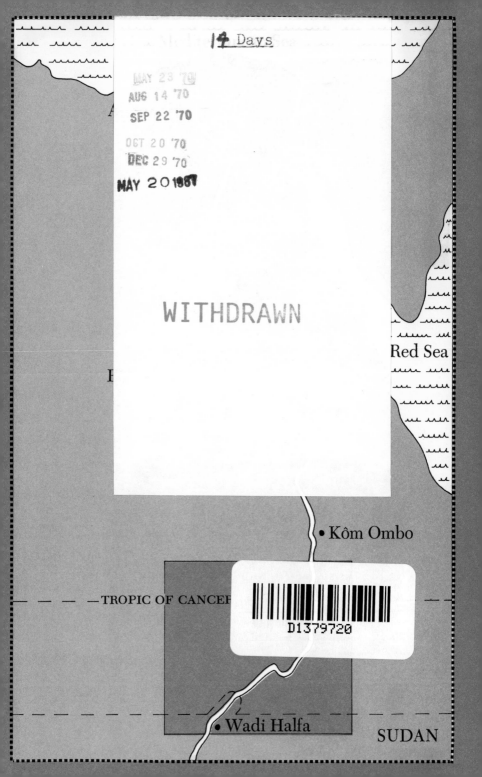

Red Sea

• Kôm Ombo

— — — — —TROPIC OF CANCER

• Wadi Halfa

SUDAN

A View of the Nile

Elizabeth Warnock Fernea

"What can I say about Egypt?" wrote Chateaubriand more than a hundred years ago. "Hasn't everyone seen it by this time?"

In a sense—through the magic of literature, painting, and photography—everyone has, if not in fact seen Egypt, felt its presence. But, Mrs. Fernea is in no doubt about what to say, and she offers here a gracefully written chronicle of what she saw and learned during six years' residence in Egypt from 1959 to 1965.

For many, Egypt is a land shrouded in exotic mystery. In these pages the reader follows Mrs. Fernea into the fascinating day-to-day life of this ancient and enigmatic nation—to teeming sophisticated Cairo; to the great Nile river itself and a voyage to the magnificent temple of Abu Simbel; to a remote Nubian village where the author and her family lived in a typical mud-built house and adapted to the

(continued on back flap)

By Elizabeth Warnock Fernea

A VIEW OF THE NILE

GUESTS OF THE SHEIK

ELIZABETH WARNOCK FERNEA

A View of the Nile

1970
Doubleday & Company, Inc., Garden City, New York

Library of Congress Catalog Card Number 71–89130
Copyright © 1970 by Elizabeth Warnock Fernea
All Rights Reserved
Printed in the United States of America
First Edition

FOR BOB

FOREWORD

My husband and I went to Egypt in 1959, intending to stay two years. We returned to America in 1965. The book which follows is a personal chronicle of those years.

The persons and places and events which I have described are all real, but I have changed most of the names, including the names of the Nubian villages. I have also merged certain personalities and situations so that no one will be embarrassed.

"What can I say about Egypt?" wrote Chateaubriand more than a hundred years ago. "Hasn't everyone seen it by this time?"

Not everyone has seen Egypt, but I would certainly agree with Chateaubriand that much has been said and written about this ancient land. I do not pretend to add anything to the scholarly studies. I can only present, as honestly as I am able, my own views of the Nile, its country and its people.

CONTENTS

CAST OF PRINCIPAL CHARACTERS

CAIRO

Susan	an American friend studying in Egypt
Nick	a friend from Chicago, doing research in Cairo
Omar	a young Egyptologist
Aziza	his sister
Dr. Laila	director of the Social Research Center, American University
Karim	research assistant to Bob
Mona	" " " "
Beryl	an American friend living in Cairo
Abbas	our cook and housekeeper
Fawzia	our nanny
Farida	" "
Madame Natalya	matron of the Coptic Hospital
Roushdi	a hospital orderly
Georgette	a nurse
Sister Angelina	an Italian nursing sister
Dr. Zaki	a gynecologist
Dr. Hanna	a pediatrician

NUBIA

In the village of Erd-Moz

   Saleh's house:

Saleh,	a retired cook and landowner
Dahiba	his wife
Hanim Ali	*" "*
Khadija	his married niece whose husband works in Sudan
Abdul Nasr	her infant son
Naima	her unmarried sister, betrothed to Jalal
Abdou	Saleh's one-legged brother

   Mohammed's house:

Mohammed	a young landowner, tambura player, well-known hunter
Nezla	his wife
Shemessa	his mother
Suffra	his married sister

   Abdulla's house:

Abdulla	village mediator, religious dignitary and barber
Fatima	his wife
Wahiba	their teen-age daughter
Gamal	their six-year-old son
Aisha	Abdulla's mother and former village midwife

   Abdul Majid's house:

Abdul Majid	village schoolteacher
Sherifa	his wife
Sitta	his wife's sister, whose husband works in London
Jalal	his brother, working in Cairo, betrothed to Naima

Widow Fatooma

Mekki, a boatman-peddler

Suliman Ali Mahmoud Haj *omda,* or governor, of Ballana province

In the village of Zingahoor

Ali Daoud	village schoolteacher, Mohammed's brother
Halima	his wife
Sayyid	his wife's uncle, retired from work in Cairo
Sekina	Sayyid's wife
Radiya	her widowed sister

THE DELTA

Hassan El Za'aty	Mona's cousin, manager of the family's Delta estate
Vera	his wife
Gulnar	his widowed aunt
Sayid Kamal El Za'aty	Mona's uncle, owner of the neighboring estate
Sitt Fatima	his wife
Zainab	fellaheen
Hamid	"

A View of the Nile

PART I

Cairo

CHAPTER 1

A WELCOMING CEREMONY

The doors of the Misr Airlines jet opened. We gasped for breath. Hot, still, heavy with alien noises and smells, the air of Egypt in September, Egypt weary at the end of a long summer, struck us, surrounded us, enfolded us.

"Passports, please! This way, *mesdames et messieurs*, ladies and gentlemen, here, *this* way, *please!*"

The blue-uniformed guide shepherded us firmly across the tarmac toward the cordoned neutral zone where we were to remain until our presence had been officially sanctioned.

I tried again to catch my breath, smoothed the front of my maternity suit for the fortieth unnecessary time, and took Bob's proffered arm to navigate the stairs, slippery with moisture from the humidity.

Yesterday, or was it the day before, all hours and days blurring together in the roar of air travel, we had been in Chicago.

"Careful!" Bob, already sweating in the heat, gripped my elbow for the last steep step to the ground.

Yesterday, Chicago. Today, Cairo.

Beyond the modern airfield where the clear sky came down to the sand, the crimson light of a desert sunset lay upon the horizon, reminding us that we had changed continents and climates in only twenty-four hours.

"We really should have come to Egypt slowly, by boat," Bob murmured. "Not such a violent change."

"But we didn't have time."

Bob had taken his Ph.D. orals yesterday; he was due at the American University in Cairo tomorrow to begin his first teaching job.

Air conditioning purred soothingly in the passenger lounge, upholstered in gray, its white walls adorned with giant travel posters. "Fly Misr Airlines! Visit the Colossus of Memnon, one of the seven wonders of the ancient world!" The pyramids were there, too, and the Sphinx, painted shining and golden against the blue posterboard sky.

"Passports, please. Health certificate? Thank you."

The official was pleasant. Egypt was encouraging foreign visitors again, seeking to restore tourism, diplomacy and trade after the upheavals of war and the changes in government of the last decade. It was 1959. Seven years had passed since King Farouk had abdicated and sailed out of Alexandria harbor, his yacht loaded with jewels and banknotes, it was said, while the crowds stood silent on the docks, watching the last scion of the Mohammed Ali dynasty depart. The officers' revolt had replaced Farouk with Colonel Gamal Abdul Nasser, son of a village postal clerk. Three years had passed since the tripartite aggression and President Nasser's nationalization of the Suez Canal.

"What is your purpose in visiting Egypt?"

What was our purpose? To work, of course, to set up a home for ourselves, our coming first-born child. But why Egypt? Why not Kansas or California? Our families and friends had asked the same question. Were we looking for Atlantis or our hearts' desire or some similar, impractical romantic nonsense? We had said we wanted to see the world before settling down into predictable academia; teaching overseas for a couple of years seemed a good way to start.

"This is your first visit to Egypt."

"No."

How well I remembered that earlier visit, a five-day

stopover on the way back to America from two years of anthropological research in an Iraqi village. The memories of Cairo in the spring had been sufficiently rich and vivid to bring us back one year later. But then it had not been so hot and oppressive. And I hadn't been seven months pregnant. However, I reminded myself briskly, we had barely arrived.

The official pressed the heavy stamps into the violet ink pads, brought them down upon our passports with a flourish.

"Welcome to the new Egypt!" he said.

We were discharged, set free into the heat again, the flat dusty area around the airport where we were besieged by porters and taxi drivers shouting at us through the dusk and haze.

No one had come to meet us. We had a message, "Sorry cannot make plane, reservation waiting for you and B.J. at Moreland House Pension."

"Nobody is ever met at the airport when beginning a new adventure," said Bob lightly. "It's just not done."

We held hands in the 1940 Fiat taxi, traveling the desert road toward the distant line of towers and trees which was Cairo. The sky was graying before us, the great city marking itself on the coming darkness with winks and flashes of light. Signals crowning the radio towers turned yellow, red. The approach lights at the edge of the darkened sand were blue.

"Damn! It's hot!" Bob took off his coat.

"Soon the breeze comes from the river, sir," said the elderly taxi driver. "Nice and cold. In one hour. You will see."

"I certainly hope so." Bob and I mopped our perspiring faces.

The taxi driver chuckled. Although his black wool beret and his upturned coat collar seemed more suitable for a rainy night in Paris than a tropical late summer evening, he sported not a single bead of perspiration.

"You English come back now, huh? Bring the wife, too. Your baby will be born in Egypt? That is good. Welcome!"

"We are *not* English," said Bob, a bit stiffly. "We are American!"

"Ahhh."

We were entering the city. Policemen in white uniforms and black berets stood atop stepladder towers in the grassy roundabouts, channeling long lines of cars, carts and bicycles into the streets, which radiated out from the central maidans like the spokes of a wheel. A Parisian had been responsible for this pattern of modern Cairo's streets, I had read. Had he studied under the man who had laid out Washington, D.C.?

"Are we in Heliopolis?" Bob asked.

"Yes," answered the driver.

I remembered driving down this avenue before, but in bright sunshine, the wide boulevard blooming pink with oleander, orange with flame trees, the procession of tall centered bushes clipped into great green goblet shapes.

The blooms were gone. But the bushes were there, as tall and mysteriously goblet shaped as ever. Along the streets on either side of us the markets stood open. Vendors hawked strings of jasmine flowers and baskets of mangoes in the sidewalk coffee shops, filled with men playing backgammon and drinking tea. Through the open windows of the cab, the noise rolled over us from all directions, a clattering, clamoring noise of animals and bells, of automobile horns and streetcar brakes, of people walking, talking, shouting.

"You Americans truly?" The taxi driver finally spoke again, after a long silence.

"Yes."

"Well, you lucky. You come to a new Egypt. Welcome!"

We had read about the new Egypt. "The stain of poverty will be erased," promised the president. "Egypt must fit herself for a new role as an independent nation . . . every man,

woman and child will be proud to call himself an Egyptian.
. . . Egypt . . ."

"Here is place!"

The taxi ground to a stop behind a slow-moving donkey
cart and we saw a familiar figure standing in a doorway,
smoking, wearing an old seersucker jacket I remembered
from University of Chicago days.

"Why, it's Nick!" cried Bob.

Nick started, stared, and ran forward to the taxi, as surprised and pleased, apparently, as we were.

"See!" The taxi driver held up a hand to touch the air.
"The breeze. Feel the breeze. It has come!"

He clicked his meter shut. No one noticed except me.
Bob was out of the cab and wringing Nicholas' hand. We
had known Nick was to be in Egypt this year doing research
in the antiquities museum. We had even known he'd be
staying in the same pension, but we had not expected to
find him so suddenly.

"Marvelous! The place is simply marvelous," Nick was
saying, clipping off his words so as not to drop the cigarette
in his mouth, helping us with bags. "Got here yesterday.
Saw the pyramids this morning."

"Forty-five piasters," announced the taxi driver, rapping
on the meter with his fist. "Feel the breeze, sir? I did tell
you."

It felt absolutely lovely, that breeze, pushing through the
thick humidity and drying the sweat on our tired faces.

"That's for the wind," Nick said gaily, putting a pre-
posterously large tip into the grubby hand of the driver,
who stared at it, then grinned and touched his beret. "Welcome!" he cried once more, backed, gunned his motor,
backed again and barreled off around the cart which still
stood there, the donkey braying loudly and agonizingly.

The wind was blowing the slender new trees in front of
the pension, blowing the huge trees ahead of us, through

which we could glimpse the movement of light on water. It was the Nile. We were really in Egypt.

"Come on, B.J., Nick has the elevator waiting," called Bob.

"Misnomer that!" Nick corrected him, laughing and pushing buttons. "That is, the thing doesn't soar or lift, it rises and drops, hardly an elevating motion."

He pushed another button and we shot up a notch, settled, then were drawn up slowly, in bumps and jerks, into the dark recesses of the pension.

"Go to the *zar* by yourself," said Bob.

"I don't want to."

"Why not?"

"Well, you know that sociology professor only asked us because they know you're an anthropologist and would be professionally interested. There's no point in my going without you."

Bob frowned.

"And also," I rushed ahead, "I don't know these people at all. Look at me, I mean, at my stomach, it moves like that at the most unpredictable times. I don't know what it's going to do next, it's embarrassing!"

Bob focused on my front, where the baby set about performing before his fascinated gaze a whole series of running turns and kicks and somersaults.

"Fantastic!" he murmured, and laughed.

"What?" I was irritated by his amusement. Little did he know how they hurt, those inside bravura turns!

"Involuntary belly dancing, that's what it suggests," he went on.

"*What?*"

He laughed again. "I meant it as a compliment, B.J. Perhaps yours are not at the moment exactly the classic *proportions* recommended for general audience appeal, but

I'm sure most belly dancers would give a lot to move their stomachs in just that capricious way!"

At my dark look, he put his arm around me. "Really," he repeated.

"So go to the *zar*," he said after a moment.

"But . . ."

"Oh, B.J., for heaven's sake!" exclaimed Bob. "What is happening to you? In Chicago, *you* were the one who was so enthusiastic about coming out here. And what have you been doing? I hardly call it adventurous to sit in the Hilton drinking lemonade."

How did he know my secret sins? After an unsuccessful apartment-hunting foray, I would often sneak into the air-conditioned Hilton Hotel to order myself something cool and familiar, and would end up sitting there for hours.

When I looked at Bob, I realized he could have profited from some of those cool lemonades, too. For despite his attempt at jolly good humor, he looked exhausted, and I knew he was, flying from the tension and work of finishing his dissertation to still another set of tensions and responsibilities. He wanted to go to the *zar* tonight, the special ceremony of exorcising evil to which we had been invited, but he couldn't because he had lectures to prepare for tomorrow's classes.

"Take notes for me," he said, in a gentler tone.

"Okay."

"And why not ask that girl who came the day before yesterday to go with you?"

"Who?"

"The tall, pretty girl from Radcliffe who's come to study Arabic. Susan."

"I don't think she is interested in such things."

"B.J. . . ."

"All right, I'll ask her."

"The *zar* is being held in a very old and interesting part of the city," pointed out Bob. "Use that as your sales talk to Susan. You girls are not likely to be invited there again for a long time."

Surprisingly, Susan agreed to go, and off we went after supper, crammed into the sociologist's open jeep, six Americans and our self-appointed guide, a student at the American University named Francis Xavier Hovanessian.

We left the jeep in a square several miles east of the pension, and walked through dark winding alleys, redolent of that classic odor found in all living cities with long histories and inadequate drains . . . an odor never forgotten, once it has been experienced.

Francis Xavier, his heavy glasses glimmering in the darkness, knocked on an apparently blank wall and we were admitted into a large courtyard.

Lanterns flared yellow along the mud-brick walls. Men turned their turbaned heads to eye us from the tops of our bare heads down the length of our bare arms, paused momentarily at our bare legs, and passed down to the toes of our American shoes.

"*Ahlan wusahlan!* Welcome!"

We were led to benches in a far corner of a lower court.

"Soon the *zar* begins," said Francis Xavier breathlessly to Susan and me. "Just to be patient!" and he dashed off.

"Well, er . . ." said Susan and stopped.

A woman had glided up to us, a woman in a *milaya-lef*, that flowing black cloak which Egyptian women have worn for centuries. She set down a brass tray on the table before us and knelt, spooning whitish powder from a small clay pot onto a saucer of smoldering charcoal.

Smoke rose from the saucer and a thick sweet scent of incense. The woman stirred the mixture carefully and murmured something in Arabic. Were we being purified so that our alien presence in this Moslem home might be less disturbing? Or perhaps the ceremony was part of every *zar*, for I remembered hearing that *zars* had flourished first among the Christians of Ethiopia.

Boom! Boom! Boom! The courts were filling with people. Near us, a fat woman dressed entirely in white was beating a skin drum with the flat of her hand, and a row of similarly dressed ladies had risen to form a line in front of the drummer.

"It is forbidden by the government to hold the *zar*," Francis Xavier was saying gleefully at my elbow. "They consider it a primitive, ignorant custom, unworthy of new Egypt."

"Then why on earth are they having one?" asked Susan.

Francis Xavier chuckled understandingly. "Oh, you Americans," he said teasingly. "Questions! Questions! Always the questions. Well, you will see, it is because the *zar* is good for people, if they feel upset or depressed. In the *zar* it comes out, and people feel better. They . . ."

"Who's *that?*"

A tall man, in a white *gullabiya* and a skullcap pleated and puffed like a miniature baker's hat, was walking through the quieting crowds toward the row of white-clad ladies. They rose and bobbed respectfully, turning so he could see what until now we had not seen, a seated figure behind them facing the wall, a cocoon-like figure wrapped tightly in a black *milaya*.

"He is the sheik who leads the *zar* and cures *her*, the one sitting in the corner," said Francis Xavier.

The sheik turned his back on his patient and, clapping his hands, set a faster beat for the drum. Through the incense, I looked over at Francis Xavier, who smiled encouragingly, demonstrating how we were to clap—so!—in time. I clapped dutifully, but Susan kept her hands folded tightly in her lap.

Almost without my realizing it, the sheik had begun to pivot slowly on the heel of his brown slipper, marking out a small circle; one of the clapping women in white followed his lead.

He was turning rather slowly, his face blank yet serene,

his arms outstretched like wings. He did not have the flair of the whirling dervishes I was to see later, in their scarlet skirts and black cone-shaped hats, whizzing faster and ever faster around the floors of the embroidered *zikr* tents. But this sheik had something else, which was probably more important in a curing ceremony—rapport with his audience. He was gradually drawing into his turning and ever-widening circle all of the ladies in white, leaving the immobile black-wrapped figure visible to everyone, hunched there, defenseless, alone, while her friends and relatives circled to the drumbeat, circled to help her in her sorrow.

Francis Xavier hissed at our side. "They say she had already lost four of her five children, and now her last daughter is dead in childbirth. She does not eat or sleep, but sits like that all day and all night. You say in English, a breaking down of the nerves, yes? But hers is quiet, more difficult."

If I had a nervous breakdown, would I want a crowd of people hovering while I went through the cure? I wondered.

"When one is sick and sad, one needs company," went on Francis Xavier, as though he had read my mind. "Just have to watch out for police!" He rapped me gaily on the shoulder and was gone.

An old man entered the court, stroked his white beard thoughtfully for a moment while he eyed the movements of the *zar*, then laid his cane against the wall and walked into the circle's center where he began to turn slowly also, timing his pivots, one to every two of the sheik's.

"He's an uncle of the sick one," whispered Francis Xavier, at our side again. "They think his dancing will help her."

Boom! Boom! Boom! Still more drums had joined the measured beat, fresh incense had been added to our saucers, the clapping was a long sharp sound. White skirts and veils of the twirling women caught the air, clouds of cloth below the clouds of incense which rose and filled the court. We had all been purified.

Suddenly the sheik tripped. In the split-second pause of the drums, a hissing intake of breath could be heard throughout the courtyard. But the sheik regained his balance, revolving with his head at his knees, then bringing himself up in a twisted, violent writhing of his whole body. His pleated cap fluttered to the floor like a dead moth.

We stared! That serene flat face had been transformed while we caught our breath. The sheik was in trance at last, his eyes wild and staring through strings of long black hair. He raised his hands higher, supplicating, the sweat ran down his face, the drums accelerated to keep pace with his quickening, rhythmic whirling around, around.

"Ahhhhh! Ahhhhh!" The women marked their turns with short, sharp cries. The incense and the insistent drumbeat and the rhythmic perpetual turning were beginning to tell.

I shook my head, fighting down a sense of giddiness. The scene had actually seemed for a moment to move backward and forward before my eyes. Beside me, Susan too fidgeted uneasily.

But is the sheik really in trance, I asked myself coldly, blinking and sitting up straighter on my narrow bench. He was moving rather deliberately, I thought, moving closer to the crouched figure against the wall, closer in his turns until in an apparently chance movement he had touched her; he had whirled away, he had whirled back and dragged her swiftly across the floor, sliding her deftly into the center of the circle, between himself and her uncle.

The patient sat, a faceless pathetic bundle, the only fixed point in the moving whirling groups in the court.

"Ahhhhh! Ahhhhh!" The women closed in, forming a protective circle of white around their friend, who began to bob back and forth, slowly, rhythmically, as though she were rocking an absent child. Above the drums and clapping, I could hear a new sound, a tearing, convulsive sobbing.

The old man turned steadily around his niece, the sheik

moved toward and away from her. Boom! Boom! The drums were deafening.

"Ahhhhh! Ahhhhhhh!"

Pivoting, pivoting, the sheik whirled upon the patient swiftly like a fury and tore open the cocoon of her black *milaya*. The circle of women in white fell back and the drums suddenly ceased.

She screamed then, into the hush, the woman kneeling there, exposed in her wrinkled cotton dress, her eyes glazed, her face swollen with weeping, her hair disheveled and wild.

"God!" she wailed. "God! O God!," and trying to stand, she fell in a crumpled heap to the floor.

The ladies in white carried her gently to a corner, cradled and comforted her and smoothed her hair while she wept bitterly and loudly and called upon God for mercy and compassion.

"The evil is coming out of her now, they think," said Francis Xavier quietly.

The old uncle, alone on the empty floor where the clouds of incense were rising skyward, took two more pivots, a final movement of an ancient quadrille, before he reclaimed his cane and walked through the dispersing crowds as calmly as though he had just completed his evening constitutional.

"Oh, madame," Francis Xavier was gasping excitedly, "the sheik wants you to come and shake his hand."

"Why me?"

"I do not know, but he asks particularly . . . and he is a famous sheik."

The sheik looked up at me, through half-closed sleepy eyes, his face smooth and serene once more, his wild hair neatly put away inside the pleated white cap. He took my hand and held it for a moment in his hot, dry one, and said something to Francis Xavier.

"What is he saying?"

Francis Xavier smiled with pure delight. "Oh, madame, he is saying you were a good omen for him."

"Me?"

"Yes, yes, pregnant women, he says, are good luck for *zars* like this woman's, what with her daughter dying in childbirth and so on." Francis Xavier stopped. "Ha! Ha!" he offered.

The sheik gave me another glance from those sleepy eyes and then looked away shyly.

"Well," said Susan, out in the alley once more, "how do you like being an omen, B.J.?"

I thought about it. "Better a good omen than a bad omen, I suppose," I answered as lightly as I could.

Children skipped around us, past the dark blind fronts of the houses, into the light of a fruit stall, still open although it was so late. The insistent sweet smell of ripe guavas reached us, triumphing over all the other odors of the alley, and I paused. The proprietor moved forward with a large cone of paper ready to hold my purchase.

"No!" Francis Xavier shouted, from behind, taking my arm and propelling me down the path away from the shop. "No!"

"I was just going to buy myself some guavas and maybe some mangoes for Bob," I explained, puzzled at his unaccountable behavior. "Why not? They were very cheap."

He paid no attention. "Look, ladies and gentlemen, look and behold quickly," he called, pointing beyond the square where the jeep was parked into the shadows of the city which lay ahead of us. "You see? You see? The big buildings across the garden."

We peered dutifully. There did seem to be something, dark outlines of large buildings, shapes of trees. But I turned back to the fruit stand framed by the night-dark walls of the narrow street. The brilliant yellow light of the pressure lamp defined the gesturing men in their striped *gullabiyas*, the frolicking children returning from the *zar*, the piles of yellow guavas and the pyramids of green lotus-shaped mangoes.

"Why do you stare at that poor street?" cried Francis Xavier. "Look instead at the noble and magnificent building in front of us. Do you realize what it is?"

"What?" we chorused like a band of school children.

"I give you a hint," said Francis Xavier. "We are near the Bab ez Zuweila, which is one of three gates of the old walled city of Cairo still remaining from tenth century. *Now* can you guess?"

"Difficult to see in the dark," offered the sociologist's wife.

"What is it?" asked Susan.

"The National Library of Egypt!" trumpeted Francis Xavier. "A great and an important thing."

We murmured appropriately.

"Now let us go quickly before policemen come to ask a question." Francis Xavier smiled. "I do hope you have enjoyed our little excursion, Mademoiselle Susan, Dr. Sir, Mrs. Sir, Mr. and Mrs. Er-Uh, and madame!"

I smiled to myself, noting that he had remembered only one of our names, that of the unmarried girl.

"Oh, yes, thank you."

"So interesting."

"Fascinating."

"Do you come often to *zars?*" asked Susan of Francis Xavier. "Do you believe in them?" The three of us were wedged with Mrs. Sir in the back seat of the jeep. The heady late September air of the Cairo evening rushed against our faces.

"What? Oh well . . ." temporized Francis Xavier, and rewarded Susan with a brilliant smile. "Here on your left, ladies and gentlemen, is the Opera House, built for the première of the famous opera of which you may have heard, *Aida*. It is exact replica, in small, of La Scala. It was when the Empress Eugénie was here that they opened it. She came for the first day of the Suez Canal."

We stared at the building, set in a small square and flanked by tall, wrought-iron lampposts, sculptured trees and a fountain.

"On your right, the Ezbekiyah Gardens, there beyond is the burned place where the old imperialist Shepheard's Hotel stood before the revolution, and . . ." he stopped, "oh, and bookstalls like you have in Paris, and there are also, as you see, fruit stands. Fruit stands! Stop! Stop!"

Mr. Er-Uh ground to a halt, nearly throwing us out of the jeep.

"What's the m-matter?" he stuttered. "Police?"

"No," answered Francis Xavier happily, "but Madame said earlier she wished to buy fruit for her husband."

I chose mangoes and guavas. Francis Xavier bargained and paid for them, and afterward, while we drove through the silent downtown streets, iron grilles pulled tightly over the fashionable luxury shops, I counted out the sum into his protesting, but not too protesting, hand.

Then I realized I had paid far more for the guavas here than I would have in the old quarter near the Bab ez Zuweila where we had witnessed the *zar*.

Why that scene at the other fruit stand? Had Francis Xavier perhaps been a bit unsure of himself back there, in the narrow street behind the National Library? It was not his neighborhood. Living as we did in one small section of westernized Cairo, it was easy to forget that this was an enormous city of five million people, with a hundred ethnic quarters and enclaves—Shia Moslems, Coptic Christians, Jews, Sunna Muslims, Armenians, Greeks, Nubians—each with its own inhabitants and shopkeepers and landmarks. Francis Xavier had rushed us back into familiar territory, where the fruit stands were owned by people he knew.

"We are now approaching the new Shepheard's Hotel," he said, "and passing through Liberation Square, so named to mark the freedom of our Egyptian people. This is the new Egypt."

We murmured again.

"A very marvelous city, Cairo," he told us. "Of course, the United States is very wonderful, too," he added politely, "but Cairo is her own, herself."

"But don't Egyptians want to visit America?" asked Dr. Er-Uh. "I certainly get that impression from the number of university students who come in to ask me help them get there."

"Oh, yes, yes, of course," Francis Xavier said. "But you know Egyptians. They go away but they want always to *return* to Egypt. They visit abroad, yes, even study abroad, but they do not leave forever. How could they?"

He gestured around him at the tall, imposing buildings, at the Nile, where people strolled late, under the banyan trees beside the river. The lights from the cafés and the pleasure boats winked back at us from the dark water.

"You are fortunate, my friends," he said, laughing, "to visit our country. *Ahlan wusahlan,* as we say in Arabic, welcome!"

He helped my ponderous self down from the jeep and then Susan, squeezing her hand ever so slightly as he said good-by.

The night was very beautiful. We sat for a moment on the bench beside the door of the pension.

"Well," said Susan, lighting a cigarette, "was it fake? Since we contributed money, I rather thought so."

"Everyone contributed money to pay the sheik," I countered. "I saw them passing the hat."

"Oh, I didn't know that," answered Susan. "I thought maybe they laid it on just for us, an exotic folk treat for foreigners."

"Bob says the *zar* is very old in this part of the world."

"Oh, but I mean, there we all were 'observing,'" went on Susan, "and that boy rushing back and forth telling us what was going to happen before it happened. I mean, really . . ."

"But the woman's withdrawal and her reaction seemed real enough, didn't you think so?"

"Maybe." Susan sounded unconvinced.

"Group therapy, sort of."

"Honestly, I don't know what I think," burst out Susan.

Across the street, on a bench identical to ours, sat two Nubian *boabs*, in white *gullabiyas* and red tarbooshes. Their voices reached us as a gentle murmur. A Mercedes Benz roadster roared past with its top down. The girl in evening clothes was laughing as her escort, dark, intense, turned his beautiful car onto the Corniche and sped up the Nile.

"*A-mo-re*, oh-ho my love!" The Italian dance band throbbed and clashed in the night club above us, on the roof top of the Semiramis Hotel.

"B.J.?" said Susan.

"Well, it's true that some things about the *zar* seemed kind of absurd to me," I finally answered. "But I guess it was all part of the scene. Maybe you have to accept it in that spirit."

"Why should I?"

"Why? Because for one thing," I found myself warming to the subject unexpectedly, "for one thing the absurdities, or what seem like absurdities to us, of the *zar* and everything else here make the place unpredictable. After coming all the way from Chicago, I think I'd be disappointed if Cairo were exactly like home. Wouldn't you?"

Susan smoked reflectively. "I see what you mean. The strangenesses add interest, right?"

"Right."

"But you've seen things like this before, B.J., in Iraq."

"Not *zars*."

"But things *like* this, places like this, people like this," persisted Susan. "I haven't. The farthest afield I've gotten before has been France. It'll take me a while to get used to it all."

"Me, too. I tell you I've never been taken for an omen before."

The *zar*, the trance, the exorcism of evil, the purification by incense, these had very little in common with the ceremonial rituals and morality plays of southern Iraq. Egypt stood at the portals of Africa, but she lay also at the center of the Middle East, that uncertain suspension bridge between East and West. Libraries on alleys, sheiks and professors at curing ceremonies, roadsters and *boabs*, where else could such apparent contradictions exist but in the Middle East, where reason and belief, wealth and poverty, squalor and splendor have lived peacefully side by side for so many millenniums?

Susan and I would hardly be able to understand the complexities of our adopted alien home simply by recognizing that contradictions and absurdities were part of the scene. But perhaps it was a point from which we could begin to discover its beauty.

"*A-mo-re*, oh-ho my love!" The Neapolitan singer was at it again.

Was he an omen too?

CHAPTER 2

A PALACE UNIVERSITY AND
A HOUSE BESIDE THE NILE

During our first days in Cairo, we passed through Maidan el Tahrir (Liberation Square) several times a day—on the way to town, to the university, to the Hilton for lemonade, to the government office building to check on the progress of our residence visas. We could not help but notice the elaborate monument in the center of the square. Curiously, the monument was unfinished, a base without a top. Perhaps, we thought, the government was waiting for a ceremonial occasion to raise here a statue of the new President, in the square he had extended and renamed. Certainly such a handsome pedestal would not remain empty for long in the traffic center of the modern city.

Weeks went by. The monument remained topless. Was President Nasser enough of an Islamic fundamentalist to forbid artistic representation of the human form? That did not seem logical, for although statues of French and British colonial figures were being taken down all over the city, these were gradually being replaced by other statues of indigenous Egyptian heroes. A bust of Saad Zaghloul, leader of the social reform Wafdist party, had been placed at the western end of Kasr el Nil Bridge; a bronze effigy of Talaat Harb, founder of the National Bank of Egypt, stood opposite Groppi's popular coffeehouse. And the colossus of Pharaoh Ramses II dominated Bab el Hadeed, the "gate of iron" of tenth-century Cairo where now train and bus terminals converged.

If Nasser was not against heroic statuary in principle, why was the monument standing empty and why were no statues of the President in evidence anywhere? It seemed strange. Replies of Egyptian friends to this rather sticky question varied in tone but agreed in substance. The officers committee which led the 1952 revolt against Farouk had indeed commissioned the empty marble pedestal in Liberation Square, intending to place upon it a statue of Colonel Nasser. He had declined. "No statues shall be raised to me," he is reported to have said, "until I am gone." One wry friend suggested the pedestal had been empty rather longer than many people had anticipated!

Just behind the controversial topless monument lay the American University in Cairo, a series of rambling yellow-brick buildings decorated with blue and yellow tiles, arched and pillared windows. Once a pasha's palace, then a cigarette factory, the property had been purchased in 1920 by the United Presbyterian Mission Board.

By the time we arrived in 1959, the Presbyterian religious emphasis had largely disappeared, for the university had passed into the hands of a secular board of regents. The American University was attempting to shed its missionary skin and emerge with a new image to meet the needs of the new Egypt. A center for Arabic studies, an expanded English Language Institute, a Social Research Center, a new department of solid state sciences: These were some of the ingredients of the new image, the new attempt to blend Eastern and Western thought to the advantage of both.

The university was offering scholarships to middle-class students, a gesture toward the more egalitarian environment of Egypt in the fifties. It was also a gesture designed to offset the university's prerevolutionary reputation as an educational oasis for the children of Christian minorities and for the daughters of wealthy Moslem families who did not care to have their girls cavorting with the 30,000 classless students at the free Cairo University.

Still, the phrase "University in a palace" has a truly romantic ring and our early impressions of the university confirmed our initial expectation. What remained of the old palace décor, the carved wood *mushrabiya* screens in the windows, the graceful stone pillars and arches in the hallways, gave the place a kind of oriental cachet and sophistication, as did the students themselves, olive-skinned, beautiful, handsomely dressed young people, largely Egyptian, with a sprinkling of Western and Far Eastern diplomats' children. Yet behind this oriental façade, we gradually came to see, lay a traditional American liberal arts college trying to adapt itself to the needs of an alien and revolutionary society.

Protected by a high wrought-iron fence that surrounded the spacious blooming grounds around the old palace, the faculty discussed academic freedom and held countless committee meetings, the students played basketball, campaigned for greater student government responsibility, presented plays in English and French. Even the cuisine of the student snack bar was resolutely Western—raisin cookies, cheese sandwiches, hot dogs, Coca-Cola. While on the campus I had to remind myself that I had really attended a *zar* only last week, that across the street in the government office building, officials were struggling for political power, that a few blocks away lived millions of people to whom the American University in Cairo was as alien as they were to me.

To our surprise, then, we found ourselves caught up in a rather familiar academic round. Between weekly doctor visits, steady apartment hunting, and the insistent social life of Americans together abroad, little time seemed left over to go looking for the Egypt I thought I had glimpsed in Bab ez Zuweila.

There was even, for example, that great old American

academic tradition, the president's annual reception for new staff. Here we met the faculty en masse, a more mixed group than the student body, American, Egyptian, British, Palestinian, German, Dutch, Lebanese. The wives, like all faculty wives, looked me up and down and commented.

"Do you attend the American Church in Maadi?" asked one.

I shook my head.

"The Scotch Presbyterian Church in Cairo?"

I shook my head.

"But you *are* Christian?"

I nodded, confused. This was not the sort of thing I had expected.

"Do you play tennis?"

I laughed. "Not now."

"Are you interested in antiques?"

"Well, I don't know much about them."

"Have you found an apartment yet?"

"No, but we need one badly. My baby is due in five weeks."

"It's your first, I think," said a very pretty, very chic woman who identified herself as Salwa Rashid, wife of the chemistry professor. Her smile was warm. "Well, let us . . . Etta, Marie, Nadia . . . come, let us try to think. Madame Fernea, as you can see, needs an apartment, and soon." She giggled, and one of the ex-missionary ladies blushed.

"Don't live anywhere but in Maadi," counseled the German lady called Etta, very tall and blonde. "It is a nice suburb, clean, very British."

"I—that's not quite what we had in mind. We'd like to be closer to—er—live in the center of town."

Etta eyed me. "I do not recommend it," she said. "It is not safe."

"Why not?" In the few weeks we had been in Cairo, I had been impressed by the calm rather than any possibility of riot or rebellion. "Isn't the government stable?"

A look passed between the other two ladies, both Egyptian.

"Everything is upset," said Etta firmly. "It is always upset in the Middle East. No one knows what will happen. It is better to live with one's own people."

My glance fluttered to the two Egyptian ladies, to Salwa's considering face. What kind of talk was this?

Salwa interrupted deftly. "You must be tired," she said to me. "The weather is so hot and the last days of pregnancy are such a bore!" She giggled again. "Come and sit down. Etta? Marie? Nadia?"

They smiled distantly, murmured something about more tea and drifted off.

"I know it seems strange to you," said Salwa, sitting beside me on a rose velvet Louis Quinze love seat in the president's beautiful living room, filled with aristocratic treasures collected during a lifetime of educational service. "Here things are all very personal. The best thing is to walk about in the quarters you like. Ask the *boabs*, I believe you call them doormen in America? The *boabs* know everything." She giggled once more, an infectious sound, and I joined her. "They know when apartments are to be free and so on."

I thanked Salwa and began to follow her advice. We had to find a place to live. And soon.

"Yes, yes, I know," muttered Bob, collapsed on the pension's lumpy bed. After a busy day of classes and committee meetings and student conferences, he found it difficult to surface from the balm of a brief postluncheon nap.

"We simply have to," I repeated, but Bob had fallen asleep, the for rent columns of the *Egyptian Gazette*, Cairo's English language daily, still propped before his closed eyes.

I knew that if I did not stand up, my resolution might wilt, along with my drip-dry maternity ensemble, and I, too, would doze on the lumpy bed until dinnertime. This baby will be born in a month, I told myself firmly, whether or not I've found an apartment.

Clang! The elevator, a remnant, I was certain, of the opening day of the Suez Canal, hit the ground, soared back up again for a few stomach-turning seconds and returned to earth. I went out on the side street, where Mr. A. Hosny, Curiosities and Antiquities of All Kinds, and Mr. Samir of the Ding Dong Bazaar no longer bothered to importune me. They knew me now; two weeks of residence and no purchases. However, being polite gentlemen, they inquired languidly after my health.

"*El Hamdillaa,* thanks be to God," I replied, "and you?" but I felt as listless as they looked in the heavy air of late afternoon.

My goal today lay on the other side of Liberation Square, the Anglo-Swiss Pension. The proprietor, who was neither Anglo nor Swiss but Greek, also owned an apartment house, and one flat was reputedly just empty. According to my trusty map, the Anglo-Swiss Pension should be just there, across the maidan, but in between were—I counted them—one, two, three, four, five streets to be crossed, streets crowded with people and thronged with noisy traffic.

"Suicide streets, they call them," a student had cheerfully told us when we first arrived. "One does not know whether the drivers of the trams and the cars will really stop at the red light or not!"

We had laughed at the time, but now I did not find the idea quite so uproarious. I watched men holding up one corner of their long full *gullabiyas* so they could run faster between the zooming cars. I looked at the shop girls, lithe and slim in their white blouses and black skirts, holding hands and shrieking gaily as they dodged the speeding, honking taxis, the motorcycles and the clattering carts.

I can't skitter like that, I told myself, I just can't, but when the light changed for the third time, I was swept along with the crowds, pushed and elbowed ahead in spite of myself. I dodged a large piece of falling plaster (the demolition workers went on a second shift after naps), and found myself standing on the corner of Rue Champollion, rumpled but intact. The murderous maidan was behind me.

"No, madame, I am sorry, the flat is taken."

The manager of the Anglo-Swiss Pension fluttered his hands. "But we have an excellent double room, full pension, bath only few steps down hall, now vacant and waiting—" he leaned forward and attempted an engaging smile, "waiting—for you, perhaps?"

I shook my head. Why move from one pension to another? What we wanted was a place by ourselves, where we could put the baby to sleep in peace and shut the door.

Outside the cavernous entrance to the Anglo-Swiss Pension a beggar stood. He was thin, so flattened against the door that in the growing darkness, which followed quickly upon the desert sunset, I did not see him until I almost stepped on his bare foot, a foot with a filthy rag tied round one toe. But I caught his dank, wretched breath full in the face as he stepped in front of me.

"Baksheesh, madame! Baksheesh! For the love of God!" he wheedled, extending a skinny dark hand.

I turned away, shuddering at that whiff of poverty and disease, that emaciated body under tattered *gullabiya*.

He followed me.

"Baksheesh!" he repeated, "baksheesh! I am hungry, madame! Hungry!"

Frightened at my own revulsion, I walked more quickly.

He came on, whistling softly, "Baksheesh! Baksheesh! I'm hungry! Take pity!" the bare feet slipping along the uneven pavement stones behind me.

I did not look at him, but I imagined, oh, how I imagined, grimy, drawn skin under the ragged *gullabiya*, sightless eyes beneath the tattered turban, the festering toe. Was he really blind? In all of my time in the Middle East, I still had not conquered my discomfort and uneasiness at the sight of the beggars. One did not see them in the villages, for there families took care of their own, but in the cities! I knew rationally that begging was an ancient institutionalized form of social security, "alms for the love of Allah," the fifth pillar of Islam, a duty required of every Moslem. But—

"Take pity! Baksheesh!" he hissed at my elbow.

I tried to go faster. I was afraid to run for fear of tripping and falling on the stones, but I shrank from the beggar's miserable breath.

"For the sake of the child you carry, madame! Alms! Baksheesh, for the sake of the child!"

I could not refuse that plea, and he must have known it, for he smiled thinly while I fumbled in my purse. A bony hand closed over the money and I shivered again at the slight dampness of his touch.

"Blessings on the child!" he whispered, and disappeared into a narrow opening between buildings.

I stopped dead on the street and took a deep breath. More crowds of people pressed around me. From the lighted clock on the tower of the Arab League Building I could see that I would be late for dinner. "Not that I will miss anything," I told myself, speculating on the evening entrée, which was called, according to the day of the week, chop, patty, cutlet or roast, but which all tasted exactly the same, inevitably of the cheap fat in which it had been cooked. The echo of my Chicago doctor's voice and my Cairo doctor's voice stirred my conscience. "You must eat," they said, "even if you don't want to, for the baby's sake!"

After dinner (a large cutlet, soggy with grease from the warming oven, saved especially for me), we drank coffee with Susan and Nick on the Victorian porch of the Semiramis Hotel.

The Nile was in flood, black and boiling, and each day it rose closer to the span of the new Kasr el Nil Bridge, which joined Liberation Square with Zamalek on the island of

Gezira. Tonight the river held no romance for me. I looked
at the moving water and felt my stomach churning with it.
The cutlet had been terrible.

"B.J. says she's upset because we still haven't found an
apartment," said Bob, "but I think it's because she had a
confrontation with a beggar in a dark alley."

His tone was conventional. I knew he was encouraging
me to talk about the beggar. I did not want to.

"What surprises me," offered Nicholas, "is how few beggars
there are. In China when my father was in the Embassy, it
seemed to me they were everywhere."

Susan said, "Even in Beirut, which looks so prosperous,
you see them."

"There were many more in Baghdad," added Bob.

I said nothing. I simply could not. I felt weary and un-
reasonably, inexplicably sad.

Bob sensed my mood, for he cleared his throat and
started again, still in that conversational tone. "They say
that Nasser has put most of the beggar children into or-
phanages and the old people into homes and has discour-
aged the rest by slapping fines on the practice."

"Unless you sell lottery tickets, penny gum, or pencils,
that is," amended Nicholas. "Well, I don't mind contributing
to social welfare that way, I must say. What about you,
Susan?"

Susan grimaced. "I can't bear beggars! They embarrass
me."

"Embarrass you!" Nicholas fairly hooted. "What you
mean, my dear girl, is not that they embarrass you but that
they make you feel guilty for being so well fed and well
clothed and well padded against life's more odious evils."

"Don't tell me how I feel, please," answered Susan in a
low angry voice. "I said they embarrass me. They do. They
don't make me feel guilty. Why should they? I didn't make
them beggars. And I didn't make myself what I am, either—
exactly, that is," she finished lamely.

Now, I thought, we all feel awful. Oh, dear.

"I think," said Bob, once more in that maddeningly lazy conversational tone, "I think Americans are made uncomfortable by the brazenness. Why," he said, looking at me, "B.J. was probably thinking unconsciously the whole time, how dare he ask me for money, why doesn't he find honest work? It's your good middle-class values that are violated, isn't that right, dear?"

"No," I said firmly. "Well, maybe or partly, but something else too." I thought of that miserable breath, that stench of despair and shuddered once more. "I was terrified of him. He *smiled* when I gave him the money. He knew he had me."

After a moment Nicholas said kindly, "Well, B.J.'s pregnant, remember? Pickles, beggars, they bother, right? It has to do with the enzyme pattern or the phases of the moon or something."

"Oh, you're all too pompous for words!" burst out Susan. "I don't notice you, Bob, laying out the coins for beggars."

Bob looked a bit abashed. "Well, I haven't seen that many when I've been with you, Susan. There are very few in Cairo compared to other places I've been."

"Isn't there *anything* else to talk about except beggars?" I found myself crying out. My stomach was churning and I was near tears.

"Let's have some more *café fransawii*," said Nick, as a gesture of peace. "No. Brandy. On me," and he beckoned to the Nubian waiter.

Afterward we strolled down the Corniche, past the new Shepheard's Hotel, its blue tiled arches and brass entry façade lighted for the evening airplane arrivals, past the empty British Embassy. Beneath the trees lovers sat on marble benches drinking Spathis lemon soda and staring at the flooding river. (This was the *new* Egypt, where girls were supposedly emancipated from the restrictions of their mothers' day.) We had been along here before. The branches of the banyans and the eucalyptus swept low, almost touching us; their roots swelled up in the rich soil and buckled the squares of asphalt. Feluccas bobbed at anchor on the cresting Nile.

"Why must you move into an apartment?" asked Nick. "Much too pleasant to bother. Stay in the pension, and Susan and I will baby-sit."

"No!" I could not visualize carrying my new baby over the threshold of the grimy pension, cranking it upstairs every day in the sinking elevator, and sitting down to postnatal meals of cutlet, patty, roast and chop.

Beside the neon sign of the Shell Oil Company's Egyptian office we followed a quiet, winding street away from the river. Dense trees rustled around us. Weak moonlight washed over tall stone houses, whitening the long fragrant branches of dark foliage which trailed over wrought-iron fences onto the pavement.

"What's that scent? Is it bougainvillea?"

"No, it's—I think it's *full*, jasmine, like they sell on the streets," I replied. "Smell, it's lovely!"

"But where are we?" inquired Susan.

"Kasr el Doubara, Garden City," replied Nick promptly. "The Doubara palace must have been here at one time. And you know something else?" Nick stopped and looked around. "I think we're lost."

"Ohhh!" shrieked Susan. "Look there!" We drew back at the glimmer of a white figure watching us from a dark garden.

Bob laughed, a little louder than necessary. "A marble Venus, no less!" he pointed out. We peered through the fence for a closer look at the life-sized statue.

"*Masaa el khayr*," said a soft voice and we jumped, all of us this time.

A policeman in his white summer uniform was watching us casually from his bicycle.

"*Masaa el khayr!* Good evening!" returned Nick and Bob.

There was a slight, strained pause.

"We're lost," explained Bob. "Can you show us the way to the Corniche, please, sir?"

"Any service, *ya ustaz,*" said the policeman.

"Thank you very much," said Nick, after we had followed the bicycle around the quiet moonlit streets until the clop-clop of horses' hoofs and the glimmer of lights on water showed us the Nile once more. "Tell me, wasn't that Kasr el Doubara?"

The policeman nodded. "Luxe district. Nice for bambino." He smiled at me.

Bob said quickly, "Are there apartments in Garden City or only houses?"

"Oh, many new flats. Good night."

He touched his black beret before pedaling off.

"Good night!" we chorused.

"I think it might be nice to live in Garden City, B.J., don't you?" Bob mused. "Quiet, not so much traffic. Why don't you look around here?"

"I'll get lost again."

"Walk along the river. How can you get lost?" I sniffed.

"B.J., you can at least try."

"All right, I'll try."

The skyscraper of Garden City rises like a white pillar so far above other buildings of the quarter that it is understandable that its construction, even its existence, might be looked upon with wonderment and suspicion by the inhabitants of the neighborhood. For that very reason, this building was my goal. We had been told that the de luxe building was almost empty.

"No structural steel," explained a young professor at the university to Bob. "People are afraid to live there. They think it will fall down. Buildings here sometimes do, you know."

Structural steel or no structural steel, a balcony with a view of the Nile seemed a pleasant prospect. In fact, by this time, any balcony seemed a pleasant prospect provided it was our own. Thus I mounted the marble steps of the skyscraper as boldly as I could, trying not to be intimidated by the imposing figures of not one but two *boabs*, one in white, one in a discreet, shining, striped *gullabiya*. They looked me up and down.

"Good morning," I offered.

"Good morning," they responded.

"Is there an unfurnished apartment for rent?" I stammered in Arabic and tried a winning smile.

The *boab* in the discreet stripe rose from the wicker chair in which he had, comfortably seated, observed my plodding ascent. Crowned with his enormous white turban, he must have been at least six foot three.

"Yessss," he said in English. "Yessss, my lady."

My heart leaped. An apartment? A place to live. A room with a view.

"But—" added the other *boab*, his finger upraised.

My heart returned to its proper place.

"Yes?" I asked sadly.

"It is on the twentieth floor and . . . er . . . uh . . ." He paused.

"Yes? What?"

"Well," both *boabs* laughed charmingly together, "the elevator not work, because Nile flood covers machine in basement."

Twenty floors.

"But soon they shall be fixed, *enshallah*," said the one in the stripe. "Perhaps this afternoon they are fixed."

We smiled at each other. They knew and I knew and they knew I knew there was not one chance in five million that the elevator would be running for at least three weeks. Yet, as good purveyors of their merchandise, they felt obliged to give me, a prospective customer, an optimistic report.

"*Enshallah*," I said. "Perhaps I shall return," and I turned down the marble steps, stepping around a pushcart of tomatoes on the pavement.

"Tomatoes! Crazy tomatoes!" bawled the peddler. "Jewels! Jewels!"

The two elegant *boabs* rustled down the steps to look at the jewels. They each picked up a less-than-perfect tomato and began to bargain loudly with the peddler. He was young and healthy looking, and his voice was even stronger than theirs.

I stood irresolute beside them. What to do now? Another morning was almost gone, and it had been totally fruitless once more.

"Crazy tomatoes! You want some, madame?"

I shook my head. A tomato was not what I needed.

"Ripe!" cried the peddler. "Very good for eating!" He bit into one, smacked his lips in appreciation of its flavor and gave me a dazzling smile.

"No, thank you," I said.

The peddler shrugged and wiped tomato juice from his mouth with the back of his wide sleeve.

"Jewels!" he cried, bumping his barrow along the street. "Crazy tomatoes! Two piasters only the kilo!"

I followed him, past the relief map of ocher stucco which covered the façade of the Italian Embassy, to a wedge of land which nosed toward the Nile. Here were trees, winding paths, a sandbox, swings. Nannies jounced babies in carriages and toddlers staggered across green lawns under the watchful eyes of mothers.

A park! Could there possibly be an apartment nearby? Then I could walk my baby in the park, like all proper mothers. To my self-image—mother pushing dimpled baby in pram—the tomato peddler, the dark brown nannies, the palm trees in the garden only added an exotic edge, like a carved frame to a picture. Here somewhere there *must* be an apartment.

So I was not really particularly surprised when the *boab* at the wide white building facing the garden nodded and led me up one flight of stairs. I tried to contain my delight, telling myself that one flight up was exactly what I had wanted all along, no more, no less, reminding myself at the same time that the rent would be too much.

"Was American office," explained the *boab*, unlocking a door with a brass number six affixed to it. "Redoing it now. Still dirty."

Painters poised on ladders began to shout at the *boab*, something about money, but I scarcely heard, for I stepped over the pale spotted paint rags, the melting blobs of plaster on the floors and wandered through large, airy, empty rooms. French doors opened outward and there, directly below me, children cavorted in the sunshine in the park. I leaned both elbows on the thick wall of the balcony and stared at that enchanting scene.

We signed the lease the next day and moved in ten days before the baby was due.

"What do you think?" Nick and Susan had come to have tea and admire the apartment.

"Please, B.J., don't tell us again that you liked the tomato peddler's face, and that's how you found the apartment," said Bob. "Spare us!"

I laughed.

"She can walk the baby in the park," pointed out Susan.

"Great location!" said Nicholas. "Close to the university, lots of room, but what will you do about furniture?" He gestured around the emptiness, the wires hanging from the ceiling where light fixtures had been torn out.

"Our things will come. We have a refrigerator and a stove and a bed and a diaper bucket," I said loftily.

Nick snorted. "And you will eat on the floor, like the noble Bedouin, no doubt. How will you explain that to your new Nubian servant? He looks as though he expects a bit more affluent frippery than a camp bed and a spirit stove."

I was silenced. Abbas, who had been recommended by elderly Egyptian friends, had the dignity and bearing of his Sudanese Nubian ancestors. In his spotless *gullabiya* and wide white turban he was obviously ready to do more than we were prepared to ask of him.

"Oh, I don't know. We sent him out to have another mattress made, and he brought back a pretty good one," said Bob. "Told me he had to get the police twice to keep the mattress makers from sneaking used wool in with the new. Full of bugs, the old wool, he explained. He seems practical enough."

"Sounds like a good man."

We sat on the camp bed and Abbas served us tea from borrowed teacups. But I did not remember having borrowed the tea tray, stainless steel and rather Swedish in design.

"Where did the tray come from?"

Abbas looked at the floor. "You did not tell me to buy it, madame, but it was only thirty piasters, a good bargain, and I cannot serve properly without a tray. I hope it is all right?"

"Yes, Abbas. Thank you."

He smiled and picked up the plates and cups from the floor with great care, as though removing Haviland from the top of a valuable marquetry table.

"Our trunks are in Alexandria," said Bob to Abbas, using, I noticed, some new words in the Egyptian Arabic dialect we were currently trying to learn. "*Enshallah* the trunks will get here before the baby does."

Abbas smiled. He treated our efforts at the new dialect with tolerance and patience. "*Enshallah*, God willing, all will be well," he observed, and headed for the kitchen.

"*Enshallah*," we replied and went to the balcony, irresistibly drawn by the cheerful noises from the park below, the cry of the kite birds in the deepening sunset and our brand-new view of the Nile.

CHAPTER 3

OUR FIRST CHILD IS BORN

The brass plate which identifies the Coptic Hospital in Cairo is barely visible behind the spiked wrought-iron fence and the dense shrubbery which help to shield patients from the noise of Ramses Street. I finally spied the door plate and trotted up the hospital stairs to reconnoiter a week before the baby was due. Dr. Zaki had suggested the visit. He had, no doubt, guessed from my set, resolutely cheerful answers to his questions that I was nervous about the forthcoming delivery. How wrong he was! I was not nervous, I was frightened out of my wits. But I was also ashamed to confess my fears to anyone, even Bob. Having one's first baby in a strange, foreign hospital, halfway around the world from home, did not seem quite as romantic now as it had at those gay farewell parties in Chicago. (Had I learned enough of the new Arabic dialect to call the nurse if I hemorrhaged in the middle of the night? What *was* that Arabic word for bedpan?)

I sat in the hospital lobby, waiting to meet Matron and be taken to view the sixteen-bed maternity ward. Nurses in white uniforms glided across the tile floors on soundless rubber soles. A large grandfather clock ticked loudly, the workaday white face contrasting oddly with its carved wooden frame.

"Yessss, modom?" It was Madame Natalya Vinogradov, the White Russian matron of this private hospital. "Good morning. You vish to see the vard? Good!"

I was shown the ward, and it looked good, at least what I could see by peering around the corners of ample Madame Natalya. I trailed along behind her, feeling small and insignificant (despite my bulging front) beside the vastness of her frame, the bristling height of her cap, the battalion-commander quality of her voice.

"You have Dr. Zaki, no? He is good, yess? Very modern, yess?"

I nodded.

"You are lucky, my little American friend. Ho! Yesss, you are lucky. Here is nursery!"

She flung open the door which was no taller than she was; it trembled at the violence of her touch.

Two nurses smiled in greeting as they went about their business, changing gowns and diapers (blue embroidered gowns for boys, pink embroidered gowns for girls), and replacing the babies in their net-covered bassinets.

Matron Natalya flung one of the mosquito nets back with a vigorous flourish and a tiny baby began to cry at the sudden rush of light and air. I sympathized with that baby.

"For bugs," said Madame Natalya, and she replaced the net. "Keeps out the many bad bugs. Sister," she boomed. "Baby is crying."

An Italian nun in a white bonnet and spectacles bobbed politely at us, took the baby into her arms, crooned to it softly.

Madame Natalya sighed. "Sister is very busy," she said. "She vorks all the time, yet she sings to the babies. She *likes* the babies. Thisss the room with the private baths, like you vant, yesss?"

"Yes."

"Ha! Ve provide vot you vant. This you vant, that you vant, you Americans; ve provide." She smiled grimly, fixed me with a relentless eye and entertained me with several hair-raising tales of childbirth on the ice-bound Russian steppes which she remembered from her girlhood. "Yesss, you are lucky," she repeated.

"Thank you," I faltered, when the grand tour was over.

"You are velcome. Ve see you soon, ve hope?" She roared with laughter, and I departed, shaken.

The hospital had seemed orderly and clean, the nurses reasonably competent, the room pleasant. I had liked the way the Italian nun had scooped up, gently and lovingly, that crying baby. But Madame Natalya?

"She won't deliver your baby or take care of you," Bob pointed out. "Forget her. She's probably only a figurehead anyway."

But it was Madame Natalya who occupied my mind when, after four hours of timing pains, we took off for the hospital one midnight. She won't be there, I told myself jubilantly, it's much too late for her. It was the most heart-warming thought I could muster as we traveled the quiet streets in a small car driven by our friend Carl Leiden, among the pushcarts clopping on the pavements, the carts sounding their donkey bells, bringing crazy tomatoes and other good country produce into Cairo for the morning markets.

"Are you all right, dear?"

"Y-yes."

The hospital night watchman shuffled into the elevator and clanged the door shut, scarcely giving us a glance. Bob held onto me, twitching in nervousness and concern. We slowly rose upward, past the carved grandfather clock in the lobby, past one dim, quiet floor after another. In the ward, Dr. Zaki was waiting with our friend Mary, the American nurse who had come to help during delivery. Somewhere a baby was wailing.

Four hours, a lot of labor and a shot of Demerol later, there was another cry, a different cry, and a dull thud.

"It's a girl!" announced Dr. Zaki.

The cry. Yes. But the thud? I tried to raise myself on my elbow and failed. "What was that? Did you drop the baby?"

"No," Mary said through her mask. "The baby's fine, but Bob was standing so close to the door the nurse hit him in the head as she went out. He'll be all right in a day or so."

"Your daughter is pretty," said the Egyptian nurse, laying the baby beside me, wrapped in a pink blanket.

And she was. Bright red, eyes screwed shut, hair still matted on her head from being born, she seemed to me, three minutes old and mine, an extremely beautiful child.

Back in the room, lemon tea was brought for Bob and broth for me. Dr. Zaki shook hands. The baby, to be named Laura Ann after Bob's pioneer grandmother, was taken away to be washed and oiled. Bob sat on beside me, his face gray with fatigue, a huge red welt ballooning up on his forehead from the impact of the delivery-room door. But he smiled with eagerness.

"Tell me about it," he said. "How did it feel, emotionally and all that?"

"I think I'm falling asleep," I answered.

Slosh. Bang. Clang. Slosh.

I sank back into half sleep. I'd had the baby and she was all right. I remembered that.

Bang. Slosh. Slu-urp. Bang.

What on earth? I raised myself on an elbow. A young man in a hospital jacket and a huge curling mustache drooping beneath his skullcap straightened up to squeeze his cleaning rag into a pail of water.

"Good morning, madame," he said in polite Arabic.

Clang went the handle against the side of the pail.

"My name is Roushdi. Congratulations on your healthy baby!"

Slosh, slither. Across the tile floor went the water, and Roushdi bent from the waist, mopping back and forth against that moving stream.

"Finished!" he announced jubilantly. He replaced the screen by my door, creak, creak, and shut the door, bang.

I sank back again into the half doze.

The sudden cry, *"Allah, Hua el Akbar!"* (God! He is Great!) startled me awake.

"Allah! Hua el Akbar!" The cry, loud and strong from scores of throats, came from the open window. What *was* it? All I could see from my bed was a rectangle of cloudless sky, the pale straw-colored sky of early morning.

"Good morning again, madame, here is your breakfast!"

Roushdi, squeaking the bed table across the still damp floor, flung the tray down expertly, squeaked the bed table even closer and cranked up my mattress.

Flat bread. Goat's milk cheese. Brown jam, for heaven's sake. And tea. This was breakfast?

"The noise," I gestured toward the window, where the chorus had changed to "Gamal! Gamal! Long live Gamal!"

Roushdi beamed.

"School," he said. "New boys' school built by our great president, Gamal Abdul Nasser."

He flexed his arms and started to demonstrate with knee bends in case I had not understood the Arabic. *"Allah,"* he began in a loud, vigorous voice, *"Hua el Akbar!* Gamal! Gamal!"

"Please, please!"

Roushdi came up from a spectacularly deep knee bend. "Yes, madame?"

"P-please close the window."

Roushdi, looking miffed, arranged his mustache, fastened the shutters, closed the windows, drew the curtains. The noise receded.

"Lovely fig jam," he cried cheerily, and noisily dragged a screen to cover the open door of my room.

I looked at my tray. Brown jam! I wasn't hungry, I decided, I was just tired. And even if I had been hungry, I didn't want goat cheese and fig jam for breakfast. My stitches hurt. Why did there have to be a new boys' school outside my window?

"*Buon giorno.*"

A spectacled face under a white bonnet appeared around the screen. Sister Angelina, the nun from the nursery, smiled, then stared disapprovingly at my untouched breakfast.

"What is this? How can your new baby, the *bel-la bambino*, eat if you do not eat?"

Good heavens, of course, how could I nurse the baby if I had no milk? I set into the until-then unwanted goat cheese (what an excellent source of milk!) and covered the flat bread with butter and with Roushdi's lovely brown fig jam.

"*Bel-la*, your new *bambino*," said Sister Angelina. She inspected my clean plate, my empty cup. "Good, good." Her rosary clinked against the bed table. "Now sleep, madame." She took the tray and glided softly out.

My eyes closed, but in a moment I opened them. There stood Roushdi once more beside my bed, his mustache quivering in eagerness. He drew from behind his back with a splendid flourish three lovely bouquets, red roses, yellow asters, pink roses. From Bob. Love from Susan. Regards, Nick.

"Now I bring milk, madame," said Roushdi happily. "Hot milk, just for you!"

And as he went out, Matron Natalya marched in and roared, "Ah ha! Here you are! They tell me you have many stitches. Dr. Zaki is very modern and adept, no? But they hurt, yes. Yesss! They hurt. Ha! That's what ve vant to hear! If they don't hurt, then ve have the trouble, the in-fec-tion!"

She tweaked the ends of my sheet, wiped her finger across the night table, flung open the shutters, banged them to.

"Every-thing iss fine, madame? The bathroom isss good?"

I nodded.

"Should you have need of some things special, call! Yes,

madame. Ha! That is vot ve have service for! Ve are here to make you more happy and com-fort-able and vithout in-fec-tion!"

She straightened her broad shoulders, tossed her head in its rigidly starched cap. Tramp, tramp, out she sailed, and as she sailed out, Dr. Zaki sailed in with Dr. Hanna, the pediatrician.

"Good morning, good morning." They smiled cheerfully. "How are things?"

"My dear Madame Fernea," said Dr. Hanna, "you have a lovely daughter, strong heart, excellent lungs, all responses normal. Congratulations!"

The two men beamed at me.

"How do the stitches feel?" asked Dr. Zaki.

"They hurt."

"Good." They beamed again. I tried to smile, but my lip quivered instead.

"She needs sleep," said Dr. Hanna.

If I had had any starch left in me, I would have beamed at *him*.

"Yes, she does," said Dr. Zaki. "Madame Natalya!"

Tramp, tramp, tramp. "Yesss, Dr. Zaki? Our new American patient, she isss good, no?"

"No."

"Vot?" thundered Madame Natalya. "Vot you mean she isss not good? I am here only moments before and she isss good."

"Mrs. Fernea needs sleep," went on Dr. Zaki smoothly. "No lunch?"

"Bring her lunch now, and then leave her alone."

"Vot?"

"Sleep," repeated Dr. Zaki. "She must sleep."

Madame Natalya inclined her head. She was a good deal taller than both men and it was quite a concession on her part.

"Yessss, Doctor," she roared. "Of course. Vot ever you say."

I laughed aloud. The two doctors stared at me. Madame Natalya stood at attention, her lips pursed.

"Rest," said the doctors.

"Humph," said Madame Natalya.

They went out and closed the door.

I slept and dreamed of Madame Natalya. "God! He is great!" she shouted, and her calisthenic accompaniment shook me even in the depths of sleep.

Breast feeding was taken for granted in the Coptic Hospital and Laura Ann was brought to nurse the day after her birth. Brought to me, and that was that. I hurriedly opened my guidebook to this strange new land of motherhood, *Baby and Child Care*, by Dr. Benjamin Spock.

"Section 27. Putting the baby to breast. 'Most babies take to the breast very well,' stated Dr. Spock. 'It's easier in the early weeks to nurse the baby lying down.'"

Well, I was lying down.

"Lay him beside you on the bed."

The nurse had done just that.

"Move closer to the baby."

I did.

The rest of the paragraph was lost because Laura Ann found exactly what she was looking for without any help from me and began nursing vigorously.

By the time I picked up the book again, I read, "During the first week it may be better to stop the baby after a few minutes if the nipples become sore."

How many minutes was a few minutes?

Laura Ann, when I looked down, had stopped nursing and was sound asleep.

"Letting the child nurse stimulates the milk supply." That sounded reasonable, and that was exactly what I had done.

The next day, Dr. Hanna said, "Mrs. Fernea, your baby is spitting up. She is getting too much milk," he added sternly.

Oh, dear, I thought.

"Try not to let her nurse so long at each time," he said. "It seems you have plenty of milk."

He smiled. I smiled. I felt terribly proud of myself.

Some of my preening self-satisfaction must have appeared on my face, for Dr. Hanna added, "You may be a little uncomfortable for the next day or so until the supply is regulated."

I nodded eagerly.

"Just be glad," he said, "that you are able to offer your baby something so valuable, something that no one but yourself can give."

Yes, yes, I thought. Isn't it wonderful? Aren't *I* wonderful? And settled down for my nap. At six P.M. Laura Ann was brought to me. Five minutes on each breast and she was removed by Nurse Georgette.

Milk was still pouring onto the sheet in a steady stream. "But—but—" I started.

"Dr. Hanna says the baby takes only a little," she explained.

By eight o'clock I was so uncomfortable I began to search through Dr. Spock once more. Let's see. Eight pages on, "If the breast milk seems insufficient." No. I flipped the pages. "Breast abscess?" No. Could it be true that Dr. Spock did not deal at length with the problem of too much milk? It *was* true. I laid the book down, crushed, and rang for the nurse.

"You shouldn't have let baby nurse so long in beginning," said Georgette.

Fine time to tell me, I thought.

By nine o'clock she and I were hard at work with the breast pump. By ten I was having hot applications. Laura Ann was brought to nurse one minute on each breast and taken away. Another session with the breast pump and I was told to sleep. Georgette smiled. But I did not. I felt absolutely miserable. Was being a natural mother worth all *this?*

"Why are you smiling?" I said.

"You are so thin. No lady in ward has so much milk." She patted me on the shoulder as though I had just run the four-minute mile. And giggled.

I did not feel like giggling.

I tried to sleep but couldn't. The milk supply was building up again. Twelve midnight. I was in agony. I rang the bell. Georgette came and we had another workout with the breast pump but it scarcely helped me at all.

"Please, please, *please* bring my baby."

"Doctor says no, baby spits."

"So much milk." I indicated my bulging breasts, which by now had become very hard and painful. "Please!"

"No. Sleep, madame."

"I can't sleep!" I cried. *"Please* bring the baby."

Georgette eyed me, shrugged and said, "I see."

In a moment she was back. "Baby asleep," she said.

"Waaaaaaa—waaaaaaa—waaaaaa!" The cry poured from the nursery.

"You see," I said. "She's awake and she's hungry."

Georgette waved her finger. "Not your baby crying. Other baby."

"Is it hungry?"

She nodded. "Mother has no milk. Mother is sick."

"Bring me that baby," I cried in desperation. "Any baby. Anything. I have to have something. I really can't stand it."

Georgette opened her sleepy eyes wide under those penciled brows.

"Rules say no."

"I say yes," I said nastily.

"You want to nurse other baby?" she persisted.

"Yes, yes, yes," I said impatiently. "Bring it. No one will ever know. And, besides, when that baby has eaten it will sleep, won't it?" I added craftily, "and stop crying. And then *you* can sleep."

Georgette returned with a thin, dark baby, screaming with hunger. I could feel the milk dripping again, and I thought I would burst with the pressure. Georgette stood by while I put the strange baby to breast. Half an hour later she took away the long, thin, dark baby, now asleep. I had never in my life experienced such immediate relief from pain. I fell asleep and when Laura Ann was brought in in the morning, Georgette was smiling again. "How are you this morning?" she asked.

"Fine." I again felt terribly proud of myself.

An hour later Madame Natalya tramped into the room.

"Modom," she said icily, "vot do I understand? That last night you nurse not your own, but one other baby in nursery?"

I nodded, smiling. "I had so much milk I was in great pain," I said. "The breast pump did no good. This was my suggestion, and it worked."

"Ve do not allow such things in thisss Coptic Hospital," enunciated Madame Natalya. "Here ve try very hard to avoid the in-fec-tion, both for the babies and for the mothers. Do you understand? Ve have the rules. You and Nurse have broken the rules." She banged her substantial fist on the bedstead.

"I'm awfully sorry. It was all my fault. The nurse didn't want to, but I insisted."

Madame Natalya drew herself up. "Modom, ve vork. Ve try to be a good hospital. Ve prefer for our patients to co-op-er-ate." Further banging on the bedstead.

"Yes," I said, pretending remorse, though I felt not the slightest twinge. "I promise I won't do it again."

"Ah, that iss good!" She patted my hand. "An ex-ample! An ex-ample! That isss what ve must be, modom."

"An example? To whom?"

"The peoples of the East, my dear modom. The peoples of the East! Ve of the Vest—"

The two Italian nuns entered, their faces grave. My evening escapade had gone the rounds. I was given another lecture. When Dr. Hanna came I tried to explain why I had done what seemed a perfectly natural thing.

"And why," I went on, gaining inspiration as I talked, "why isn't that other poor baby on formula or something if its mother can't nurse? Do they leave it without anything to eat?"

Dr. Hanna sat down. He took off his glasses, put his thumb and forefinger over his eyes for a moment, opened his eyes and replaced his glasses.

"Mrs. Fernea," he said. "You know we are not in America. Here in Egypt we have also our problems."

"That baby—"

"His mother is sick. She cannot nurse." He sighed. "In this country that is a catastrophe."

"But surely they can make a formula." I had seen all brands of powdered milk in our neighborhood pharmacy.

"Yes, but the baby's father does not want that done." Dr. Hanna sighed once more. "He feels it is an unnatural mode of feeding. He believes the child will grow up stunted, both physically and emotionally, if it does not have mother's milk, the warmth of being held and nursed."

"So he will let the child die instead?" I began to feel quite righteous and angry.

"No, Mrs. Fernea, no, no. He—" he paused.

"He what?"

"He is looking for a wet nurse for the child."

I opened and shut my mouth.

"So you see."

I nodded.

"I also understand the mother's need," he went on in a brisk professional tone, "to expel excess milk. But it is best if you limit yourself to the breast pump."

As the day wore on, it seemed that an unusual number of people paused outside my door. Late in the afternoon, I looked up from a book to meet the eyes of a small boy peering at me over the top of the screen. It was most unnerving. How had he gotten there? I rang the bell.

"Oh, that," said Georgette. "Well." She smiled. "Everyone wants a look at the American lady who has so much milk. They can't believe it."

"Why?"

"Well, you're so thin. And then—"

"Then what?"

"Many people think American ladies don't nurse babies because it is too much bother. So they use cans. This is difficult to understand, for with cans of milk, how can one be sure the milk is *right* for the baby? So they find *you* strange."

The reactions of my friends to this incident were rather surprising. Bob laughed. Nick and Susan smiled in embarrassment. Several of the kind faculty wives told me it was better not to "get involved," whatever that meant. Most people just stared as though I had just told a slightly inappropriate joke. For them, what *I* had done was *not* the "natural" thing. Yet to the father of the child I had nursed for one evening, simply to assuage my own discomfort, what I had done was obviously the "natural" thing. Who was right?

I posed the problem to Dr. Hanna, who gave what seems to me a classically practical answer to all such questions.

"Consider the child first," he said. "Whatever is best for the child is the natural thing to do."

Bob escorted his new daughter and her proud mama home through Cairo in a taxi.

"Everything looks different," I said, looking out at the passing city, "and—" adding quickly at the amused and skeptical look in his eyes, "it's not just because I'm a mother now and I wasn't before."

"Autumn perhaps," suggested Bob. "The days and nights have become much cooler suddenly. And it's not so smoggy."

"Yes, it is cooler. And the light is different."

When I entered the hospital the city had still lain under the spell of summer, its trees thick with dust, the planes of buildings distorted in the glare of fierce and constant sunlight. In a single week, the north wind, blowing hard from the Mediterranean, had brought fall, brushing the leaves clean, dispelling the haze. The sky was as bright blue as the airport posters had painted it, and the granite colossus of Pharaoh Ramses II before the railway station glinted in the clear light.

"Bob, look at Laura Ann," I murmured fatuously. "She's sleeping so peacefully."

Bob looked. He smiled.

By the time we had turned along the Corniche toward Garden City the sun was lower and the river, calm in the wake of the receding flood, gleamed like molten pewter. The tea hour was over, and families strolled beside the Nile. The afternoon nap effectively cut the day in two, and people emerged refreshed, ready for another session of work or pleasure.

"Full! Full!" A half-grown boy waved his armload of delicate threaded jasmine blossoms in our direction.

"Here," said Bob, passing a coin out the cab window and handing me the bracelets of flowers. "It's the last of the season, B.J."

Past the Semiramis Hotel, the Coca-Cola peddlers and the shoeshine boys were plying their trade, and out on the water a felucca had caught the wind in its sails. Work boats hugged close to the banks, heading south with fish or north with a cargo of stone for Alexandria.

We turned in from the river, around the park where the children were having a last turn on the swings. I looked down at the sleeping baby on my arm, her face curled and quiet.

"I was worried," I confessed, "thought she'd throw up or scream on the way home. It's been very easy and pleasant, really."

"Don't speak too soon," cautioned Bob. "Remember the fun's just beginning. Look at your welcoming committee."

Our two *boabs* each opened a taxi door.

"*Ahlan! Ahlan!* Welcome, madame!"

"*Hamdilla bisalaama!* Thanks to God you have returned safely!"

They shook hands and peered at Laura Ann's face with delighted smiles.

Up the stairs we went into the apartment, where Abbas waited with the new nanny, Fawzia. They congratulated us, they oohed and aahed to even my vain motherly satisfaction, at the undeniable and obvious beauty of my week-old daughter!

Abbas had switched on the lights in every room; I sensed he had done this to make the still half-empty apartment seem more warm and inviting, and I silently thanked him for his thoughtfulness.

A change of season, a change in the family, a change forever. We were home.

CHAPTER 4

THE GANEENA

Our view of the Nile included the *ganeena,* that wedge-shaped park to which, happily, the tomato peddler had led me months before. In any big city but especially in Cairo, where the strip of cultivatable land is so narrow, private gardens are rare, and we felt fortunate to have outside our living-room window, in the middle of the crowded city, not other apartment windows and walls but a pleasant panorama: palm and casuarina and cottonwood trees shading white marble benches, children's swings and sandboxes, green circles of lawn bordered with carefully tended seasonal flowers.

"Yes, the apartment comes with a garden," Bob wrote home, only half jokingly, for we anticipated spending afternoons and evenings with our new child, on one of those marble benches beneath the nodding green foliage beside the river.

The *ganeena* did become "ours" in the next months, although not quite in the ways we had expected. Years later in America, Laura Ann, reading aloud from the latest adventure of the children's favorite fairy-tale character Babar, suddenly stopped in mid-sentence and announced, "Why, Babar's garden of pleasure is a *ganeena!*"

"*Ganeena!* What's a *ganeena?*"

"Don't you remember the *ganeena* where we used to play every single day in Cairo?"

The other children allowed that they did remember.

"Well," went on Laura Ann, "the president made it, just like Babar made the garden of pleasure."

"What president? President Johnson?" murmured the others, who had been younger when we left Egypt.

"What president?" returned Laura Ann. "Gamal Abdul Nasser, the president of Egypt. He *made* our *ganeena.*"

In a sense, Laura Ann was right. The president did not lay out the original garden with his own hands (that had been done by the gardener of the pasha to whom the land belonged once upon a time), but the president was responsible for opening it to the public.

The Garden City *ganeena* was not the only one which the president "made." One of his most popular first acts was to transform the private palaces and gardens of the rich into public museums and parks and children's playgrounds.

Ex-King Farouk's opulent Abdine Palace, Mohammed Ali's Manyial Palace with its ancient banyan trees, the royal family's summer palace in Alexandria are all museums now. Princess Fawzia's garden in Zamalek is a children's playground; her showpiece avenue of magnificent white royal palms leads today to the tower of Cairo.

Along the river the changes are even more dramatic. Standing on the steps of the Museum of Antiquities, it is difficult to imagine that the view across Liberation Square to the river did not exist twenty years ago, that this central section of modern Cairo was occupied by the British Army. By cutting a riverside highway through the old army compound and building beside the highway the pleasant tree-shaded esplanade of the Corniche, the president gave to his people the view and the freedom of the Nile banks, which had once been reserved for a few British officials and titled Egyptians. He extended Maidan Ismailia across the British parade grounds, planted trees and grass and flowers, erected mobile film screens, folk art museums. In a decade the focus of the modern city has shifted to this maidan, renamed Liberation Square; a cluster of new buildings has risen to encircle it. Beside the old Museum of Antiquities, long still pools reflect the blue and orange mosaic tiles flaring across the façade of the Nile Hilton; nearby stand the Arab League headquarters, the new Shepheard's Hotel, the Cairo town hall, and the Egyptian radio and television studios.

He may not have realized it, but President Nasser was only carrying one step further the tradition of other leaders and conquerors throughout the history of the Near East, who in times of peace have used their power to create gardens, surroundings of beauty in which to enjoy their leisure. The Arabic word for paradise is *El Genneh,* literally, the garden, and what could be more heavenly than a lush garden in a region of the world where eighty percent of the land is dry, arid desert?

In the past, of course, the leaders pleasured only themselves. As early as the sixth century, in Fustat, the original army camp from which Cairo proper grew, Khumarawayh, son of Ibn Tulun, was busy silvering and gilding the trees in his palace grounds.

The Mameluke lord, Emir Ezbek, home from the wars in the fifteenth century, built a pleasure lake in Cairo, where "floated the flowers of the yellow water lily." Later, beside this lake Napoleon set up his headquarters and here the first Shepheard's Hotel of whodunit fame was eventually built.

It was the great Albanian Mohammed Ali who was responsible for the first "public" garden. He filled in the lake, landscaped it and opened it to the fashionable citizens of Victorian Cairo.

But the Ezbekiyah Gardens, commemorating the old emir who watched the yellow water lilies, charged an entrance fee, which effectively screened its clientele. President Nasser's idea of free gardens for everyone's enjoyment is

relatively modern; we were glad that one such garden was
so close to us.

Bob, in the early months of his teaching, had no leisure
hours to sit in the *ganeena*, but I took Laura Ann there
every day.

In the mornings, after Abbas had departed for the market
with his daily shopping list, I would leave Fawzia to wash
and iron, and with Laura Ann freshly bathed and dressed,
would set out upon my journey to the outside world of
the park. The early morning rituals in the *ganeena* we had
already witnessed from the balcony, Bob and I, while we
drank our breakfast coffee. The twittering hoopoes (crested
with the golden feathers which King Solomon legendarily
bequeathed to them) had finished their morning toilette
on the lawn of the Indonesian Embassy garden next door.
Abu Ali, the *ganeena's* gardener, had said his prayers in
the empty park, his head bowed in the direction of Mecca.
He had watered the lawns, settled the dust on the paths between the play areas, weeded the flower beds. His wife,
Um Ali, had scrubbed the public lavatories, which, since
they were accessible from both park and street sides, were
a great convenience of the neighborhood.

While Bob and I drank our second cup of coffee, Um Ali
and Abu Ali ate their breakfast together on the grass,
bread bought hot from the vendor passing on his bicycle,
tea from the tea vendor (spirit stove, teakettle, spoons and
cups rattling on his back).

The municipal garbage truck usually arrived at the same
moment Bob was climbing into his customary taxi at the
taxi stand and a few confused seconds would ensue. The
taxi driver did not want to waste precious expensive gas
going around the block so he would back and turn carefully
in the small space, guided by the tea vendor, the bread
vendor and the garbage collector himself.

"Watch! Watch it! Careful!" the garbage man shouted,
from his lofty eminence atop the enormous truck, into the

maw of which was gathered and ground all the garbage collected on the street corner. Considering how many households were represented, it was a surprisingly small amount of trash, already combed through by individual garbage men for anything of possible use.

Bob would zoom off in his cab, Laura Ann and I waving good-by from the balcony. The roar of the garbage truck would cease, and the old street sweeper would pad along, pushing at the bits of remaining rubbish. Abu Ali would disappear for the day, and Um Ali would station herself at her customary post near the lavatory.

"Don't forget to wash your hands!" she would cry to the first child who entered, an admonition she repeated all day long, for the *ganeena* was now officially open: Am Mohammed, the custodian, had arrived and unlocked the gates.

In those first months, the *ganeena* was a double luxury to me. Not only was it a convenient place to air my new baby and enjoy the gentle midwinter sunlight, but it provided an interesting outlet from the agreeable but restricted oasis of the American University. The *ganeena*, I decided, was an ideal place to meet Egyptian mothers and find my own way into the community of Cairo.

Thus I would arrange myself on a marble bench, well situated for both sun and shade, not too close yet not so far from the next marble bench as to preclude a friendly conversation, should it occur. I would open my newspaper or my Arabic text, rock Laura Ann in her carriage, and wait.

Am Mohammed would always amble over to greet me and bestow a few phrases of Arabic baby talk upon Laura Ann before limping back to his favorite marble bench, far from mine, beneath a cottonwood tree by the fence where, without moving from his station, he could gossip with the tea vendor, the newspaper boy in his kiosk, the policeman on his rounds, the local taxi driver back from taking Bob to the university.

With his wooden leg and his good-natured, rather silly countenance, Am Mohammed obviously had obtained his job as park custodian through someone's charitable tampering with the mechanisms of the lower echelon civil service. His vaguely threatening air was reinforced by a trachoma-whitened eye and by his slovenly appearance (rumpled *gullabiya*, covered in winter by a hideous hand-me-down lady's tweed overcoat and a Princeton scarf!). But the children knew better than that. Am Mohammed called most of them by name, he joked with them and told them stories. He was stern, I noticed, only with the half-grown boys who dared to snatch the swings from smaller children, and for these bullies he had a thick stick which he had no compunctions about using on their backs.

Am Mohammed had one other responsibility which he took seriously: keeping men out! This came as somewhat of a disappointment to Bob, who, on the first occasion he found to stroll in the *ganeena*, was politely but firmly evicted by two sheepish policemen, summoned at Am Mohammed's behest. No men were allowed in the *ganeena*, not even fathers!

"But why?" Bob asked of Omar, a new Egyptian acquaintance. We turned to Omar a good deal for guidance and Omar was always helpful. A University of Chicago Ph.D. himself, he had returned to Egypt recently enough to be aware of some of the more puzzling differences between Egyptian and American life. He was young and bright, eagerly applying his Egyptological training to his new job in the Museum of Antiquities.

"For a very good reason, which you should be able to guess, since you've been in the Middle East before," answered Omar.

"What is it?"

"Well, Bob, you know that in this country a woman's reputation is the honor of her family."

"Yes, but—"

"Rich women can evade importuning, but who is to protect the poor girl who must work for a living as a nanny or a servant? In this small garden she is safe. Everyone in Cairo knows this *ganeena* is for women and children only, so if a girl is seen here, no one will talk."

"Yes, that makes sense, I guess," Bob admitted, and resigned himself to observing rather than participating in the life of the *ganeena*.

I did not then confess to him that, although I was allowed into the park, for some reason I did not yet understand, I was no nearer to becoming a member of its particular society than if I had remained sitting with him on the balcony. In fact, I scarcely spoke with a soul from one day to the next except Am Mohammed.

The *ganeena* certainly *looked* like an American park, with its shade trees and play equipment. It was true that the children who played there were of all colors and nationalities, that they wore *gullabiyas* and smocked French dresses in addition to blue jeans, and built minarets as well as castles in the sand.

But it wasn't only the children that were different from those in the parks where I had played as a child in America. The *ganeena* seemed to be primarily the province, not of mothers, but of nannies. Some came early, some came late, some even came without children, for the *ganeena*, it turned out, was also an unofficial servants' employment exchange. A nanny in need of a job, a nanny who had been instructed to "look out" for a laundry woman, all these converged in the *ganeena*. Many of these ladies, young, old, middle-aged, in blue or white uniforms and prim caps, or wearing the conservative *milaya*, smiled at Laura Ann, but they offered no such greeting to me. I was only a mother, a *sitt* ("a lady

of the house"), and my presence in the *ganeena* apparently
puzzled them.

Morning after morning I sat in isolation on a bench
apart, studying Arabic or reading a book I told myself
I was dying to read. I could not resist, however, glancing up frequently, not only to check on Laura Ann, but to
eye the spirited conversations among the nannies, and to
envy slightly their comradely joy in sharing lumps of goat
cheese or patties of beans along with (I supposed) the
secrets of their mistresses' boudoirs.

Was I lonely? Yes, I admitted to myself, I was, a bit.
Being a mother and a *sitt* took a little getting used to,
after my years as a career girl, a working wife and a com-
panion-helper to my husband in his research. I sat there in
unaccustomed leisure, and while the children shouted on
the swings and the nannies scolded them and wiped their
noses and kept them out of the drinking fountain and
gossiped, the lush produce of the Delta and the services of
the city were hawked along the street and carried up and
down the back stairs of the apartment houses fronting the
ganeena.

"Crazy tomatoes! Jewels! Jewels!" Yes, the tomato peddler came and the lettuce vendors, crying, *"Khass! Khass!
Fresh lettuce!"* for although open-air markets, grocery stores
and government food cooperatives are found throughout
Cairo, the individual peddlers still make the rounds, hoping
for a tiny profit on a barrow of produce, bought early in
the morning on the outskirts of the city from the carts arriving from the countryside.

Onions, potatoes, radishes (*"Fijl! Fijl!"*), garlands of
garlic, braces of pigeons, crates of live chickens, tiny eggs
in grass baskets were offered for sale on our street and,
in season, fresh artichokes and narrow, sweet strawberries.
Oranges and grapefruit came in the winter, pomegranates
and prickly pear in the spring, with Persian melons and
mangoes, and in early summer, the great red watermelons

for which Egypt is justly famous. Our children still call watermelon by its Arabic name, *batika*, to the bewilderment of supermarket personnel.

I enjoyed watching this mobile market and had justified my idleness to do so by telling myself I might pick up some bargains. But this, it seemed, was not my province. The first day I purchased guavas from a *ganeena*-side peddler, I discovered to my chagrin that, according to Abbas, I had paid far too much.

"They see you're a foreigner and don't know how to bargain, so they overcharge you," insisted Abbas. "Leave the shopping to me. I can save you money."

I did so. I concentrated on planning the meals and teaching Abbas to cook. As Abbas and I came to appreciate and trust each other, he would ask me to purchase specialty foodstuffs not available from the passing vendors or in the stores owned by Nubians whom he knew—the coffee, tea and jam, the fresh cream and sausages and ravioli, the choice European cuts of meat which could be found at Groppi or one of the downtown Greek grocers.

I had one other important function in this new kind of household, to telephone the butagaz company, a "modern" organization that preferred to receive its orders, not from the servant, but from the mistress of the house. After my call in the early morning, the company's official bicycle would appear and a man in a neat green uniform would haul up a "bomb" of butagaz to fuel our stove.

"*Pre-moos!*" The cry of the primus stove repairman was followed by the knife sharpener, the pot mender, the basket vendor, the old clothes, old bottles man shouting, "*Bakeeya! Bakeeya!*" in a hoarse and strangulated voice.

The flower peddlers came at morning's end, in hope of selling a bouquet to grace the lunch table (no doubt guests were expected and the cook had a few piasters of his shopping allowance left).

"*Ward! Ward!*" they called. "Lovely rose, ladeee?" and

soon the nannies began taking the children home for lunch, and I departed, pushing Laura Ann, with my Arabic plurals in order for tomorrow's lesson.

I fed Laura Ann, gave her to Fawzia to put down for a nap, washed my face and waited, as all the other wives in all the other apartments waited, for my husband to come home from the office.

The *ganeena* was deserted at this hour except for the very poor women who had no work, who could not afford nursemaids, and whose husbands had to work from dawn to dark rather than take the civilized break for lunch and nap in midafternoon.

These few women, lunching with their children on snacks in the shade, were the only Egyptian mothers I had ever seen in the park. After a single abortive conversational attempt with one of the tired-looking ladies in worn *milayas*, I stopped trying. (She had looked startled, peered around carefully to make sure it was to her I was addressing my remarks, then rose and quickly left the *ganeena*, apparently under the impression that I was telling her to go away.)

All that was left was Amina, the *ganeena* regular, who had no qualms about speaking to anyone, for, absolutely destitute as she was, she had no other choice. Yet what could I say to poor Amina? She bobbed at me in a way that made me vaguely uncomfortable; obviously I was supposed to provide clothes for her and her two children, not converse with her about the weather. Amina, Fawzia finally confessed to me, wondered *why* I wanted to talk to her. Did I want to know her story and perhaps contribute? If so, she, Fawzia, would tell me. It was less embarrassing for Amina.

Hunger had forced Amina to the garden one day, penniless, deserted by her husband, far from her village home in the northern Delta, and without any way of transporting herself back home or of supporting herself in the city. She could not write; she had no money for a letter writer; how could she communicate with her family? They would not have wanted her to come home anyway, she had confided to Fawzia; three more mouths to feed, how could her old crippled father manage that with his scrap of land?

Amina was proud to say that she did have a place to sleep; a cousin of her mother's brother by marriage lived in a room in the Sayida Zeinab district and Amina was allowed to sleep there with her children. However, they could not stay during the day (someone else slept in the narrow space then), and the cousin could not feed them.

On Amina's first day in the *ganeena*, a pair of nannies, good-hearted girls from the country themselves, had given the two children bread and cheese from their own lunches. Next day Amina came again, and from then on, every day when the *ganeena* opened, she appeared, to live there until the *ganeena* closed. The nannies took turns feeding her and her children. Many people contributed clothes and food to Amina and within two years, her children were prospering on a decent diet. Before the end of the third year of this good fortune, Amina's husband came back, took her off to a rented room in Shubra and there, we heard, she bore a baby who died. We never saw her again.

After several weeks of *ganeena*-sitting, I began to feel a bit foolish. I compromised by sending Fawzia with Laura Ann in the mornings, and took the baby to the park myself in the afternoons. Fawzia was pleased, but I could not entirely squelch the pangs of guilt which came unbidden at the thought that my first-born child was being cared for, loved and shown off by a stranger!

"Is there some rule that you have to be with your baby every minute of the day to prove you care for her?" Bob asked when I voiced my feelings.

"No, but . . ."

"You don't mind letting Fawzia wash the dirty diapers, I notice."

"That's right. I don't mind at all."

"So what's bothering you?

I couldn't explain it to Bob in rational terms, but it was there.

"If you don't think Fawzia cares for Laura Ann properly," went on Bob, "if you think she is even slightly unreliable or will mistreat or neglect the baby, then fire her!"

"It's not that, Bob. I think Fawzia is fine. I do trust her, honestly."

"Well, then, B.J., thank the gods you're lucky enough to have a healthy baby and some free time, too."

"Yes, but . . ."

Bob threw down his newspaper.

"American women!" he cried. "I will never understand them, I swear! At home my sister complains that the baby is so much work, and here you complain because you aren't busy enough. Ah, our Puritan ancestors!"

He eyed me for a moment. "Ah ha!" he mused, smiling a bit. "Are you afraid, my dear, that your daughter will end up loving Fawzia more than you?"

"Well . . . er . . ." that last thrust had stung a bit. How had he been able to define so well that tinge of worry on the edge of my consciousness? I hadn't even stated it to myself.

Abbas came in to refill our coffee cups.

"The baby ate a good lunch today, some mashed banana, some squash," he said approvingly. "She grows, God protect her," he added, indicating, between thumb and forefinger, the exact diameter of the fattening forearm of my daughter. "She even laughed at me today!"

When Abbas had gone, Bob said quietly, "Abbas is very fond of Laura Ann. Does that bother you also?"

"No, Bob, of course it doesn't."

"I think," said Bob, "that it's wonderful for a child to have lots of attention and have lots of people loving it when it's small, and not just its mother. After all, even in America in pioneer days there were people around the house: grandmothers, maiden aunts, hired men. Do you think a child can get too much love?"

I shook my head no.

"Well, I don't either. I think every bit it can get is so much the better."

I had to agree. Laura Ann seemed pleased with her life, with Mama and Baba, with her kindhearted nanny, with Abbas, with the chuckings under the chin which she received daily from the *boabs*, with the jouncing from Fawzia's nanny friends. Hadn't Dr. Hanna said, "What is best for the child is the natural thing to do?" It was obviously mother, not baby, that was having troubles.

Gradually my uneasiness receded, and I began to enjoy my free mornings. With Salwa Rashid, I went to coffees, I listened to lectures about developing social services in Egypt. Perhaps I could volunteer to help at one of the new day-care centers?

"Furnish the apartment first," said Bob firmly. "Make me comfortable before you start helping other people. And don't tell me you don't know where to start. Omar says his sister Aziza will show you the shops and the upholsterers, that sort of thing, anytime you want."

Thus Aziza appeared in my life, proud and beautiful, sometime student at the American University, who had obviously shown many American ladies through the labyrinth of shops and antique stores in modern and old Cairo.

She intimidated me in the beginning, Aziza, she seemed so knowing, so sophisticated for her twenty years. But Aziza, beneath that beautiful polished exterior, had a warm heart; she enjoyed trotting foreigners through her beloved native city, showing them secret nooks and hidden bargain shops known only to herself.

My guilty pangs at thoughts of Laura Ann and Fawzia in the *ganeena* came less often. It was true, I had to furnish the apartment somehow, and thus I justified those pleasant sunny mornings with Aziza, shopping, followed by coffee in Groppi's garden. Home I would go for an hour's play with Laura Ann and lunch with Bob, prepared by Abbas. This was my lot instead of household chores and baby care. What was I complaining about?

I still held out for my afternoons in the *ganeena* with Laura Ann, afternoons of play and diversion. Laura Ann was growing, she jumped up and down in my lap as though she, too, anticipated, with the other children, the appearance of the balloon man, the cotton-candy man, the man with his trained baboon.

First came Fadhil, Fadhil the nut vendor. Being a man, of course, he was not allowed inside the *ganeena,* but he set up shop beside the fence and built a tiny charcoal fire in the grill, which he had ingeniously fitted onto the superstructure of a discarded baby carriage. With shouts and flourishes he fanned the flames and soon a tantalizing aroma would bring the nannies and children to bargain for an ear of corn on a stick or a handful of nuts dispensed in a cone of paper, cones which Fadhil rolled in idle moments and stacked in the corners of his wagon like tall stalks of ever-blooming paper flowers.

"Dum-da-da-dum-da-da-dum!"

The faint tinkling notes announced the organ grinder, a tiny old man bent double under the weight of his enormous instrument, a lacquered black hand organ, decorated with turn-of-the-century Italian ladies (the rose in the cleft of the bosom, the Spanish comb in the pompadoured hair). The organ was lowered gently onto a portable three-legged stool, and gradually, as the nostalgic melody of "Never on Sunday," warmed and mellowed by the soft air, floated across the *ganeena,* children would gather at the fence and gentlemen and ladies taking tea in the salons of the apartments would drift onto their balconies to listen. Just before the music had reached its climax, the little old man would stop and whip off his dusty black beret to solicit contributions. If not enough coins were forthcoming to satisfy him, he would spit in the street and depart, his song unfinished. But if the audience was appreciative, he would grind through "Never on Sunday" again and then favor us with the only other selection in his repertoire, "Arrivaderci Roma."

Oh, and there were puppeteers, what puppeteers!

"*Ara-goz! Ara-goz!*" they bawled, trudging toward the *ganeena* with a tattered screen folded on their backs, hand puppets sticking from their pockets, ready to begin at a moment's notice the drama of the old lady and the policeman and the cruel husband, or the adventures of Emad ed Din and his donkey. We hired them to perform on Laura Ann's second birthday, and the children hung over the balcony in their starched dresses and new hair ribbons, clutched firmly from behind by their nannies, and squealing with satisfaction while the puppet policeman gave the nasty husband yet one more thump on his turbaned head.

Child acrobats came, to perform for their more fortunate peers, thin pale children in shiny cotton tights and shirts, who could twist their bodies into unbelievable contortions on the bare pavement. There was an adolescent boy who played "Jalousie" over and over again on a jazz trumpet, a crippled man who sold homemade reed flutes and three-stringed violins. On feast days there were donkeys to ride and sometimes during Ramadan an old, blind Koran singer, who would chant, in a high sonorous voice, the sacred verses, reminding the faithful of the world beyond that of the *ganeena*'s pleasures. It was only to this singer that I ever saw Abbas give a piaster of his hard-earned money.

And always there was Am Ashu, who sat quietly, humbly at the gate of the garden, beside a basket of penny gum and candy. Laura Ann learned his name almost as soon as she knew Fawzia's and took great pride in passing her scalloped copper piaster into his gnarled old hand in exchange for a stick of bubble gum.

They were great fun, those afternoons, Laura Ann trying

to talk, constant entertainment around us, the winter light, paling toward sunset, turning the trees sharp and bright, the river golden.

I watched the East European mothers come and go, thinking, aha, they will not find anyone to talk to in the *ganeena*, either. But they were looking for different things than I. In those days, the Czechoslovakian ladies from their Embassy on the edge of the garden, were either under orders not to fraternize or simply did not find non-Czechs to their taste, and thus they sat very close together on one marble bench, occupying every inch of space so that no non-Eastern bloc lady would be tempted to sit down and try to strike up a conversation, which might prove inconvenient or embarrassing. Elbow to elbow, they sat and knitted steadily, scarcely raising their eyes except to warn a straying child or to look at the angle of the sun and try to guess if it was time to go home.

The Sudanese ladies were different, large and plump in filmy *milayas* of snowy white, pink or black voile wrapped about them like saris. They smiled at everyone, including me, but they also tended to cling together on one bench, patting their beautiful bronze children, and nursing their white-swaddled babies lovingly. My one or two tentative sallies in Arabic to these friendly looking mothers were met with surprised giggles. They looked at each other, at the ground, but not at me. I felt awkward. They felt awkward. I retreated.

I reflected that perhaps I had been using my excursions to the *ganeena* as an escape during my first lonely days as a new mother in a strange city. Now, had they not become merely an excuse for my unwillingness to look outward, to make the effort to try to learn something about the country I was living in? What did all my vague notions about international friendship among mothers amount to? Friendship requires something more than the shared fact of motherhood. I had known that. As for my reluctance to let Laura Ann be loved by Fawzia as well as me, what was that except an expression of my own uncertainty as a new mother, my own doubts about this unfamiliar society in which we had come to live. Yes, I admitted to myself, I was, according to my mother's rather Puritan definition, an idle lady, but what to do? Act as though we were in Iowa rather than in Cairo? It was clearly ridiculous to resist, rather than accept gracefully, the advantages which this society had to offer.

Sunset was approaching while I vowed to mend my ways. It was almost time to pick up my things and wheel Laura Ann home. Abu Ali was saying his evening prayers and the day's procession of peddlers and entertainers was coming to an end.

"Groppi!" The local Good-Humor man on his bicycle had come with his blue and gold freezer of ice cream specialties.

The nannies looked at their watches. Was there time for a mango ice cream bar or a cardboard cup of pistachio sherbet?

"Grop-pi!" The ice cream man called for the last time and circled slowly, temptingly around the garden.

Abu Ali began to water the flowers, Am Mohammed was shooing us all out of the *ganeena*. Amina and her pathetic brood headed sadly to their square of cousin's floor. Am Ashu crept away with his basket of penny candies. Fadhil went on to greater sales, presumably, pushing his baby-carriage-cum-barbecue along the Corniche, its tower of paper cones wobbling in the evening breezes.

Laura Ann splashed in her nightly bath, Abu and Um Ali had departed, and Am Mohammed, with a long pointed stick, had finished spearing desultorily the bits of paper on the empty lawns and paths that were the only remnants of the day's activities. The *ganeena* was closed.

We sat on the balcony before dinner, Bob and I, watching the street lights turning on, the kite birds winding home to their nests in the darkened shade of the cottonwood trees. The Nile shone silver through the empty garden, and taxis rushed up and down the Corniche. The long, lovely night of Cairo was beginning; it was time for children to be in bed.

Only once did we ever see anyone in the *ganeena* after dark. Susan and Nick and Aziza were visiting us, and suddenly Nick said, "Look, Bob, isn't that someone moving? I thought the *ganeena* closed at sundown."

"It does."

We stared over the balcony railing. Someone was in the *ganeena,* all right.

"Should we call the police, maybe?" I ventured. I did not relish the thought of an interloper making off with the swings and the teeter-totter boards which the children loved so much.

"Shhhh!" warned Susan. "It *is* a policeman."

"But someone else is with him," whispered Bob.

For a moment we watched in silence the policeman, his white summer uniform glimmering in the shadows, while he pushed his children up and down on the swings. The children made no sound, but when the great forbidden treat was finished and the policeman lifted his son and daughter over the fence to the street, he kissed them each, loudly, and we heard his own low laugh of pleasure and happiness.

"Ah," said Aziza, "when my mother was a child, no policeman would have *dared* enter that garden. *Tout ça change,*" she mourned.

"But Aziza," I pointed out, "the rest of that proverb is '*tout ce que reste la meme chose.*'"

"It's not true!" she cried. "Everything has changed. It will never be the same."

And interpreting our silence correctly, she added, "Of course I agree with you that perhaps many of the changes are for the best, but still one cannot help regretting some things that are gone."

"Like what?" asked Nick idly.

She looked at him. "Oh, Nick, I mean different things than you. You Americans must be tolerant of other people's strange attitudes. You expect *us* to be tolerant of *you*. The Indonesian Embassy garden used to be a delightful gorgeous forest, and here, B.J., around this very house where you now live, there were nightingales. Garden City was truly named then. Now it is only a mélange."

"I rather like it this way," put in Bob.

"Oh, I do, too," answered Aziza, "and though I complain, I love my country dearly. I would not want to live anywhere but in our mélange, with or without nightingales." She giggled at her own bon mot.

Garden City was a mixture, reflecting more sedately and pleasantly than other parts of the city the changes taking place in Egypt. Only a few old pashas, a cousin of King Farouk's among them, lived on as reminders of the past beside foreign embassies, beside the nouveau riche and the other classless families in the apartment houses, facing the *ganeena*, the garden which the president had opened to everyone, but which, was open, without reservation, only to children. Laura Ann, and in later years our other children, were accepted into the little society of the *ganeena*, but I, as a mother, never was.

"B.J.?" Aziza drew me up.

"Yes."

"I know your afternoons are your times in the *ganeena*, my dear, but could you come to tea on Friday? Susan is coming too; my sister is home from Paris for her sculpture show in that little gallery near Groppi. Do come!"

"Just once, B.J., Laura Ann will be all right," urged Susan.

Where were my wits? Where was that single bright, carelessly gay remark with which I could, at one stroke, announce the end of my *ganeena* vigils, proclaim that I had seen the light?

"Uh-er," I stumbled, "er-uh, Aziza, thank you, I'd love

to come, that is, I'm sort of giving up the *ganeena,* I think,"
I ended lamely, and tried to laugh.

"Bravo!" cried Bob. "At last! At last!"

"I knew you'd come around," offered Nick. "Realize how
lucky you are to live in a place where you can be an
ornamental lady and raise your children in a civilized manner."

Had Nick said "civilized"? Nick who announced loftily
that children should be raised in Skinner boxes filled with
sawdust until they had reached the age of reason? "Civilized!" I felt myself bristling, but Aziza's sudden peal of
laughter stopped me.

Aziza, her pure lovely Pharaonic profile below the
smooth dark hair broken up with mirth, finally gasped out,
"Oh, my dear, forgive me, but you are so funny, B.J. All
Americans are. I just cannot understand them."

"Our strangenesses, don't they make us more interesting?"
said Susan quietly, with a side glance at me.

"Oh, Susie, of course, interesting, but so amusing, too."
She sat up and wiped her eyes. "I mean, Cairo is not a
village. And when I think of poor B.J. sitting out there
day after day with the nannies in the silly dull old park
when she could be visiting the mosque of Ibn Tulun or
climbing up the old caravanserai in the Mouski, or coming
to my aunt's salon—if your French were only better, that is,"
she qualified.

"I'm ready," I said. "Let's go. I'll even start up my French
again."

"You'll come with Susie, then? At five on Friday. Good.
My mother will be so pleased."

She indulged in one more giggle before bussing me
soundly on both cheeks. I felt as though I had just gradu-
ated from something, but what?

"Did I pass?" I asked her, amused.

"Ah, *ces Américains . . .*"

Aziza, I reflected later, was absolutely right. Cairo was

not a village nor an American town nor a European city. As Francis Xavier had said long ago, it was itself. Now it was time for me to face what Aziza would call my provincial American attitude and try to enlarge my view, to look beyond the little society of the *ganeena* and the oasis of the university.

The months passed, we were adjusting to our adopted home, our new way of life. We were changing.

CHAPTER 5

THE CITY

"What one sees in a dream surpasses reality," wrote a student to his teacher Ibn Khaldun, the great Arab historian-philosopher of the Middle Ages, "but all that one could dream about Cairo would not approach the truth."

This was the way we felt as the scope and variety of the city in which we had chosen to live and work began to unfold before us. Cairo was scarcely an uninterrupted dream of magnificence and perfection; its changing moods and its unpredictable people alternately delighted and drove us to despair.

Yet, as in the dream of Ibn Khaldun, we were tantalized by it. The city stirred us deeply.

"It isn't what I expected at all," I confessed to Bob.

"Cairo? Well, what *did* you expect?" returned Bob, sensibly enough. "Another Baghdad?"

"Well, it's more—er—European."

Bob laughed. "I'm sure people like Aziza whose family owned a town house in Cairo when Paris was only a peasant village would find your reaction, how would she characterize it—amusing," he said.

"I mean, there are all kinds of people and cultures, so of course it isn't European or even Western, but . . ."

"What you mean, dear, is that it is cosmopolitan."

"No. That's not what I mean."

"Yes," argued Bob. "It is cosmopolitan in the original sense of the word, 'composed of elements gathered from all or various parts of the world,' see, here is the definition, that's it exactly. Besides, neither of us knew much about Egypt before we came, so almost everything is a surprise."

We had certainly known very little, and what had we expected? The pyramids and the Sphinx, deserts and camels and peasants toiling in picturesque costumes along the banks of the Nile, as in a *National Geographic* feature. "The Nile is the second longest river in the world," read some old school geography book of mine. "Egypt is literally the gift of the Nile, for without its water, the land would be dry as the Sahara."

What else had we known? *Caesar and Cleopatra* with Vivian Leigh. Lawrence Durrell's *Alexandria Quartet. Suez* on the late, late show, with a young and handsome Tyrone Power building the Canal all by himself.

No one who has ever lived in Cairo fails to respond to the city. Some people are appalled, like the elderly ladies who were friends of friends of my mother's. They refused to leave the Hilton until the taxi came from American Express to take them to the airport and the next stop on their world tour. The wife of one American University faculty member kept her two toddler children inside their apartment the entire year they were in Egypt. They had no servant. Each day she scrubbed the rooms herself. She boiled all their food and all their clothes and allowed no one to touch them but herself and their father (after he had washed his hands). Those of us who were not so rigid in our hygiene were secretly amused, I think, to discover that she *and* her children were constantly ill, whereas ours were sometimes sick, usually well, following a pattern not too different from the children of our friends and relatives in America.

One middle-aged lady from Florida reacted quite differently. "Oh," she told us breathlessly as we sipped tea with her in the garden of the Mena House Hotel, a stone's throw from the Giza Pyramids, "I just love Egypt, especially the dear, dear pyramids."

Susan and I looked at each other.

"The pyramids?" we echoed foolishly.

The lady from Florida, wearing beige linen, uncrossed her tanned legs, threw back her blonde hair, and gestured dramatically toward the three pyramids, which stood behind us like a painted backdrop. "Of course I love the pyramids!" she cried. "They are just my color!"

We discovered, to our surprise since we often complained ourselves, that we were becoming partisan to our adopted home and would spring quickly to its defense, often unnecessarily, in gatherings of foreigners whose response to life in Cairo was not as enthusiastic as our own.

"You mean you had your baby here, in an Egyptian hospital?" women would demand in amazement. "Was it clean? Were there nurses?"

I said that it was and that there were.

One woman, after glancing around to make sure no one was listening, leaned down and whispered, "Did they have real bedpans?"

In the books that we read, as we tried to become acquainted with the history and the literature of Egypt, we found the same mixture of reactions. Champollion confesses: "For Egypt I feel only horror and pity." Ibn Khaldun rhapsodized: "A paradise extends on each bank of the Nile; the flow of its water replaces for the inhabitants the water from the sky, while the fruit and the wealth of the earth offer them their salutations."

No one could argue with Captain Lyons of early Baedeker fame, who, in his advice to new arrivals, noted, "The blue, cloudless sky, the powerful sunlight and the dry warm air are among the first facts that strike the traveler on his arrival in Egypt and his surprise increases when he observes that the conditions remain uniform day after day and are, in short, so generally the rule that the weather ceases to be a topic of conversation."

We reveled in that blue cloudless sky, and Laura Ann was thriving in the sunlight and the dry warm air. Bob and Susan and Nick went horseback riding over the desert by moonlight to the Step Pyramid at Sakkara, the ancient city of Memphis. We took Laura Ann in her car bed and picnicked at Giza. With Nicholas, we stumbled up and into the pyramids themselves.

"Two and a quarter million," Nick would mutter.

"What?"

"Two and a quarter million blocks of stone in the great pyramid of Giza alone! Think of it! A hundred thousand men took maybe twenty years to build this one tomb for the god-Pharaoh Khufu!"

In the bazaars of Sharia el Muski and Khan el Khalili, Susan and I wondered among old Islamic houses, mosques and lovely gateways, feeling romantic and reading Ibn Khaldun again, "I walked through the crowded streets of this capital and through its markets, which burst with all the delights of this life."

The way to Khan el Khalili was through the perfume market. "Sandal! Sandal!" called the merchants, "At—tar of rose. Very rare, modom!" urging on us perfumes "beyond price," but we passed on to the spice markets where the crooked twigs and roots were displayed in open sacks on the doorsills of the narrow shops. Would we like powdered baby crocodile skin to rub on warts? Or a bag of herbs to assure safe delivery of a child?

We headed for "our" spice shop and sat down on stools to wait while "our" friendly, plump clerk, who lisped beneath a pleated skullcap and whose ragged sweater sleeves showed beneath his striped *gullabiya*, measured into brass scales wrinkled black peppercorns, round whole nutmegs, and splintered strips of cinnamon bark, or pounded the yellow turmeric root to a fine powder in a brass mortar.

When my shopping bag was filled with aromatic packets, each wrapped in coarse pink paper and tied with an excess of string, we would proceed to Ibn Khaldun's "delights," the silk and carpet bazaars, the jewels, the antiquities.

"My workmen make the best fake scarabs to be found in Egypt," asserted one old merchant proudly. He had a narrow domed head, completely bald, which shone like one of the alabaster statues he offered for sale. "You would like a scarab for how much? Five piasters, ten piasters, twenty-five? Now the ones for two pounds" (he displayed a green specimen between two long yellow fingers) "like this, cannot be distinguished from the real thing except by a trained expert." He smiled. "Like me."

"You have real scarabs, too?" we asked eagerly.

The old man's face shone like the rest of his head and he drew from a locked safe tiny drawers filled with tinier boxes. Within each tiny box, bedded in cotton wool, lay the carved sacred scarabs or dung beetles, the hiero-glyphic sign for the sun god, worn by the ancients as amulets and often found in their tombs. Of jade, steatite, malachite, jasper, some no bigger than a fingernail, they each bore a sign, an engraved cartouche clue to their date of manufacture.

On the "Street of Gold," we peered like school children at the dazzle of precious metal, pressing our noses against the brassbound glass display cases.

"You want earrings?" Susan would say jestingly.

There were hundreds of pairs, crescents of heavy worked gold, droplets of seed pearls. There were bracelets and gold beads, charms to hang about the necks of newborn babies, golden miniatures of the Koran, which opened like lockets, crosses and Coptic "key-of-life" symbols on delicate chains.

"What would you like for Christmas?" I would ask Susan, and we would choose fanciful jewelry collections for our-selves from the dozens of shops.

Next to the goldsmiths were the silversmiths, who often

had a few antique pieces of silver Bedouin jewelry, jewelry that was going out of fashion now; the Bedouin women wanted gold like the city women. In between, on the gold and silver street, were the discreet shops of the diamond and gem merchants (seats for customers, velvet pads on the counter from which to admire the jewels at close range). In one of these we were shown peridot.

Aziza had told us about peridot. "It is very rare," she had said. "A pale green stone, like a drop of sea water. A good buy in Egypt, like turquoise."

"Is very rare, peridot," repeated the jeweler, as though he had heard Aziza's sales talk. He fussed around us, stroking his head with its few remaining hairs brilliantined carefully down upon its bald surface, pushing up his striped shirt sleeves which were held in place by old-fashioned arm bands. He spent a long time pretending to calculate, by gazing through the jeweler's glass fixed into one dark, faded eye, the exact price he would accept for this pale green drop of peridot.

"Comes from one island only, this stone."

"Where?"

"Island in the Red Sea."

The Red Sea. Moses. Susan and I looked at each other and shivered appreciatively.

We fingered, exclaimed and admired, but we did not buy much those first years. We were disappointing customers, I am sure, staring not only at the merchandise but at the streets and the passersby and the shops themselves, which often bore in their structures old stones from Roman aqueducts or Fatimid mosques, the worn lettering sometimes still discernible on the scratched surfaces.

In the beginning, we could not help feeling standard thrills when we heard the ping of little hammers resounding on brass trays, copper pots, and candlesticks, which, sitting in the sunlight before their minuscule shops, the artisans fashioned by hand.

There were many kinds of artisans, of course. We were escorting a group of American visiting wives through the bazaar one day when one elderly lady in a Davidow suit stopped and said, "What is this good man making? It looks very interesting and resourceful."

I looked. It was resourceful, all right. He was making new douche bags out of old douche bags and, delighted to have an audience, proceeded to show us in detail how he did it.

On the sunny side of the narrow streets, the tentmakers sat, catching the clearest light in which to stitch onto cotton complex abstract designs in orange and red and blue, designs that covered the walls of the funeral tents, erected near the mosques to receive official mourners after death.

"Oh, B.J., look!" Susan murmured. "Shades of Sheherazade!" The old man before us was manipulating, with his toe, a string on a bow of wood, miraculously producing before our eyes *mushrabiya*, the carved wood screening that did provide window coverings for the harem quarters in the time of Sheherazade.

Turning, we would lose ourselves in a new set of winding, covered streets, lined with shops offering us Turkish silver, modern Egyptian rugs, Chinese antique celadon, mother-of-pearl inlaid boxes, silver filigree, candles, old Persian hangings, sugar dolls for the feasts, polished cotton, until we found an unexpected twist and came out suddenly upon the square where the minarets of El Azhar University were etched black on Captain Lyons' cloudless blue sky.

We could never resist pausing at the door of El Azhar itself, "the oldest university in the world," murmured Susan, reading from the guidebook again, "founded in 900 A.D."

Our Egyptian friends were vociferous in their remarks about El Azhar. "The past! The past! Egypt is drowning in the past," Omar had cried. "El Azhar teaches jurisprudence, rhetoric, when we need science and engineering. They hold back progress, the sheiks!"

But we were from a new young country, we told Omar, and El Azhar was something we had never seen before, like the pyramids and the Sphinx.

Here groups of students in *gullabiyas* and turbans clustered about the scholar-sheiks still lecturing in the medieval manner; an old man sat against the pillar of a graceful stone archway, his face to the sun. His eyes were closed, his garments threadbare, a shapeless bundle of belongings lay beside him on the stones. Was it romantic and impractical to hope that in the rush of change the old man might be left in peace here, upon the stones among the scholar-sheiks, contemplating the divine? Did it really matter to the thousands of Egyptian and Afro-Asian students who thronged to the free public universities, Cairo, Ein Shams, Alexandria, Assiut, and the new branches of El Azhar, on the hills above the city?

Gradually the first tourist thrills receded. The city stirred but also lulled us, and we began to feel we knew all about Egypt, at least all about Cairo. After all, hadn't we been here nearly six months? Hadn't we read, asked questions, wandered, tried to learn the language? But each time this mood came over us, something jolting would happen to remind us that Egypt was six thousand years old and we were not yet thirty.

After Christmas, the doctor suggested a vacation for Bob, recovering from hepatitis, and we took the train south to Luxor to visit our friends at Chicago House, the University of Chicago archeological expedition's permanent headquarters. In Luxor, site of the ancient city of Thebes, the pace was more leisurely, the sun warmer, the feluccas more majestic, the river, well, it was different somehow.

"One remembers one's in Africa here," commented Bob, with some satisfaction.

Our archeologist friends were talking about spending the coming season digging in Nubia.

"Nubia?"

"Stretch of land south of Aswan, lots of temples and ruins to be covered by the backwaters of the High Dam. You've heard of Abu Simbel probably."

"Vaguely," answered Bob. "The land is uninhabited?"

"No, I've seen some small villages of Nubians," replied Dr. Hughes, director of Chicago House. "The people are to be resettled by the government, at least that's what I hear."

"Are they old villages?" asked Bob.

"Very old settlements, it seems."

"And you'll set up camp in one of them?" persisted Bob. I stared at him. What was he getting at?

"No, we've already signed a contract for the season with a boat," said Dr. Hughes. "The villages are small. I don't know really what we could expect to find in them in the way of supplies; the boat is easier in the long run."

Bob paused, and then said lightly, "Maybe you need an anthropologist to go along?"

"Oh, sure," said our friend Jim. "Come for the ride."

"Could I cadge a bunk on your boat if I could find a way to pay my way, Dr. Hughes?" Bob said.

"Well . . ." Dr. Hughes looked at Jim and back at Bob. "I don't know why not. You'd have to check it out with John Wilson, when he comes from Chicago for the UNESCO meetings in May. But you're not serious, Bob?"

"I might be. I don't know. I hadn't thought of it before."

"More cake, B.J.?" Mrs. Hughes was officiating at afternoon tea in the garden, the same garden, I told myself, where James Henry Breasted had no doubt plotted his monumental history of the ancient world. Had the stupendous discoveries of King Tut's tomb first been whispered here over the tea tables, while the crows cried from the palm trees and the oleanders bloomed pink and white?

"Hussain would know that," smiled Mrs. Hughes. "He has been at Chicago House for at least forty years. He is really

too old to work, but what would happen to him if we were
to let him go?"

Hussain limped over and leaned down to hear my question. He shook his head. He couldn't remember about those
days. He was getting old, he said, and then asked me
whether Bob was a doctor, too.

"No," said Mrs. Hughes, smiling. "No, Hussain."

"A doctor?" I queried.

"Hussain sometimes gets the days muddled," explained
Mrs. Hughes. "We had a team of American doctors to
tea a week or so ago, from Planned Parenthood. They
became quite annoyed when Hussain told them he thought
planned parenthood was a big mistake."

"But why? Is birth control against Islam?"

"No, madame." It was kind Dr. Mohammed, the Luxor
resident representative of the Egyptian Ministry of Antiquities. "But the problem is a bit more complex. Sometimes
you Americans . . ."

"Are naïve," I finished with what I hoped was a friendly
smile.

Dr. Mohammed smiled, too, a bit ruefully. "Well, madame, perhaps not *you,* or Mrs. Hughes" (a bow to our
hostess), "but you see these American doctors . . ." he
paused, groping for an explanation that perhaps we would
understand and not be offended by. He caught sight of
Hussain, who had returned to his place in the shade of the
covered walk, near the oleanders, where he could view the
court and make sure that the outdoor tea party was proceeding properly.

"*Effundum!*" answered Hussain briskly, at a gesture from
Dr. Mohammed, hurrying forward and limping around the
softly plashing fountain.

"How many children do you have, Hussain?"

The old man's expectant face fell. "One daughter," he
said sadly, "but we had many lovely ones, my two wives
and I. They died. God knows best."

"How many died?"

"Seventeen."

I gasped. "Seventeen?"

"Yes, madame," answered Hussain. "My first born was a daughter, just as beautiful as your own, may God preserve *her*. Ours did not live a year."

My heart jumped. I looked down at Laura Ann, whose health I found I was beginning to take for granted. The possibility of her death had not entered my head until that moment. My instinctive clutching of my baby must have been obvious to everyone except Hussain, whose eyesight was bad. He went on describing in detail the illnesses of each of his children, what color their hair had been, how they had lisped his name.

"You will live with your daughter when you can no longer work?" asked Dr. Mohammed.

"Yes," sighed Hussain, "but who can be sure of anything in this world except God's will? If only one other child were alive, my heart would be easier."

"God is merciful," quoted Dr. Mohammed.

"God is merciful!" repeated Hussain. He leaned down and looked at Laura Ann closely once more. "Oh, the first born, she was so beautiful, just like Madame's baby here, may God protect her."

Straightening up, he took out a large handkerchief and blew his nose loudly before he began to remove the tea things.

"You see why I say the problem of birth control is complicated," continued Dr. Mohammed. "If Hussain could, he would marry tomorrow and try to father another child, for the sake of his own security. Until the government can demonstrate to the poor people of Egypt that their children will live, not die, they will go on bearing children."

"Yes, I see," I answered, a bit sheepishly, holding Laura Ann more tightly than I needed to. She strained and fidgeted in my arms. "But how can that be demonstrated?"

Dr. Mohammed raised his eyebrows.

"How indeed?" he asked. "Think that fifty years ago the population of Egypt was a mere eleven million. Today it is twenty-eight million!"

"Twenty-eight million!" echoed Mrs. Hughes. "I had no idea it was increasing at that rate. Why doesn't the government do something?"

"They are trying," said Dr. Mohammed. "Nasser has instituted a social security plan. They say he may make a speech in favor of birth control before too long. But one does not legislate against children, madame, at least not here."

We visited the temple of Karnak by moonlight, leaving Laura Ann asleep under the kind and watchful eye of Mrs. Hughes.

"Karnak seemed to me a dwelling place of giants," wrote Flaubert, "giants who in the daytime were served, on plates of gold, whole men en brochette, like roasted larks."

We walked through the forest of columns leading to the sacred lake and looked at the moon. It seemed very small above those immense stone pillars, a mere bauble in the clear sky, yet its reflection widened and yellowed in the quiet waters of the lake.

El Azhar and the scholar-sheiks and the aged, threadbare man upon the stones; thousands of students clamoring for modern learning in the new universities; Hussain with his one living daughter and seventeen dead children; Luxor and Karnak and the Valley of the Kings.

Had things been simpler then, in the days of Pharaohs?

CHAPTER 6

OUR THOUGHTS TURN SOUTH

"You want to hear the story?"
"Yes!"
"The real story, the true story?"
"Yes! Yes, we do!"
"Well, this is the beginning, and this is how we did it!"
(Cheers in the background, and drums)
"We built the High Dam!"

The popular voice of Abdul Halim Hafez singing "Sud el Ali, the Story of the High Dam," against a well-produced background of chorus and drums, was a hit record throughout Egypt that winter and spring of 1960. However, my mind was hardly on the High Dam. I was pregnant again, Laura Ann was teething, Fawzia's family had opened marriage negotiations with her first cousin's father (and where would I find another good nanny, I worried to myself). Bob had become fascinated with the idea of doing salvage anthropology in Nubia. That casual conversation in the garden of Chicago House at Luxor had been like a stone dropped into a deep pool; the circles widened every day.

But whether or not I wanted to think about the High Dam, it was with me everywhere I went. Taxi drivers turned their radios to full volume when Abdul Halim Hafez' voice signaled the beginning of "Sud el Ali." The choruses resounded from the coffee shops and record stores along Talaat Harb Street. "You want to hear the story, the true story?" came piping from the transistor radios propped up among the pyramids of pomegranates and the baskets of artichokes in the stalls of Bab el Loukh market. On 26th of July Street, the television sets displayed in Cicurel and Sednauoui department stores featured Abdul Halim Hafez in person, singing "The Story of the High Dam" on the Cairo television channel. Little queues of people gathered before this projection of the popular singer to watch, but also sometimes to clap in time.

At home, the Nubian *boabs* in our apartment building sported, under their white turbans, skullcaps decorated with the new High Dam design, a pattern in yellow and green and orange thread created by a Nubian housewife.

In the cinemas, the features varied: the new Egyptian film *Do'a el Karwaan,* based on a classic novel by Taha Hussein; an American hit, *The Guns of Navarone;* Russia's *The Cranes Are Flying.* But the short subject was always the same, a new documentary called, not surprisingly, *The Story of the High Dam!*

"Let's face it," Bob said to Nicholas. "The High Dam may change *our* lives, too, as well as the Egyptians."

"How?" I asked.

"Well, I mean, if I do get some money to do research and Nicholas does get a grant to lead an expedition . . ."

"I didn't realize Nicholas was thinking of going to Nubia."

Nicholas laughed. "Who knows? One must think large thoughts these days. That's what the President is doing."

"And it seems to be working," put in Bob.

President Nasser was embarked on many projects to improve the individual's standard of living, to lift Egypt from nineteenth-century dependence on Europe to economic self-reliance. But the High Dam was the grandest of them all. He had taken Germany's offer to build an iron and steel plant, he had signed a contract with American engineers to develop new water sources in the oases, he concluded an agreement with the Fiat company to ship auto parts from

Italy and assemble them in Egypt. Factories were being built and consumer goods appeared: drugs, cosmetics, plastic dishes, refrigerators, all with the proud label "Made in Egypt."

But none of these achievements had the popular appeal of the High Dam. More land—two million more acres of land— could be placed under cultivation when the dam was finished. That made sense to a people who knew from thousands of years of bitter experience just how many bushels of grain could be raised on a tiny strip of Nile-silted soil. Electricity, ten billion kilowatts of electricity, were promised. That made sense, too, to light the dim village houses, to power the television, the refrigerators, the radios that were to come with the new prosperity.

Think grand thoughts, Nicholas had said. Well . . .

"If you do go to Nubia, couldn't I come?" I asked.

"See," said Nicholas, "she's getting the bug, too."

"How could you?" asked Bob. "Bring the babies and live on a boat! Impossible!"

"Why couldn't we live in a village house?"

"B.J., I don't have the money to do *anything* yet. Nobody at Chicago House has even agreed I could bunk on their boat if I *did* have the money. Let's just wait and see."

I began to pay more attention to the daily news accounts of the High Dam's progress, to the government speeches about plans for the development of the city of Aswan. (Maybe I could live there with the children if Bob went to Nubia. It would be 750 miles closer than Cairo.)

Abbas was a Nubian. I asked him about the countryside, about the houses in the villages south of Aswan. Could I manage to live with two babies in one of those houses?

"They are nice houses," said Abbas doubtfully, "but they're made of mud and have no running water, and . . . well, madame, I don't know."

I didn't know whether I could do it either, but I was willing to try. If the Nubian people were anything like

Abbas, I was certain I would like them and enjoy living among them. I even began to listen more closely to "The Song," as we began to call it.

The curious thing about "The Song" was that it completely neglected to mention the Russian role.

"We built the dam, we built it with our hands, we built it with our money, yes, we built it, the High Dam!" sang Abdul Halim Hafez. I often wondered what the Russian Information Agency made of all this. Officially, the Egyptian cotton crop, main source of cash income, was mortgaged to the Russians for millennial years to pay for all those bright yellow bulldozers, for the Russian engineers and advisers, for the master plan of the largest earth-fill dam that had ever been attempted in the world.

But the Soviets got not so much as a footnote of popular appreciation in the songs and the stories that circulated throughout Egypt. It was true that the average Egyptian had almost no contact with the Russians, who arrived, planeload after planeload, and then seemed to disappear. They went directly onto the through train to Aswan, we were told, where they lived in a special housing project somewhat apart from the city of Aswan. If they stayed in Cairo for special duty at the closely guarded and walled Soviet Embassy, they still were not seen much in public, for they had their separate "leisure" compound.

We'd seen that compound. Its picket fence, which had allowed such interesting glimpses of the Russian children and their mamas, was now bricked in. Within its confines, we were told, were a social club, a dining hall, a school and a cinema. The Russians were required to spend most of their leisure there and were bused from home to embassy duties to compound in Soviet-hired vehicles. They did not even have servants, who could have gossiped about them. The ambassador had brought his staff with him from Moscow. The rest presumably needed none.

I saw Russian ladies in the markets in homemade cotton

house dresses, their hair crimped and permanented, trying desperately to determine, through a dense language barrier, the prices of turnips, potatoes, cabbages, onions, beets.

"Parlez français? Ingleezie? Yonani?" The vendor would go through his five or six languages to no avail.

Occasionally I saw those ladies standing for long, silent moments in front of shop windows on Kasr el Nil and 26th of July Street, shop windows which Egyptians insisted were empty in comparison to the displays of previous years, but which apparently did not seem so to the consumer-goods-hungry Russians. And they sweated, how they sweated in the heat! Several years later, when Khrushchev made his official visit to Egypt, he was met at the Aswan airport by a solid mass of his fellow countrymen. One middle-aged Russian lady broke ranks when she saw him mopping his sweating brow, and bursting into tears, ran forward, crying, "The weather! The weather! Isn't it awful, Comrade Khrushchev?"

The privately circulated memoir of a Russian engineer who came to Egypt with the first contingent of technicians reported that he and his colleagues were "stunned" to be met at the Luxor railroad station by a crowd of enthusiastic Egyptians bearing placards lettered WELCOME BACK, OUR AMERICAN FRIENDS! At the Winter Palace Hotel, the multi-lingual bartender did not understand the Russians' carefully pronounced Arabic and was heard later remarking to one of the waiters, "What is the empire coming to when the British pashas drink vodka and cannot even speak proper English?"

The Russian Embassy was taking steps, it appeared, to bridge the cultural gap between the East and the Middle East. Dar el Shark Bookstore opened in the center of town, its windows decorated with photographs of Marx, Lenin and Engels. Translations of Russian books were offered at very low prices, and we enjoyed ourselves poking through the books and the inexpensive long-playing records, many still unavailable in the United States. The bookstore had soft carpets, cool whirring fans and reading tables where students might sit and browse. Yet it remained nearly empty, and oddly enough, there was scarcely a Russian in sight. All the clerks were Egyptian.

The Odeon Cinema, which advertised Russian films, was almost always empty. It was said that the ushers took down names or descriptions of all Egyptians seen entering the theatre, under orders from the secret police. The less dramatic reason given for low attendance at the Odeon was that the Russian films were not amusing.

"Dem-el-thegeel awii!" explained Omar, using the Arabic expression that sums up an attitude of life particularly alien to the Egyptian temperament; literally, it means heavy-blooded. If one has the opposite kind of blood, *dem-el-khafeef,* one is *sympatico,* gay, lighthearted, and can be counted upon to bear the vicissitudes of this life with a laugh, rather than a groan. It is, from an Egyptian, a high compliment.

"Certainly I am glad the Russians bring their heavy machines to build the dam," agreed Omar, when we pressed him, "but does that mean I have to sit and listen to their heavy-handed jokes?"

Perhaps it was only we Americans who were so super-curious about the Russians. Our Egyptian friends did not seem unduly interested, but then, they were not particularly interested in any foreigners as foreigners.

"I probably wouldn't see so much of you, if Bob and I hadn't both gone to the University of Chicago," said Omar, whose attitude was common. "Cairo has five million people," he would explain to me paternally. "The city has always been full of foreigners. Today it is full of foreigners from places I have never heard of. So? So."

The brief hiatus in international diplomatic and economic life, which came with the nationalization of the Suez

Canal, was certainly over. Cairo, ancient crossroads of trade between East and West, was open for business as usual.

"Fascinating," Nick went around saying to anyone who would listen. "Look at the different combinations of people. History, history, all is history. A thousand years ago there were Syrian and Indian princes, even Chinese; five hundred years ago, Turks and Frenchmen. Now we are in a new phase. Africans. And the Chinese are coming back."

The Red Chinese were indeed coming back. Nicholas, who had spent his childhood in China with his foreign-service-officer father, visited with glee the newly opened Chinese restaurants, not one but two, and tried out his few words of remembered Chinese on the puzzled head waiter. (He had come from Peking to serve Arabs, not Americans, his expression seemed to say.)

We heard that the Red Chinese Embassy staff had increased from three to ten people. The next week rumors insisted that a staff of two hundred and twenty was handling stepped-up diplomatic relations. The week after that we were given to understand that more than three hundred Chinese specialists were infiltrating the Arab Socialist Union and sitting on mats in village courtyards, explaining Mao Tse-tung to the fellaheen.

"No, no, no!" protested an American Embassy political secretary. "Everyone knows the Egyptian Communist party is illegal, and no Red Chinese employees are even allowed to leave Cairo! Think of what would happen if they got to Aswan unannounced. Sino-Soviet friction here? That is hardly what President Nasser has in mind."

We saw President Nasser for the first time when he returned from his visit to the United Nations in New York. Busloads of fellaheen, shouting, "Ya Gamal! Ya Gamal!" had been arriving all day in the city, brought in from the country, it was said, and given lunch at government expense to swell the crowds. But such measures did not seem to be really needed, at least in Liberation Square, where the sidewalks were jammed with people, the windows and the roofs facing on the maidan were crowded with on-lookers, and even the lampposts were topped with small boys, waving happily from their precarious perches. We stood on the balconies of the American University and lis-tened to the wailing of the sirens, heralding the approach of the *polis el negda,* official motorcycle escort of the president.

"*Ya* Gamal! *Ya* Gamal!" chanted some of the onlookers. A loud spatter of steady applause erupted as the President drove past, standing up in the open car, hatless, a tall man in a dark pin-stripe suit, smiling and waving to the people, whose pride he had restored and whose stains of poverty he had promised to erase.

But how could he do it? The problems were so gargan-tuan, the balance between a small amount of land and an enormous population so uneven.

Yet those were the years when it seemed possible. The High Dam was under way at last, and the UNESCO cam-paign to save Abu Simbel Temple from the dam's back-waters was focusing international attention on Egypt and its problems. The most cynical of our Egyptian friends ad-mitted to a cautious optimism, and Nasser's enthusiasm was communicating itself to his people and to the foreigners who had come to Egypt.

The oasis of the American University was widening to include Japanese businessmen and African exchange stu-dents studying Arabic, young Egyptian clerks learning Eng-lish in the extension evening classes. The parties we went to were marvelous cosmopolitan conglomerate gatherings of cultures and races, of political ideas and multilingual jokes. Even the *ganeena* had its share of thrills; the children and nannies would run to the fence to watch the motorcades roar by along the Corniche bringing President Sukarno of Indonesia, Ben Bella of Algeria, Prime Minister Nehru of

India, or Marshal Tito of Yugoslavia in state to the President's house.

Gay and hopeful, confusing and amusing, they were, as Omar said, "Real *dem-el-khafeef* [light-blooded] days." And always, now at the back of my mind, lay that magic image—Nubia!

"Come with us, Susan," I would say, without thinking.

"Come where?"

"To Nubia, of course."

"Why not?" Susan would answer.

"I thought your esteemed husband was only planning a tiny piece of research," Nick would put in.

"You're the one who encouraged me to think big, Nick," Bob would say. "I'm putting together a proposal to show Professor Wilson when he comes."

"Oh?"

"Yes," Bob answered eagerly.

He, too, was thinking about Nubia all the time. The more he had inquired about those "few, small" Nubian villages, the more interested he had become.

One hundred thousand people were to be moved from their homes and resettled. Very little was known about them. Some work had been done on the Nubian language, and the Egyptian archeologist Ahmed Fakhry had gathered informal notes about Nubian customs and superstitions. But anthropological studies? Ecological studies? Nothing.

Bob assembled as many facts as he could, made some rough cost estimates, and went to see Dr. Laila, director of the Social Research Center at the American University and an anthropologist herself. If he could get bed and board on the Oriental Institute boat, would the Social Research Center be willing to sponsor a small bit of salvage anthropology on the Nubian people?

"Yes," said Dr. Laila. "Most definitely, yes. When will you know? I have to submit budgets, too."

"Professor John Wilson can give us a reasonably definite

answer," said Bob. "He's coming from Chicago for the UNESCO commission meeting on the Save Abu Simbel campaign. Can you come to dinner then?"

Dr. Laila could.

The suffocating warmth of an early summer night in Cairo is mitigated and finally dispelled by the natural air conditioning of Mediterranean winds, fresh and sea-laden, which arrive regularly from the north each evening about dusk. But, of course, on this particular evening, with Professor John Wilson and twenty other guests coming for dinner, no breeze had yet come. Bob suggested closing the shutters again—the shutters we fastened tight in the morning to keep out the heat and opened in the evening to take advantage of the winds. We closed the shutters and turned on the fans. Then we opened the shutters again and tried putting the fans in the windows. Neither ploy helped. It was as hot and close outside as it was inside, the air pressing on one with an irritating close breath of its own.

"Maybe we'll have a *khamseen* tonight just to make everything lovely," Bob said cheerily. "Do you think so, Abbas?" It was *khamseen* season all right, when the hot, dry winds came from the desert, bringing sandstorms with them.

"No," said Abbas. "*Khamseens* don't start at dusk."

Laura Ann, crowing in her bath, seemed the only comfortable one in the house, though Abbas, in a fresh white *gullabiya* and turban, looked unruffled, as did Mohammed, his cousin, brought in to help for the occasion. Fawzia didn't look too harassed either, I thought. It was only Bob and me, fussing.

"Why tonight?" I muttered to myself as I walked around the apartment, checking ash trays, nut dishes, straightening cushions. The hot rooms were filled with the insistent scent of a great bouquet of creamy white tuberoses standing up stiffly in a brass urn in the dining room. Nothing moved in the apartment, not the spiked leaves of the tuberoses, nor the filmy bedroom curtains, not even the paper lantern in the hall.

"What time is it?"

"Seven," answered Abbas.

"We have an hour. Maybe the breeze will get here by then."

"If it doesn't the party will be ruined!" pronounced Bob in his own special voice of doom. He had already showered and dressed and was pacing up and down the length of the apartment. "No one will want to stay in this hot box for a fraction of a second longer than they absolutely have to for politeness' sake. How awful it is!" He marked off a few more paces.

Laura Ann was brought out, cool and happy in a batiste nightgown, kissed and jounced and taken to bed.

"Oh *where* is that wind?" cried Bob. He was on the balcony now, staring up and down, searching the air for sound, looking for the wind, but only the rude honking of taxis on the Corniche and the beat of the cha-cha-cha, carried across the still river from the night club on the opposite bank, answered him. That and the hushed conversation of all our neighbors, who were also out on their balconies looking, like Bob, for the wind.

"It will come," said Abbas shortly. He and his cousin Mohammed moved the dining table to a more central location for the buffet, the table draped in our best tablecloth for UNESCO. Abbas knew all about UNESCO and he had heard bits of Bob's plans to "do something" on the Nubians. After all, Abbas himself was a Nubian, from the Sudan. He had known the great temple of Kerma as a child, which was more than any of us could say, as Nick pointed out. Abbas had even heard of John Wilson.

"Maybe you should take those flowers out," suggested Bob.

"The tuberoses? But why? They have a lovely scent."

"Maybe too lovely. Why suffocate on hot, scented air rather than on just plain . . ." Bob mopped his forehead. "Really, B.J., I . . ."

The doorbell rang. Abbas opened the door to admit Professor Wilson and Omar. The party had begun. The wind had not come, and even a plentiful supply of gin-and-tonics was no proper substitute.

"When shall I serve dinner?" Abbas asked me. "Everything's ready."

I glanced about at our guests, who by now filled the rooms and seemed to make them even hotter than before. There was nothing I wanted less at that moment than food, and I was sure they felt the same. And yet the lamb wouldn't wait forever, nor would the rice and Abbas' good casserole of squash and lentils and tomatoes and onions. The salad would wilt, the rolls dry up and the wine grow warm in the heat! I could have wept when I thought of the hours of preparation Abbas and I had put into that meal. A slight hush had descended on the crowd. They are trying to think of a polite way of leaving, I thought bitterly.

Abbas held up his hand.

It was a very slight movement, a faint whisper from the dusty leaves of the casuarina trees in the *ganeena*, taken up and passed like a message through the drooping foliage of the cottonwoods.

We waited.

Another whisper, another flutter.

"It is the breeze," announced Abbas with certainty.

Everyone rushed onto the balcony to watch the leaves move, the branches sway. We gulped the delightful air. In a quarter of an hour the temperature had dropped ten degrees and the breeze continued to blow. The guests sailed back into the dining room and consumed all the food and drained the wine, poured by Abbas (though with compressed lips—a good Moslem, he never touched alcohol himself). Laughter and conversation filled the apartment.

Dr. Laila, in a white and silver dress which set off her vivid coloring, sat with John Wilson and Bob in the living room, talking animatedly and gesturing. The two men talked, too, and gestured, on the couch under the windows where gusts of that cool sea air wafted through, ruffling in an attractive way Dr. Laila's dark shining coiffure, moving the tuberoses in the hall and actually blowing up the corners of the tablecloth!

"We're not the only people partying," Susan pointed out.

The roof of the Czechoslovakian Embassy across the *ganeena,* so tightly closed and guarded by day, was ablaze with light. The beat of a folk dance boomed into the night, and the Czechs polka-ed and laughed and slapped their knees, little knowing that the wind brought each slap and guffaw across to us in blasts of sound. Next door the colored lights strung about the Indonesian Embassy garden glinted on the silver of the ladies' saris, on golden epaulets and campaign medals and ceremonial swords. The ambassador was having his military evening, decorous and quiet except for military marches performed in unfamiliar Southeast Asian rhythms.

Laila and Bob and Professor Wilson talked on.

During dessert, the almond soufflé that was Abbas' specialty (he had been given the secret instructions by the landlady's cook in exchange for his bread recipe), I could not keep myself from that animated trio under the window any longer. What were they deciding about our future?

Professor Wilson smiled. "I think I've persuaded Bob and Laila," he said, "that their plans should be made on a grander scale."

"The idea," said Laila in a rush, "is that the Ford Foundation should be asked to support a long-term project to record Nubian culture."

"Salvage anthropology, but also cooperation with the ministry that's resettling the Nubians," explained Bob, "and training graduate students."

"What you should stress, I think," said Professor Wilson, "is the international cooperation in the social sciences angle, just as the archeologists are collaborating to save Abu Simbel. The Nubians, after all, are an ancient and proud people, one must remember that. They're mentioned in Pharaonic sources, they are painted on the walls of tombs."

"Do you think the Ford Foundation would be really interested?" I asked.

"It seems a natural to me," answered John Wilson, "with all the attention Nubia and Aswan are getting these days. Nobody has yet given much scholarly thought to the people. Why not you and Laila?"

"If Ford isn't interested, there are other foundations," said Bob.

"B.J. can bring the family down and set up housekeeping like she did in Iraq," went on Professor Wilson.

"I can?" I looked at Bob.

"Let's try anyway, Laila," said Bob. "We've nothing to lose."

"Exactly!" agreed Laila. "And potentially who knows what we might gain?"

Professor Wilson shook hands. We parted.

Would all these possibilities have arisen if the evening breeze from the Mediterranean had not chosen to blow up the Nile that early summer evening? Sometimes I have seriously doubted it.

CHAPTER 7

NUBIAN ADVENTURES BEGIN

Nubian fever gripped us all that autumn. Bob and Dr. Laila submitted a formal proposal to the Ford Foundation for a Nubian ethnological survey. It would be, as envisioned, a three-year program covering a great many aspects of this soon-to-be-lost culture. Nicholas had decided, after talking with ministry officials and with other archeologists, that the American Research Center in Egypt, his sponsor, could very well apply for one of the permits being issued by the Ministry of Antiquities to excavate Nubia.

"If the Poles, the Dutch, the Russians and the Austrians can do it, why can't we?"

"Why not?" asked Bob. "Nicholas, I have a great idea, a kind of interdisciplinary plan."

"Now what?"

"If you excavate near one of the villages where we will do long-term community studies, perhaps we could even compare data later on."

"Ho-ho, my good friend!" responded Nicholas. "Capital! The compleat history of the area from prehistory to 1960!"

We toasted, in Stella beer, that particular inspiration.

"You should see those villages," Omar exulted.

Omar dominated every gathering of Nubia-philes because, although we all talked about Nubia, he was the only one of us who had been there. The Ministry of Antiquities had sent him with a group of archeologists to survey major temples to be recorded and photographed for posterity. Then, should the UNESCO campaign fail, history would still have some record of the drowned monuments.

"At first I could not believe that simple people had built such sophisticated dwellings—and of mud!" continued Omar.

"Tut, tut, Omar! Your prejudices are showing," chuckled Nick.

Omar did not laugh. He was tall and dark and elegant and joked most of the time, but at this moment he did not laugh. "You must see the villages for yourself," he said. "I'm glad, Bob, that you're going to study these people. I had no idea there was a culture like this within the boundaries of my own country."

"Can you find me a job in Nubia so I can come?" asked Susan.

"Me, too," chimed in Aziza.

"Aziza! You in a village!" Omar did laugh now. "You'd be no good at all. You'd only slow them down; where, my dear, would you have your hair done?"

Aziza rapped her brother on the shoulder. "I could take an anthropology course," she suggested gaily. "It might be fun!"

"Well," said Bob, "plenty of time to decide. We won't be going for a while. Even if we hear about the grant by Christmas, there is much to be done before we actually go down."

Yes, I thought, planning on many levels to be done. Our second child was due before Christmas and if all went well, Bob planned to leave for Nubia in January and get settled in a village by late spring; he was determined to do a community study himself rather than stay in Cairo and administer the proposed project, as everyone expected him to.

Next fall, with Laura Ann two and the new baby nearly

a year old, I would take the children and join him in the village.

"All we can do now is wait," said Bob.

But our new baby, it seemed, did not feel like waiting. He had indicated rather firmly his intention to arrive before his time.

"Hurry, can't you tell the driver to hurry, I don't know what's going on, it's not at all like Laura Ann," I wailed to Bob as we whizzed along the Corniche at midnight on our way to the hospital.

Dark, it was much too dark. The coffee shops had snuffed out their colored lights, the slender minarets of the Zamalek mosque library, without their garlands of electric blossoms, had become only shadows, mere frightening ghosts of minarets in the shadows. The Nile was still, only a dark, scarcely rippling path between the two banks.

"Oh, no!"

"What?" said Bob in concern.

"Oh, look, on the curb."

Were those vagabond boys planning to descend on the lone vendor up the street? He started to move, evidently thinking so too, pushing his lighted glass shop-on-a-cart ahead of him home, and with each bump in the street, my stomach jerked, the pains flashed, and the peddler's white enamel bowls of rice pudding and jello, the brown clay pots of yogurt rattled and banged against the walls of the van, walls painted in lurid colors and topped with cuttin curlicues and towers.

"Bob!" I cried.

"What?"

"Nothing. Really, it's nothing."

Had it been only a year since the doorkeeper ushered us into the Coptic Hospital for the first time? Where would we be this time next year?

Our second child came into the world in silence, and in

the several lengthened ticking seconds before the silence became a muffled gurgling and finally erupted into a full-fledged human cry, my mind wandered again, panic-stricken, over those darkened whizzing scenes which we had passed in our midnight race to the hospital. The dark, smooth, rippling path of the Nile, the frightened peddler bumping his cart, the dark, nameless boys in the gutter after him, armed with broken sticks.

"Congratulations, Mrs. Fernea!" cried Dr. Zaki. "It's a boy. We're lucky. The cord was tight around the baby's neck. If your labor had been longer, he might have strangled."

But from the piercing wail now emerging nonstop from my newborn son, strangling did not seem an imminent danger, and my midnight fantasies receded. I thanked God for the strength and timbre of that cry.

Little did I know that the wail would go on and on. Many times in the following months I had to remind myself how grateful I was that the baby's lungs were clear and well formed. The only visitor that David Karim's bellow did not send scurrying out was Abbas, come with a loaf of bread and a sponge cake to dispel the monotony of hospital food.

"Oh," he said cheerfully, blinking at the volume tiny David seemed capable of producing ad infinitum, "this boy is a strong one, may God protect him!"

We brought our son and heir home to a veritable phalanx of neighborhood greeters. Bob, for the first time in years, seemed embarrassed.

"Did they all expect a *baksheesh*, Abbas?" he asked afterward.

Abbas shrugged. "Well, if you'd given them one, they wouldn't have said no," he answered. His face softened. "But everyone likes babies," he added. "They are gifts from God. Everybody wants to see a new boy."

After three weeks of nonstop crying, we visited Dr. Hanna.

"Just relax," he said calmly. "The child had a bad time coming into the world. Didn't you just about lose him twice? He simply has an unusually severe case of colic."

"But . . ." said Bob wearily, passing a hand over his eyes. He had his son to worry about now as well as Nubia. "Dr. Hanna, isn't there something you can give him to stop the crying?"

Dr. Hanna smiled. "You might try a weak infusion of caraway seed, with a bit of sugar. Or tilleul which is only lime flowers."

I stared. "Fawzia suggested that, but I didn't pay any attention. I thought it was some old wives' remedy."

"Usually my American patients expect a more scientific answer," said Dr. Hanna smoothly, "and if I were to say that a simple infusion, such as is used by the very poor, would help, they might think that I, a doctor in an under-developed country (isn't that the phrase?), was ignorant of recent advances in international medicine. Tilleul and caraway tea are not things I learned to prescribe in American medical schools, but American mothers, as I'm sure you have realized by now, madame, have different problems than Egyptian mothers."

He smiled and we shook hands.

In the following weeks of Davy's life, I was very grateful for tilleul and caraway tea. It had been so simple with Laura Ann, who nursed and ate well, slept, smiled, grew round and pink with scarcely any effort. I had felt pleased (a bit too pleased) with myself when I wheeled her along, past mothers with unpleasant cross children and whining unattractive babies.

"Really," I had said aloud more times than I care to remember, "all one needs to do is relax. Simply a matter of a calm environment."

Along had come Davy to end my smug theories. The

tilleul didn't work miracles but it helped, and Davy was gaining weight. "Food and mother's milk and tilleul," twinkled Dr. Hanna and I nodded humbly.

The new year passed. Bob was depressed and worried. It was difficult to say whether Davy's problems made Bob more edgy over not hearing anything definite about the Nubian project, or whether they merely substituted an immediate, somewhat remediable problem for one that had no ready solution.

He fretted. Dr. Laila fretted. The Ford Foundation office in New York seemed a long way from Cairo.

"What we're up against," said Bob, as we sat in Dr. Laila's garden with the local Ford Foundation representative, "is time!"

"The first group of Nubians, you see," explained Laila, "has to be moved to new houses before the Nile is diverted into the side channel."

"And how long is that?"

"Two, two and a half years at most," said Bob. "If we're going to do this thing, we must do it quickly."

"What do you suggest?" asked the Ford representative.

Bob looked blank for a moment. "Well, er, rather than waste valuable time just sitting and waiting, maybe I could do a quick preliminary survey of Nubia for six weeks or two months."

"Alone?"

"No, I could take Karim with me. None of us actually knows what the situation is, you know," went on Bob, warming to his subject. "Will we be able to rent houses in the villages? Or will we need tents? How many people for each community study? Which communities, for that matter? Will we need motorboats? Donkeys? Water filters?"

"But how can you do such a survey, Bob?" interrupted the Ford representative. "You've told me yourself the Sudan Railways steamboat is the only public transportation in the area and it only stops in three or four places. This would hardly provide you with the information you say you need."

"Well—" said Bob, and he sat up suddenly and the words tumbled out of him, "we could hire a felucca in Aswan."

He smiled and I realized he was absolutely delighted at the thought.

"A sailboat could pull in any place along the river, and we could stay wherever we wanted as long as we needed to. Why not? It couldn't be that expensive to hire a tourist sailboat. At the end of the trip we can take the Sudan Railways express boat back from Wadi Halfa or Ballan."

"Where will you *sleep* and eat, for that matter?" asked Laila.

"On the boat," said Bob quickly. "On the boat. We'll get a sack of rice and a primus stove and sleeping bags . . ."

"Shades of Alan Villiers!" cried Nick in glee. "Two hundred miles in a felucca! You're not serious, Bob!"

"Of course I'm serious," answered Bob.

I realized the idea had just come to him in the past several minutes, but already it was taking shape in his mind, and he could visualize himself at the prow of a felucca (wearing a *gullabiya*, perhaps, and a pith helmet), sailing up the Nile with his primus stove, his typewriter and his Swiss army knife.

I had to laugh. I couldn't help it. Then I realized ruefully why I was laughing.

"She laughs," said Bob to Nick. "Ha! She laughs, but she is just jealous."

"Excellent idea!" cried Laila. She was laughing, too, and I fancied she wouldn't mind going along on the felucca, either. "Wait until Karim hears about this."

Susan reported that when told of his role in the forthcoming Nile expedition, Karim, one of the bright younger research assistants in the Center, turned pale. Any comment he might have made was drowned in the excited clamor of the office staff.

I wondered about Karim, a nervous and intense young man. He was intelligent and well educated, but had never lived outside a city, and the cultural milieu within which he grew up did not include summer camps. Those were for poor orphan boys whose families could not afford vacations on the beaches of Alexandria. Thus Karim had no nostalgia for the great outdoors. But he said nothing. He bought supplies and began to fill, systematically, a metal first-aid kit the size of a suitcase.

Bob scoffed. "For heaven's sake, Karim, we'll never use all those medicines up in fifteen years!"

"I am thinking in broader terms, D-Dr. Fernea," stuttered Karim. "This is for the big project, eventually, for all three camps."

"Oh, good," answered Bob, "but there won't be room for it on the felucca. Take out everything except aspirin, entrovioform, sulfa powder, a few basics."

Karim peered doubtfully after Bob's receding back. I bent over and helped remove the vials and jars and bottles.

"But we must have the anti-snakebite serum," insisted Karim, "and the anti-scorpion medicine. I got it with a special permit from the Ministry of Health."

"Well, if you think so," I said doubtfully.

"Yes, and the penicillin and the splints and the malaria medicine . . ." He looked at me and said quickly, "I'll carry it all with my luggage, and Dr. Fernea won't have to bother about it."

On a cold, dank February evening, Bob and Karim departed for Nubia, Bob with his mind full of ideas and plans and his briefcase full of papers. Karim had arrived early and stowed the first-aid suitcase under the seat of the Cairo-Aswan sleeper, I noted.

"Beni Suef, Assiut, Luxor, Aswan!" called the conductor.

"Karim's mother asked me just now if I would ask you to be kind to her son," I whispered to Bob.

"He can only eat, apparently, the special food she cooks for him, and she's worried," added Susan.

Bob stared. He looked at Karim, jumping about nervously in the huge crowd of friends and relatives who had come down to see him off.

"Kind?" he said, amazed. "Why on earth would I be unkind?"

The train began to move. Bob and Karim climbed aboard.

"God go with you!" cried the crowd of well-wishers.

"Wear your scarf all the time, dear!" begged Karim's mother.

"Don't drink the water!" called someone.

The crowd laughed loudly. Steam rose around us. Karim's mother dabbed at her eyes as the train chugged out of the station. The Nubian adventure had begun.

"Nubia," wrote architect Hassan Fathi, "was like a world so new, so fresh in invention and artistry that we were enchanted . . . we could not believe it to be true. Most of us" (artists sent by the Ministry of Culture to record impressions of Nubia for posterity) "had never visited this part of our own country, and the clearness of the architectural purpose, the procession of glistening white houses on the banks of these ancient shores, was like a dream from another age."

We awaited letters in like vein from Bob and Karim. But traveling, as Hassan Fathi had, on a well-staffed luxury boat was rather different from Bob and Karim's plans to hire a garden-variety felucca and drop anchor at every village along the way.

"Well," wrote Bob finally and brusquely, "we're setting off at last. Four days in Aswan to line up a felucca and crew. No one seems to want to make such an unorthodox trip, the local Nubian sailors are unwilling to give up transporting tourists around the cataracts. Infuriating waste of time. We go through the locks at Aswan tomorrow before sunrise, and then on to Nubia!"

Karim wrote, "Can you believe, dear friends in the Center, that we are actually on the river almost all the time, Dr. Fernea and me? The boat is very small, I must say. We bobbed up and down in the locks like a cork! It makes one rather nervous. I sleep on the boards on top of the boat, like the sailors in old-fashioned English novels. My transistor radio has run out of batteries. I feel very far from Cairo and my friends, from the coffee shops and the tea garden of Groppi."

"*Le pauvre!*" enunciated a pretty research assistant, as this letter was read aloud to the breathless office staff.

"Now Bob's new letter," prompted Susan, who was working part time in the Center.

"The river is trickier than one would think," Bob had typed. "For instance, yesterday we came very close to grinding a hole in the bottom of the boat, on a submerged tree. There are hundreds of them, especially along the shores, trees that were covered by the flood after the 1933 raising of the dam. I suggested we steer a course closer to the main stream of the river, but the boatmen absolutely refuse, say it's dangerous and so on. I suppose they know what they're doing, that's what I hired them for, after all, but I'm beginning to wonder."

The girls stifled tiny yawns.

"Is that all?" asked the pretty researcher.

"Well, oh yes, here's a nice part. 'The villages are quite something, very clean, some houses have porches with pillars, like southern mansions. Yesterday we found a whitewashed staircase coming right down to the water line; we moored the boat and walked straight up to tea. We've seen sculpture in mud brick, very good some of it, decorating the houses, and also colorful paintings on the walls and doors. By the way, how are the children?"

The girls oohed and aahed. I felt a pang which I tried unsuccessfully to suppress. Whitewashed pillars and sculpture along the quiet Nile. A long procession of days in the warm winter sun and nights sleeping under the stars. I wouldn't have thought of leaving the children, and yet . . .

Abbas was in good form these days, as manager and protector of the household. From years of living and traveling on the river, he knew it well, and each evening after we had gone over the daily accounts, he found occasion to tell me some story about the Nile, the first cataract at Aswan, the second at the Sudanese border, and the third and final cataract of the river near his own home of Kerma in New Dongola. His eyes shone as he talked and I wondered again what we were all doing up here in Cairo when we could be trail-breaking along the second greatest river in the world. Then I shook myself and wrote a long letter to Bob, full of the children's newest words and accomplishments.

The next thing that happened was a telegram.

"Don't worry!" the transcriber of the cable had typed, suitably punctuating the phrase to alert me at once. Don't worry about what? "We are o. k. will cable when more news love Bob."

Had the boat sunk? Had they been attacked by scorpions or chomped upon by crocodiles?

"Don't worry," repeated Abbas. "Probably they went aground. The Aswan boatmen don't know the southern channels."

Abbas' tone was brisk and his advice seemed sensible. Not to worry. But how could I help it when I had no idea where Bob was or what had happened to him?

Four days passed without word. "They may have to wait three or four days, a week maybe if they are aground," cautioned Abbas.

"Why?"

"Till a bigger boat comes along to pull them off," he answered.

"But the steamboat goes past every three days!"

"Yes," said Abbas, "but the steamboat doesn't stop for every felucca that goes aground. They might be in an empty place or in a cove, out of sight."

Empty! Now in my dreams, footage of the river and the stars combined with a frame of Bob and Karim, stretched on the sand in the classic lost-in-the-desert pose. I knew this was perfect nonsense, but still. . . . Did they have water canteens with them, I wondered, and sat up in bed in the middle of the night. Why hadn't they written or sent another cable? A week had gone by, eight days.

"Dear friends in the Center," Karim's letter brought me down to the office posthaste in a taxi to hear it read aloud. "I know you will not believe it, but I think I have gained several pounds on Dr. Fernea's cooking. It is horrible, but rice and bully beef are filling. I do not even take my sleeping pills and aspirin before bed as I am so tired I fall asleep at dark and there is no radio to keep me awake."

The girls babbled all at once.

"Karim fat?"

"Incroyable!"

"Karim without his pills?"

"Can Dr. Fernea cook?"

"Oh," sighed the pretty research assistant, "he was so thin and elegant, Karim. I shall have to plan a small *regime* for him when he returns." And she giggled.

This letter did not make sense in relation to the "Don't worry" cable. I pored over the postmark after the girls had gone back to work and finally realized the letter had been mailed before the cable was sent, so was not actually news at all.

Then where were they?

"Two weeks," I said to Susan, who was staying with me

while Bob was gone. "Two weeks is a long time not to hear a word. He could have sent a cable."

"Maybe there's no place to send a cable from."

"Don't worry, madame," repeated Abbas.

Next morning the letter did finally arrive. I skimmed over the beginning, he did seem to be all right, and yet . . .

"Yesterday," wrote Bob (the letter was dated more than two weeks before), "we were skidding along the edge of the river again as usual when we ran over a submerged palm, just as I had predicted days before, and tore a hole in the bottom of our boat. Water poured in, great confusion. It wasn't very serious, as it turned out, and we easily made it to shore but as far as our sailors were concerned, that was that. They put us and our belongings ashore, turned the boat upside down and announced that as soon as it was repaired they were heading back to Aswan! We could go to hell and so could our 'agreement'! We're currently bargaining with a vendor of salted fish and other salables to abandon his trade for a time and take us on for a month as passengers. Here's hoping we're successful, as I don't fancy spending the next month in this particular village, though there are interesting things about it.

"When we first arrived we were taken to one elderly man who addressed us in good English with a strong southern accent. While Karim and I sat there with our mouths open, he told us his tale; he'd worked as a steward on a merchant ship out of Suez, had jumped ship in New Orleans and lived there for twelve years. He even married a New Orleans woman and they ran a restaurant together. One day, it appeared he got homesick for Nubia and for his Nubian wife and family, and got an Egyptian ship to take him on again. Sounds like an unlikely story, doesn't it, but he certainly knew New Orleans inside and out. Seems the Nubians are going to offer us plenty of surprises of this kind. I mean, one might not be too amazed in Cairo, but imagine finding a man who knew all about the restaurants in New Orleans living happily in a little village on the Nile halfway through the Sahara desert!"

Susan and I looked at each other appreciatively.

"Is there more?" she asked.

I nodded.

"I don't fancy going on in this other boat either, smells of rotten fish from stem to stern, but we're stuck, and we will be lucky if we can get them to take us on. The post boat is coming soon so I want to mail this letter. Will let you know what happens next time I get a chance."

Next morning, not only was Abbas grinning from ear to ear for having diagnosed the situation correctly from the beginning, but two more explanatory letters arrived, together.

I took the children for a walk along the Corniche, trying to feel virtuous and motherly. It was not a success. "All I need now," I told myself, "is a truly lyrical letter about Abu Simbel."

Eventually that letter arrived, too.

"The yellow acacia tree is in flower, it provides a nice foreground for the temple."

Could that really be Bob writing?

"We spent the night sleeping on shore in front of the four mighty colossi of Ramses. At dawn, just as the books say, the rays of the sun do strike the inner sanctuary of the temple. The light was a bit off the altar though, since we are past whatever day the sunrise is supposed to strike full center.

"Actually, sleeping on the sandy shore sounds romantic, but it was most uncomfortable because of the insects, which reminds me, don't forget to send us some more insect repellent, c/o Dr. Riad at Sebua, we will pick it up at the post office."

Yes, that was Bob writing. But there was more.

"Karim and I took the day off to look at the temple, the big one dedicated to Ramses, and the smaller one, his queen's. One feels one knows a bit what the earlier explorers of the Nile must have felt like. Here we are, all alone, the river, the empty sand, everything so quiet, and this great monumental temple just standing here. The place is most memorable. You must see it."

Yes, I thought, I'd like to very much.

In the office, the girls were once more agog over Karim's prose in praise of Abu Simbel.

"They all want to go to Nubia," said Dr. Laila. "And when I think that two years ago, we couldn't have paid enough to one of those girls or to the boys either, to go to a village, any village and work. . . ."

She paused. "Egypt is really changing," she said. "The only problem is, well, you know."

Yes, I knew. Money. There still had been no definite word from Ford.

The bright, clear days of February passed. Ramadan began, and special preparations were under way in the kitchen each day for the *iftar*, or breaking of the fast. Abbas jounced Laura Ann and now Davy, who had passed his howling days and except for a stubborn cold seemed finally to be enjoying life for the first time.

Bob wrote about the temple of Derr, the pottery-makers of Sebua, of the village near Abu Simbel where he hoped to base one of the community studies, of Faras on the Sudanese border where archeologists were uncovering medieval Christian churches with Byzantine frescoes. "Karim and I seem to be thriving in this air. I can understand why the Pharaohs used to come to Upper Egypt for their health. WHAT GIVES WITH FORD?"

What indeed? I did not know. Neither did Laila or the Ford office in Cairo.

Could Ford say no? Of course they could. And then what would happen to the Nubian idea? A little piece of research, perhaps, one man on the University of Chicago expedition boat, as Bob had originally envisaged it. It would be all right. Not so grandiose, but useful and interesting. Things had gotten beyond that stage, however, and we all entertained bigger ideas. Setting up field camps. Spinning up and down the river in motorboats. Seminars with the Ministry of Social Affairs, which was handling the Nubian resettlement. A chance to be of some real service perhaps. UNESCO cooperation.

I met Laila at a large cocktail party for an NBC correspondent in Cairo on his way back from filming the Upper Nile.

"Everybody in New York wants to see Abu Simbel these days," he explained. "So we have to give the public what it wants. Vince Halliday. How do you do?" He was ruddy faced and his thickening chin above the fashionable shirt hinted at middle age, his boyish shock of graying hair brushed the top of heavy horn-rimmed spectacles.

"You've just come from Abu Simbel?" I asked eagerly.

"Yes," said Vince. "New York won't believe what Roger and I went through to get this footage . . . just to hire the boat, I mean."

Laila and I looked at each other.

"Fantastic place, though," went on Vince. "Worth it all. And we ran into a couple of guys traveling by sailboat. Like to do that myself if I were twenty years younger."

"Really?" I began. There couldn't be that many people traveling coursing up the Nile in a sailboat, could there? "Who were they?"

"Nubians told us the tall thin blond with the stringy beard was a Swede, and the other, a chubby dark fellow with a big bush of a beard, an Ethiopian."

"Were they?"

Laila giggled. Vince looked at her. "Well, no," he said. "We got them to give us a live interview, which we sold to the 'Today' show. Quite an interesting bit. Bush Beard was a Palestinian and Thin Beard was, honest-to-pete, ladies, an American. I discovered I'd been working in Chicago when he was there, and they ended up staying to lunch. Can you believe it? In the middle of the desert?"

Next morning Laila telephoned.

"I've just sent a cable to Thin Beard," she said.

"Asking him to give up the lie he's been leading all these years and send in his Swedish passport for validation?"

"B.J.!" cried Laila, exasperated. "Listen to me! This is the cable. 'Ford has given us the grant!' Did you hear that?"

"Yes."

"Well, say something. Isn't it wonderful? *El Hamdillaa!* Thanks be to God!"

The Nubian Ethnological Survey was about to become an actuality.

"We'll be here three more years," I told Abbas.

He grinned. "Nubia is a fine place," he said.

Three more years. Three more years of our lives to be lived abroad, in Egypt, three more years of our children's lives. We had not thought this far in advance when we'd come from America less than two years ago. But now it seemed a fine thing. What would my mother say, and Bob's mother? Their grandchildren raised in foreign climes? Why? Well, why not?

"It seems that Thin Beard has triumphed at last," I told Susan at suppertime.

"*El Hamdillaa!*" she pronounced. "You'll take the children and go down in the fall, then, as planned."

"Yes, if Davy gets over this stubborn cold."

"A cold! For heaven's sake, B.J., don't turn into a fussing mother just when we're about to embark on our Nubian adventure," said Susan lightly, and added, "I'm sure he'll be fine in a few days."

"You're probably right."

We sat on the balcony, watching the lights wink along the Nile, and thinking of Bob and Karim, sitting beside this same beautiful river, but closer, far closer to its source.

PART II

Nubia

CHAPTER 8

UP THE NILE
TO ABU SIMBEL

The ancient Egyptians believed the Nile to be the center of the world and that the source of this great river lay in a narrow rocky gorge near Aswan. Within the gorge, the myths say, the mysterious Spirit of the Nile, the god Hapy, unleased the miraculous waters which flooded the land with rich loam and "divine sweat" and allowed men to survive in the desert.

As usual, the myths bore some resemblance to reality. For the first cataract of the Nile is at Aswan, the last natural obstruction in the river's three thousand miles of wanderings from its source in the mountains and lakes of central Africa. And the Nile, as it rushes through the cataract, does seem to be beginning, to be gathering momentum and strength for the remainder of its journey to the Mediterranean Sea.

From the canopied veranda of the Old Cataract Hotel in Aswan, high on the sandstone cliffs above the riverbanks, one can see occasional quiet pools, reflecting the golds and reds and darknesses of the wide, clear sky. More often the river boils and froths, surging around islands of palm trees and whitewashed houses and Pharaonic temple ruins, around granite boulders polished and worn into curious shapes by centuries of the passage of these foaming waters.

The Nile winds, as it has always wound, above and below

the cataract, but a railroad has never been finished beyond Aswan. The only overland traffic which pushed south into Nubia was that of the caravans, the camels and donkeys of the Bishareen nomads who circumnavigated the rocks along the riverbanks and traveled inland along the desert of the valley floor. Today even this traffic is thinning, as the Aswan Dam rises and its backwaters are slowly covering Nubia with a vast lake. Most southbound passengers are now flying south or taking a circuitous ocean route through the Red Sea and the Gulf of Aden.

But before the days of the High Dam, passengers could go on by water, as Bob and Karim had done earlier in their hired felucca. The river was the main highway through Egyptian Nubia, a three-hundred mile stretch of country between Aswan and Wadi Halfa, in the Sudan. Feluccas sailed up and down the Nile with loads of dates and grain, with sheep and goats, salted fish, straw mats, produce to be traded in Aswan or Halfa for cloth, tea, tobacco, pots and pans and gold. Smaller feluccas ferried the Nubian people across the river to grind grain at the mill, to see the government doctor, to visit friends, to celebrate feasts. For more affluent travelers, the Sudan Railways operated a twice-weekly steamer, an unpretentious but cheerful riverboat, with an adequate sun deck, a dining room and small but well-kept cabins. At Wadi Halfa the voyager could, if he wished, connect with the train to Khartoum and Juba, on the edge of Uganda and the Congo, near the source of the Nile.

It was this Sudan Railways steamer we boarded one January morning, after a bumpy night on the Cairo-Aswan sleeper. We stood on the dock at the little port of Shellal in the crowd of gesticulating Nubians, shouting porters, a handful of tourists and a few harassed-looking Egyptian customs officials in wrinkled white uniforms. Bob and Susan and I, with Laura Ann and David, were bound for Nubia at last.

"A pleasant trip for all of us," Bob had predicted. "Abu

Simbel's the last stop before Halfa, we'll wait at the temple and someone from the village can come pick us up. Two days and a night with nothing to do! What more could one ask? Riverboat travel is very relaxing."

Well, we can all use some of that, I thought, feeling suddenly tired although it was not yet noon. Bob, too, had a harried look. Only Susan appeared her normal calm self, holding Laura Ann by the hand and pointing out the exciting parts of the steamboat we were about to board.

"See, Laura Ann, that little white platform is the bridge, and the man with the gold shoulder tassels calling through the megaphone is the captain. Those are the lifesavers if we fall in the river."

"Fall in river?" Laura Ann pulled forward to the edge of the dock where the shining water dropped to unknown depths. Susan pulled her gently back.

"And there," cried Susan, "look at the big wheels in back turning, they'll push us up the river!"

The science of paddle steamers seemed beyond the ken of two-and-a-half-year-old Laura Ann, but Aunt Susan's enthusiastic tone was bound to rivet her attention. She stared in fascination at the big wheels at the rear of the boat which were, indeed, beginning to turn in the depths of the Nile.

It had been many months since Ford had given the money for the Nubian project, and Bob had been back and forth between village and city ever since. Davy's stubborn cold had developed into what the doctor called allergic asthma; he had sprouted various fungus infections and was losing weight; Dr. Hanna had begun treating him with cortisone. I was pregnant. For a time it had been give-and-take whether I would get to Nubia with the children at all. Finally, Dr. Hanna admitted that Nubia's dry climate might help Davy, since he was not improving in Cairo. Dr. Zaki had agreed that if there had been no trouble by the beginning of my fifth month, I could go to Nubia (provided

I did nothing foolish, he said firmly; I had laughed to myself at that). Yet here I was, already tired, not the proper beginning at all for such a long-anticipated and momentous journey.

"Oh!" I cried. "Oh, no!"

A huge wooden box teetering dangerously on the bent porter's back missed Laura Ann's head by a quarter of an inch. I turned away so she would not hear my involuntary cry, and found myself staring at a young tourist couple. Slender, smooth-skinned, they smiled and held hands, obviously honeymooners.

How gladly, for one moment, I would have traded in my ponderous self for the lighthearted slimness of the girl, would have exchanged my diaper bag and our other odd-shaped pieces of luggage (water filters, kerosene lanterns, cans of powdered milk, motorboat parts, sleeping bags) for the chic compactness of their single suitcase, their cameras on narrow straps.

"Where are the vaccination certificates, B.J.?" shouted Bob above the noise.

Oh, dear, where are they, I wondered. I passed Davy to Susan while I rummaged, in the midst of the crush, in my catchall purse.

Shellal, although still in Egypt proper, was the official border crossing point into the Sudan.

I'd expected the extensive baggage searches in progress; Bob had explained that much petty smuggling went on between the two countries. But I'd forgotten that health checks were made here, too. *Where* were those certificates, ah, at last.

We were scheduled to sail at eleven. It was now past noon and the customs officials were still combing through the bags and bundles piled on the dock. They were looking for something or someone, Bob whispered; he'd never been held up this long.

Our valises, I noticed, did not have the neatness of

those carefully sewn cloth bundles which the white-robed and turbaned Nubian fathers carried on their shoulders, leaving a hand free to hold a child. The little girls, wearing red-fringed head shawls over bright flannelette dresses, a warm red to set off their dark brown skin, stared with round eyes at Laura Ann's big baby doll, clutched to the bosom of her blue sweater. The boys were not so distinctive; they wore the casual *gullabiya* found throughout Egypt; only the design and color of their hand-made skullcaps showed they were Nubian.

Like me, many of the Nubian women carried a baby, but more resourceful than I, they also managed their luggage at the same time, big baskets of beige, purple and orange, which they balanced as easily as hats on their black-veiled heads.

"Maaaa! Maaa!"

The protesting bleat of hobbled goats and sheep tore through the din. People were beginning to board. Crates of clucking poultry were being passed into the hold, and sacks of sugar and tea marked with the sign of the government cooperative stores. Mailbags came last, precious mailbags containing money from fathers working in the cities to their families in rural Nubia.

Bells clanged, motors roared, the paddle wheels turned the river to froth. The customs search had apparently been fruitless, for the signal had been given to depart, and the gangplank was hoisted up. We were on our way to the little village of Erd-Moz, where Bob had begun his community study.

"How many people will be able to say, my dears," Bob joked to Susan and me, "that they lived when young beside the drowned temple of Abu Simbel?"

Laura Ann's blonde head did not quite touch the top of the ship's rail, where she stood with her father, watching the shoreline while we steamed slowly upriver. The granite boulders, which had seemed so picturesque in the changing light of Aswan, were bleak here, strewn high upon each bank and tumbling down crazily and seemingly haphazardly to the lapping river.

"I thought Nubia would be just sand," I ventured.

"Nonsense," said Bob crisply. "Why?"

"Well, it's a desert, isn't it?"

"Yes, but a mountainous desert, and it's all around you now. Over there to the west is the Sahara and to the east the mountains and valleys go on until you reach the Red Sea. There is no habitable land anywhere except this bit along the water's edge."

And that doesn't look like much, I thought to myself. In Cairo the strip of cultivated land was wide and lush; one was not as aware of the hovering presence of the desert. Here in northern Nubia the riverside vegetation had been covered by the waters of the first Aswan Dam, erected in 1933; all that remained was this waste of rock and coarse sand.

Earlier, we had passed a few villages where, Bob had said, the population consisted almost entirely of women and children; the men had gone to work in the cities.

"I can see why," said Susan. "How could *anything* grow here?"

There was obviously no source of livelihood left on the barren shores. The houses stood up among the rocks, small and bravely whitewashed but these, too, we had passed, for the landscape became more empty and silent with each mile we traveled south toward the Sudan.

Davy, in Susan's arms, strained upward toward a white bird with long, lazily drooping legs and wide wings. The bird swooped and rose, swooped and rose with the gentle undulations of the churning steamer.

"Davy'd like to fly, too, I think," said Susan.

Davy was still not walking. "He's weakened from the

months of coughing, remember," Dr. Hanna had said. "When he is strong enough to walk, he will walk."

"Is that a stork?" I asked.

"Could be," said Bob.

"Yes, a stork," volunteered a small bearded gentleman standing near us at the rail. "Gurf Hussein," he added, and pointed to a mound of broken stones in the distance. "Perhaps you would care to see?" and he offered us his binoculars.

He smiled in a friendly, one-passenger-to-another way. "What you see is the remains of the colonnaded court which stood before the rock temple."

I could not find anything too remarkable in the cluster of broken stones but the little man was awaiting a reply.

"So many antiquities in Nubia!" I remarked rather stupidly. "I had no idea of that. I suppose it's because Abu Simbel gets all the publicity."

David sat on the deck at my feet. He held onto the iron netting which fenced the rail, pulled himself upright for a moment, sank down wearily. Bob picked him up. Laura Ann and Susan began a game of hide-and-seek between the canvas deck chairs.

"Ah, dear madame," the little man spoke with a distinct French accent, "Nubia is a veritable treasure house of the past."

With a sweeping gesture he encompassed the tumbling white wake of the boat, the vast empty stretches of rock-strewn desert land on either side of us, the disappearing broken remains of the Gurf Hussein Temple. "Pharaonic, Greek, Roman, Byzantine, Islamic, the entire panorama of history before the Middle Ages has left its traces here."

"Really?"

"Yes, but all these records will soon be under water, lost to humanity forever!" he declaimed. "Because of one dam."

Bob handed Davy to me. "The whole country is full of antiquities," he pointed out. "Nubia is not unique."

"We do not know," admitted the little man, stroking his beard. "I, with some others, believe that if Nubia were to be explored thoroughly, our whole idea of the history of Egypt would change."

"The dam, though," put in Bob, "is very important if the Egyptian economy is to survive."

"Perhaps," the little man allowed.

We took turns looking through his proffered binoculars at the distant mountain, the changing landscape. Occasionally, clusters of palms and light fringes of grass appeared softening the harshness of the rocks. Was it because we were leaving that section of Nubia which had been flooded by the first dam? I turned to ask Bob, but he was listening to the Frenchman who, with gestures and little quick nods of his bearded profile, was delivering a brief lecture.

"The Nubian kings rose to power," I heard him say. "They had waited a long time." Battles, slaves, caravans of ivory and ebony and spices, gold mines opened, resumption of trade with Africa. "Greek soldiers actually wrote their names in the temple of Abu Simbel," he said, his voice rising. "That is how we know the campaign came so far south. You will see the stone."

"I have seen it," said Bob.

The little Frenchman paused, but not for long.

"And then we come to Juvenal."

"Juvenal, the Roman satirist?" I was jolted from my reverie. I had not pictured Juvenal, somehow, in this wild, remote land.

The Frenchman chuckled. "I can see, madame, that you indeed are not aware of the extent of Nubia's place in ancient history. Yes, Juvenal"—wagging a finger at me—"was banished to the most remote frontier of the Roman Empire, that is, to Syene, near Aswan, as punishment for his biting attacks on the Roman court. That is interesting, no?"

Laura Ann rushed toward us, and I was afraid she

would bump into the Frenchman with her hard little head. Whoops! She did.

He looked offended.

"Here, on this side, Laura Ann, run to Aunt Susan."

But our shipboard acquaintance, though shaken, had not been deflected from his course. "Romans, the Nubian Christian kingdoms and bishoprics . . ."

I watched Laura Ann out of the corner of my eye as she crept up on Susan from behind, barely able to contain her excitement.

"Byzantium!" declared the Frenchman, raising his hand as if to bless us.

I shifted Davy from one shoulder to the other. "Long after the fall of Constantinople, Byzantium flourished here in Nubia, madame."

Laura Ann ran, shrieking, toward us again. Short yellow hair flying, brown eyes sparkling, she was a sturdy, pretty child.

She smiled at the Frenchman.

He beamed. "You are taking your children, madame, to see the ancient temple of Abu Simbel?"

"Well, not exactly," I answered, looking about for Bob who had drifted away down the rail. Antiquities had never been his number-one nor even number-two interest in life.

"Excellent," replied Monsieur, as though I had not spoken, "for when this young lady is grown, she will be able to tell her children she saw the temple before the Nile covered it."

"I thought they were hoping to save it."

A wave of his small, compact hand. A scarab ring set in gold flashed in the sun. "Fantasy. Sheer fantasy," he answered. "This hydraulic lifting process, you mean? Hmph! One millimeter of a mistake, and the entire temple will lie in ruins. It is impossible!"

"That's not what John Wilson says."

Our French shipmate looked closely at me. "Your husband

is an archeologist? I don't believe I have had the pleasure . . ."

We exchanged handshakes and names. Gaudet. Archeologue. Fernea. Anthropologist.

Bob came back.

"I'm making an ethnological survey, yes, in a village with my wife and children . . . oh, the village houses are quite adequate for us. . . . We are planning a study of each of the three different linguistic areas of Nubia. . . . Actually, we know almost nothing of Nubian culture . . . yes, of course there is a culture. . . . No, I prefer to call the southern dialect Mahasi, not Fedicha. . . ."

Again I was only half listening, watching my son in the arms of Susan, Susan who had volunteered to spend her winter vacation helping me in the village. Dr. Zaki had said I could not go without help, and taking Fawzia was not the solution, Bob had decided. The Nubian women did not work for others and would have patronized poor Fawzia; this would have created tensions before we had even begun our work, Bob felt.

Now Susan had made Davy smile. And he smiled so seldom these days. He . . . what if he . . .

"Are we not scheduled to reach Abu Simbel tomorrow afternoon?" M. Gaudet was asking.

"If the weather stays calm," Bob answered. His mouth was tight with worry. I knew why. Would the boat from Erd-Moz be at the temple to meet us? Was the village house Bob had rented going to be adequate? What had Karim accomplished while Bob had come to Cairo to bring us all down? What would he, Bob, do should something go wrong suddenly in my pregnancy? Would Davy be all right?

I glanced away, but the little Frenchman stepped forward and touched Bob's arm.

"M'sieu," he said gently, "do not look like that. To see the mighty rock temples for the first time at sunset, in their natural setting, approaching slowly up the river, as the ancients must have done, on their way to the great religious celebrations—ah, this is a rare opportunity which you are providing for your family and Mademoiselle Susan, an opportunity . . ."

The gong sounded.

"An opportunity," went on M. Gaudet, undeterred, "that they will not forget!"

He snapped his binoculars into their worn leather case, patted Laura Ann on her shining head, and we went into lunch.

The calm weather held. By the next afternoon we had left behind the empty, rocky landscape of lower Nubia and had reached a different land. In the south the countryside had been less affected by the first dam's flooding. Grain grew green in square plots on the western bank, below the wooden arms of water wheels thrusting diagonally across the wide sky.

"Are those flowers I see painted on the walls of the houses?" asked Susan in amazement.

"Yes," answered Bob. "They are. The women decorate their houses. Some villages have only white designs, in other villages they use every color of the rainbow."

"And I," added M. Gaudet, joining in, "have even seen pillars on the verandas which the people must have copied from the temples. The ancients have had their influence," he said, stroking his beard thoughtfully, "incredible really, pillars made of mud brick in the old mold, and finely carved."

Near the clusters of low houses stood palm trees, their height and luxuriance a testimony to the long history of these southern villages. The afternoon sun poured light on the dark green palms, on the river and on the mountains of the eastern shore, mountains higher than any we had seen, lying like dark islands in yellow lakes of sand.

"*Voilà!*" M. Gaudet pointed toward the shadowed western bank where a great elbow of rock narrowed the upstream path of the Nile. "That, *mes amis,* is the backbone of the temple of Abu Simbel." He spoke the phrase like an incantation.

Upon the bridge of the riverboat a bell clanged shrilly. The tourists, cameras ready, were assembling at the rail.

"Slow—ly it comes now!" breathed M. Gaudet at my side.

"Mama!" Laura Ann, sensing the general air of excitement, jumped up and down beside me.

Davy, too, reached forward, in Susan's arms, again toward a bird skimming the shining path of water leading to the mountain ahead.

A bell shrilled again and the engines were cut. The ship seemed to pause momentarily in midstream before drifting slowly forward toward the mountain which was being transformed before our eyes. Giant sculptured heads, shoulders, knees emerged from the natural surface of the stone.

"Ramses II, Pharaoh, Beloved of Amun-Ra," chanted M. Gaudet, "King of Upper and Lower Egypt, Lord of the Two Lands, the Living Horus. It was he who immortalized himself thus four thousand years ago. Can it be imagined or encompassed by the mind, that?"

Susan and I were silent before the spectacle of the changing mountain, mighty stone figures taking shape as we approached, giant hands folded peaceably in stone laps, stone feet on the edge of the moving water.

"Great! Isn't it great?" The voice of the young honeymoon husband came to us down the rail.

"He, too, even senses it," M. Gaudet pointed out happily. "Would you like to view through the binoculars? Perhaps M'sieu Fernea . . ."

But Bob had moved away, to the far end of the rail where he peered intently toward shore, shading his eyes with both hands against the afternoon sun.

"He's looking for the Nubians who are coming from the

village to meet us," I explained. "Knowing my husband, he'll worry until we've actually reached the village."

I tried to laugh. It was not a success. What if the Nubians don't come, I asked myself. There was no rest house, no hotel at Abu Simbel, no telephone to the village. Where would we spend the night after the steamboat had gone on? In the temple?

"As many times as I have seen it, the temple, as many times," M. Gaudet said, "I am always moved by the natural splendor of the setting.

"The great builder, Ramses was called. The great egoist might be a better sobriquet, don't you think?" M. Gaudet was chattering on, more to himself than to us. "Imagine building not one, but four colossal statues of oneself, each more than sixty feet high!"

Susan chuckled politely. I watched Bob. He did not seem to have picked out any familiar figures yet.

"Queen Nefertari's temple, as you see, faces inward, toward that of her king and lord," M. Gaudet said. "A charming invention on the part of Ramses' architect."

"They're here, there's Mohammed," cried Bob, coming down the deck at a trot, his face momentarily cleared in relief. "See, there," and he pointed to four men on the sand, near the dock where the Department of Antiquities boat was moored, and next to it, a small felucca.

"We're going on in that felucca?" asked Susan. "I thought there was to be a motorboat."

"No," said Bob. "They couldn't run the boat without the part we picked up in Aswan. Never mind, it's all right. There's a wind blowing. We should easily reach Erd-Moz before dark.

"So, Monsieur Gaudet," said Bob, "it has been a pleasure."

M. Gaudet shook hands solemnly. "Since you are a non-archeologue," he said, "I would like your assessment of Abu Simbel."

"Impressive," said Bob, "but only a monument, when all is said and done."

"*Mon Dieu!*" ejaculated Monsieur Gaudet. "What is the world coming to when one of the great achievements of ancient civilization can be dismissed with the word that it is 'only a monument!'"

Bob stared. "What are we coming to, indeed," he returned, "when millions of dollars are spent to raise a monument of stone, and scarcely a fraction of that is spent on the thousands of people who must go the way of the monument!"

M. Gaudet stroked his beard a moment. "It is a point of view, I grant you," he allowed with a smile. "A point of view. *Au revoir.*" He patted Laura Ann on the head.

"*Au revoir.*"

We crossed the gangplank onto the sand, and in the shade of the yellow-blossomed acacia tree between the king's temple and the queen's temple, we were introduced to the four Nubian gentlemen: Abdul Majid, the village schoolteacher; Saleh, a retired, middle-aged man from whom Bob was renting a house; Abdou, Saleh's one-legged brother; and Mohammed, young, handsome, and, Bob said lightly, in his obvious pleasure at seeing them all again, "Mohammed is the best tambura player and the most famous duck hunter in the whole Abu Simbel area."

The colossal sandstone figures of Ramses Pharaoh glared white in the brilliant sun, almost as white as the towering turbans and flowing *gullabiyas* of our dignified Nubian escorts, who were gaily greeting the children.

"*Ya,* Daoud!"

"Lor-Ann!"

Mohammed picked up Laura Ann first; she squealed with delight. Then he threw David up in the air and tossed him to his father while I held my breath.

In the background I could hear the resident guide beginning his piece. "The edifice, ladies and gentlemen, is

181 feet long, carved directly into the living rock. There are eight main chambers, some as high as . . ."

Bob caught me looking wistfully after the tourists filing into the temple.

"Come on, B.J.," he said. "We'll come back and look at Abu Simbel later, when we can have it all to ourselves."

Sails billowed out on the felucca from Erd-Moz. It looked very small beside the colossal temple cut out of the towering mountain. Children and bags were passed hand to hand, and I climbed, after Susan, unsteadily into the swaying boat. Waves rocked us from side to side. Davy buried his face in my shoulder. Susan held onto squirming Laura Ann, Bob gripped the rudder, and Mohammed steadied the yard. The two small boys who had helped push off stared at us in a rather friendly, curious way, but the Nubian men sat impassively in the stern, their hands placed carefully and formally upon their knees, like the statues of Ramses II, Beloved of Amun-Ra.

We crossed the choppy water to the center of the Nile, Mohammed and Bob tacking skillfully until our sails caught the evening breeze blowing from Egypt south to the Sudan.

"We should make it to Erd-Moz in record time with this wind," shouted Bob.

He was actually smiling.

The sky, clear and wide and uncluttered as far as I could see around and before us, was pale and luminous. The river—Pop! A strategic button on my woolen maternity jumper broke from its moorings and clattered to the sloshing bottom of the felucca.

The Nubian men opened their eyes, Bob tried not to notice, and Laura Ann, escaping from Susan's grasp, retrieved the button.

"See, Mama!" She was very proud of herself, and I tried to smile, sitting there, annoyed, holding that button foolishly in my hand, examining with great care the beveled edge, the four holes with the bit of wet thread hanging from them.

Here we were, in a romantic lateen-sailed felucca on the
Upper Nile, leaving behind the world-famous temple of
Abu Simbel, and the only emotion I seemed able to summon
was irritation at the fates for loosening the thread on a
single, small button! What was the matter with me? I took a
deep breath, guided Laura Ann across the watery boat
bottom to Susan, and shifted Davy forward on my lap,
using him as a shield while I covered that gap across my
middle with a large safety pin.

"Stop *wiggling!*" I whispered.

"Ah—ooooooooo!" My human shield let out a blood-cur-
dling yell.

He had shifted at the wrong moment. I knew it had hurt
because I had gotten the pin full in the finger.

"Davy!" Susan took him, and I rummaged, cursing, in the
purse for a handkerchief, a scarf, anything to wrap around
my bleeding finger. But when I caught sight of Bob, I had
a mad impulse to laugh. For there he sat, looking steadily
out at the palm trees, the remote dark mountains, the water
reflecting that glorious luminous sky, trying, it appeared, to
establish a mood of patient tolerance that would get
him through the last of this journey. Why, that stiffly
dignified back seemed to ask, had he *ever* urged me to
come down to Nubia, a pregnant mama so clumsy she
allowed her son to sit down on the point of a safety pin in
the middle of the Nile? Why, indeed? I was beginning to
wonder myself. At least nothing *else* can happen, that stiff
back seemed also to convey, and I agreed.

We were wrong. The brisk wind died and we were
becalmed. Becalmed is not quite what *we* were; the boat
was becalmed, but the children were restless and noisy.
They were hungry; it was hours now since lunch, and our
stores of biscuits long since finished. I sensed both Davy
and Laura Ann were working up to a good cross cry, and
I did not really blame them, while we waited and waited

for the flapping sails to be furled, the oars to be fitted in the oarlocks, the rowing to begin.

The sun was sinking, the sky was reddening slowly. I rummaged in my purse, but alas, not even a dusty date could be found in its depths. Susan rescued us all by producing lumps of sugar from her pocketbook and popping them in the children's mouths as we slowly forged ahead on the still river.

"Hobby of mine," she announced briskly, with a professional smile. "Collecting sugar, I mean."

The marvelous quiet produced by those paper twists of sugar (packets marked Sudan Railways, Nile Hilton, Semiramis Hotel) was broken only by the creak of the locks, the steady splash and drip of water from the oars and Bob's conversation with Saleh.

"Has the house been cleaned?"

"Yes."

"Is the bed ready, that I ordered for the baby, and the chairs?"

"Yes, Karim has arranged everything."

Six or seven sugar lumps later, we tied up at a little stone wall built into the riverbank where Karim waved and some children waited for us, shouting and calling, "*Ahlan! Ahlan! Ahlan wusahlan!*"

"Where's the house?" I looked toward a grove of palm trees into which our bundles and bags seemed to be disappearing, each in the hand of a different half-grown Nubian boy.

"We have a little walk," said Bob heartily. "Up to the dune ridge."

"UP?" I remembered Dr. Zaki's last warning, "Promise me you won't try to climb any hills," and my blissfully ignorant reply, "Oh, there aren't any hills in Nubia, only sand."

Bob must have been thinking the same thing, for he

added quickly, "You don't have to do it in one sprint. Go up slowly, zigzag."

Laura Ann, delighted to be out of the confines of the boat, skipped along the narrow mud footpath, jumping over the tiny feeder canals with Susan's help, the canals cut from the riverbank which watered the grove of date palms, the small orchard of fruit trees and the grain growing in every inch of free soil between. Davy jogged happily ahead in Karim's arms.

Several Nubian girls passed me, balancing on their heads shiny kerosene cans filled to the brim with river water. One of them was pregnant. They were not going up, zigzag, like me, they were heading straight up, up the dune to the row of long, low mud-brick houses on the topmost ridge above. I knew that I did not have the strength to do that, even without a heavy can of water on my head, and I felt again that surge of unreasoning weariness that had come over me on the dock at Aswan. Was I going to have to climb up and down this hill every day?

Maybe Dr. Zaki was right, and I shouldn't have tried to come. What if I turned out to be more trouble than I was worth? That would hardly speed the progress of Bob's work. For the first time, I felt apprehensive and also very sorry for myself. Stop it, I told myself, watching the straight-backed Nubian girls mounting easily the hill before me. Stop it and start walking. You wanted to come. You know it will be worth it.

"You all right, B.J.?" Susan called.

"Yes, just want to look at the view."

Women had assembled at the top of the dune. They sat in front of their houses, or stood, eyes shaded against the sunset glare, to watch my slow ascent. Bob had been in the village off and on for nearly five months; he had told me the men as well as the women were eager to look over his family. I needed a moment, not only to catch my breath, but to compose myself before the introductions began, to the Nubian ladies I would live among during the coming months.

The table-topped mountains on the eastern shore were clearly outlined against the bronze sky. The sand had darkened. But the river was still alight, and it turned southward in a shining arc around the mountain where the architect of Ramses II had declared to the workmen that here, just here, in that fold of hills, the temple of Abu Simbel would be carved out of the solid rock. It was a magnificent scene, the grandeur of the natural landscape complemented by the inspiration and workmanship of the architect and the sculptor, and while I absorbed its beauty and harmony, I tried to quiet the turbulence in my mind, the pounding of my tired heart.

"Come *on!*" called Bob.

The seated women rose as I reached the last ridge of dunes. They came forward in their long, black, full-sleeved garments, trains dragging over the sand behind them like court dresses. They smiled, flashing teeth in dark faces, and shook hands, some of the older women wrapping their hands in their veils before clasping mine. They nodded at Susan, pinched Davy's cheeks, stared at Laura Ann, as curiously as she stared at them, and gazed with undisguised interest at my safety-pin-covered bulging stomach, my black tights and loafers, my uncovered brown hair.

"*Mascagna!*" cried several of the women together.

"It's a Nubian welcome," said Bob, who was watching carefully, I noticed, the impression his family was making.

With several Nubian men, he stood to one side, not exactly mixing with the women but not exactly excluded from their presence, either. This was apparently going to be a different situation than in Iraq, where the village men and women were socially segregated.

"The women speak Arabic less than their husbands, but you can reply in Arabic. Most of them will understand," he prompted.

I did, and that was the language in which we conversed for the rest of my stay in Erd-Moz.

"Come and see your house!" offered a young woman. She was very pretty and she carried on her hip a son almost the same size as Davy.

"*Your* house!" echoed another woman sarcastically, an older woman with buck teeth in a thin, middle-aged face. "Listen to her!" she mocked the younger. "Come and see the part of *our* house which we are renting to you," she announced ungraciously to me.

"I will take them in," said Saleh.

He led us across the colonnaded veranda to a heavy door where a design in brass nails surrounded the carved wooden lock. Three flowered china plates had been unexpectedly set into the lintel above the door.

"Is that Meissen?" asked Susan. "And why is it above the door?"

"It's symbolic," answered Karim, who seemed glad to be our tour guide in Nubia, more at ease here than he was in the Center at the American University in Cairo. "The plates above the door mean the man of the house is alive, Susan. If Saleh were to die tomorrow, his women would break the plates."

The house was large and well laid out, a series of open spaces surrounded with rooms, some entirely enclosed, some partially shaded by half roofs. The floors were of sand, the roof beams were of palm wood, and a paved walkway circled the central court, which was wide and open to the sky.

"We have camp cots in our room," said Bob. "Surprisingly comfortable. Susan and Laura Ann have the two wooden bedsteads in this room. And how do you like the crib I had made for Davy? Interesting process. They split the palm wood into different widths, and sort of weave it together in various patterns."

So little light seeped into the windowless children's bedroom (cooler in summer that way, fewer drafts in winter,

Bob explained) that I could scarcely see the crib, but it appeared adequate.

"A nice house, don't you think so?" Bob ventured.

It *was* a nice house. Everything seemed neat, orderly and well-planned, though obviously not planned for us, but for some other mode of living with which we were not at all familiar. Different things took place in these houses, different schedules had been organized. A clay water jar suspended in a wooden frame had a tight wooden lid to keep out the flies, a drip pan beneath it to catch the evaporating moisture. Several squat storage jars the size of bushel baskets, of clay and painted in different colors, lined a shaded wall. A container of water with a spigot and basin stood on a small table beside the porcelain water filter, which I recognized as part of the expedition gear. These objects, with our beds, comprised the sum total of the house's furniture.

The last rays of sun shining through the woven, rush half roofs created pleasing patterns of shadow on the floor of the court, but there was little other decoration to be seen. Three kerosene lanterns hung on nails, a tin cup hung above the water jar.

"Wait till you see the *diwani,* though," said Karim. "The bride's room really. The bride and groom sleep together for the first time in the little bedroom there, and then they come into the *diwani* in the morning to receive guests and presents and entertainment, and to eat their special wedding breakfast."

At the entrance to the *diwani* we stood in silence for a moment.

"But it's quite beautiful!" exclaimed Susan in surprise.

"Why are you so surprised?" returned Karim. "The Nubians have very good taste."

I looked at him. For an Egyptian city boy to make such a remark about his peasant countrymen was rather startling, but Karim was obviously sincere.

What limited resources were available to the Nubian

housewife with a flair for interior decoration had been used here in ingenious ways that would never have occurred to me. The family's collection of reed plates, locally woven of palm fiber dyed in various hues, had been hung at eye level in a neat row, rather like an ornate wallpaper border on the walls, walls whose smooth matt gray mud surface provided an ideal background for the display of design and color.

"But aren't those the plates they clean the grain from the chaff with?" I asked. Bob had mentioned noticing these plates, which I had seen used similarly in Iraq.

Karim smiled. "Oh, they have plain ones for work," he said. "These are just to be looked at for pleasure."

The palm fiber strips, in orange and purple or wine and natural pale-straw colors, had been used to weave a whole series of variations in design on the plates: whorls and diagonals, circles and squares, and below the plates, on the mud-paved floor, reed mats of the same colors had been laid. From the beams in the ceiling were suspended, like a series of chandeliers, scores of painted bowls and china plates, each nested in a swing of plaited leather. The mock chandeliers were decorated with streamers of the same plaited leather, ornamented with clusters of white shells. Wind stirred the shells to a mild clacking, reminding me of the oriental wind chimes which my aunt had hung in her Chicago garden.

"Where do we bathe?" inquired Susan.

"Oh, you can bring a couple of buckets of water into the *diwani* and lock the door. Nice ambiance in that room for baths, eh, Karim?"

Karim and Bob smiled at each other obliquely but Susan, used to a shower a day, did not appear amused. She did not comment, however.

The total effect of my rented Nubian house (except for the riot of color in the *diwani*) was austere, even bare, but pleasing. In another mood, say that of the slim tourist bride on the steamboat, I would have been enthusiastic about the simplicity and functionalism of the basic design. But foremost in my mind now was not design, but the need to establish my own routine in this alien place. Boiling water to mix with powdered milk, mashing baby food, washing diapers, where were these tasks to be accomplished? The shells clacked softly once more above me, the sound was soothing; surely something could be arranged. Put a table there, and . . .

"Where do you sit down?"

Bob smiled. "On mats, of course, on the floor just as you saw in the *diwani*. There are some rolled up in the bedrooms. You can bring them out when you like. The women sweep them off and roll them up to keep them clean."

"You eat and type and so on, on the *mats?*" I contemplated getting my ponderous self up and down from the sandy floor forty times a day; my natural childbirth exercises seemed built into this situation; I decided I would worry about them no longer.

Bob smiled once more, to himself. "I was putting you on, B.J. We do have a table and chairs in the *mendara*, the guest room. It has its own separate entrance from outside, so the house is more or less private for you and Susan and the children. Karim sleeps in the *mendara* and only comes here to wash his face and go to the toilet."

I looked around for some evidence of such a facility, but found none.

"The Nubians are very clever about everything," said Bob.

He took me to the innermost court, where a long open stairway led up to a closed door on the brink of the roof.

"*Voilà*, as our friend M. Gaudet would say," Bob said. "Right up at the top of the stairs. Open to the air, but shut off from the rest of the house. Chilly at night, but very sanitary."

A cold wind swept through the almost empty rooms. I

shivered. M. Gaudet. Had it really been only this afternoon that he had entertained us with his gentle, courtly lectures about ancient Egypt? It seemed in another age, another world. Darkness was almost upon us; it lay in pools of shadow in the central courtyard, where Davy and Laura Ann played, happy to find at the end of the long trip the surprise of a built-in sandbox.

"Come into the *mendara*. Susan and I have set the table." Karim stood at the door with the lamps, the Coleman hissing white, the kerosene lanterns flickering yellow.

Saleh brought in a tureen of vegetables and meat. The steam rose upward from the aluminum camp table to the dark beams of the ceiling, and we ate the thick soup gratefully, eagerly.

It had been years since I had eaten by lamplight. The children felt the strangeness, too; they clung tightly.

"Where's house, Mama?" asked Laura Ann, thinking, I was sure, of our warm, electrically lighted apartment in Cairo, which seemed thousands of miles from this little oasis where we ate soup by lantern light and Karim fiddled with the tape recorder, finally triumphantly producing a faint recording of a Bach double piano concerto.

"Our house is still there in Cairo, but we're going to stay here for a while, with Baba," I explained.

She slurped a little soup. Her eyes drooped.

"Where's my bed, Mama?" she asked, and her lip quivered.

Bob went out suddenly and came back with suitcases. Susan and I put on the children's sleepers, went through the motions of washing hands and faces in half a basin of cold water, and carried them, wrapped in blankets to the bedroom, Davy snuffling and sneezing, Laura Ann almost asleep.

> "I gave my love a cherry
> without a stone."

I went through the lullaby ritual and covered the children with all their blankets against the cold which grew with the darkness.

Bob was waiting in the court with a lantern. "I'll stay here," I said.

"You don't need to, B.J. Saleh's women sleep just the other side of the wall and can hear every breath the children draw. We can, too, for that matter, since there's little intervening noise. Come have some tea. It will warm you up."

We stood on the veranda for a moment. The night sky lay above the river and the mountains like a vast splendid coverlet, the stars so thick I could scarcely distinguish one from another in the blaze of light.

"I'm awfully glad you're here, but it won't be easy, you know," said Bob in a worried undertone, the timbre of his voice at odd variance with the serenity of the sky and the river, the stillness of the sleeping village, dark except for faint flickers of lantern light from a house down the hill, silent except for a peeping of Bach from Karim's tape recorder, a bawling of a calf for its mother.

"I knew that before I came."

Susan coughed from behind the closed shutters of the *mendara*.

"There's a doctor at the temple and one at Benha. You must tell me if you feel bad, have strange pains or anything."

"I will."

"The boat stops at Abu Simbel twice a week, and you should plan on leaving anytime you want to, any time the going seems too much. I want you to share Nubia with me; it is a beautiful place, but I don't want you down here if it will damage your health or Davy's."

"Yes," I said, and we went in and sat in the *mendara*, listening to the Bach on Karim's tape until sleep reached us.

CHAPTER 9

THE VILLAGE OF ERD-MOZ

The houses in Erd-Moz commanded their fine view of the river and the mountains, not by chance, but by design. Erd-Moz was a planned village in the ideal sense of the word, planned by the occupants, each house designed and constructed by its owner, with the help of local mud-brick masons and wood carvers.

Half a century ago Erd-Moz had been a compact cluster of smaller houses closer to the shore of the Nile, in the midst of palm groves and strips of the cultivated land. The villagers traveled up to the hills only to look for fuel, to graze their goats and sheep on the tender camel's-thorn, to bury their dead under piles of the flinty stones which littered the mountains behind the dunes.

"My great-grandmother did not have to go so far for water," I was told by Khadija, the young and beautiful niece of our landlord Saleh. "Our people were frightened of these hills then."

Moving the village to high ground had taken place long before Khadija was born, in 1900, after the first Aswan Dam flooded land in northern Nubia. The southern area near Abu Simbel had been scarcely touched by the waters, but Khadija's ancestors had been prudent men.

"If we have to move now, we may have to move again," they reasoned. "Who knows what the British will do to the river next?"

Thus the village was laid out on the highest ridge of

dunes, and in 1933 when the first dam was heightened for
the third time, the people of Erd-Moz received cash com-
pensation for their flooded land. With this money added to
their average annual income (which was probably not more
than $250), they built larger and more elaborate houses.
The women plastered the walkways smooth with mud,
painted walls, doors and shutters with designs in bright
colors; they decorated the lintels of their doorways with
china plates set into the plaster, those dainty plates that
would be smashed if the man of the house were to die.

Compared to the French-Oriental villas of Cairo, Nubian
houses like the one in which we were living were simple
dwellings. But compared to the huts in the Delta where
lived fellaheen of similar income and status, or even to the
average two-bedroom California ranch house, these Nileside
homes were mansions—spacious and neat, well arranged
for comfort in both summer heat and winter cold. A large
central courtyard, surrounded by bedrooms, a *diwani*, or
bride's room, a *mendara*, or guest room, a storage room, a
summer kitchen and a winter kitchen, a separate toilet room,
an outside fenced shelter for the animals: These were basic
features of almost every house in Erd-Moz. Inner courts,
covered walkways and patios, wide porches with benches
upon which one could sit and admire the view—these were
added, depending on the needs of the family, the size of its
income.

We lived in half of a semidetached dwelling, which Saleh
had designed to keep his two wives content in separate
domains and at the smallest possible expense (most men had
settled their wives in separate homes, often even in separate
villages, which raised the cost considerably). I remembered
buck-toothed Dahiba's ungracious welcome. Since she was
the displaced wife, it was hardly surprising that she was the
least friendly of the occupants of Saleh's house: Hanim Ali
and Dahiba, his wives; Khadija and Naima, his nieces; and
Abdul Nasr, Khadija's infant son. Hanim Ali and Dahiba

were childless, but they lavished affection on Abdul Nasr, whose father worked in Khartoum. Khadija and Naima's own father was also reportedly in the Sudan. A disgraced younger brother of Saleh's, he had disappeared after being accused of some crime.

"We heard your son coughing all night long," Khadija reported two or three mornings after our arrival. "Did he get that awful cold on the express boat?"

"He was sick before we came."

I sat on a straw mat beside the sunny courtyard wall. Khadija offered me tea while Davy's lunch cooked and drinking water boiled (we had no stove in our house). David and Khadija's son, Abdul Nasr, had been born the same week, we discovered.

"Was yours a difficult labor?" she asked.

"Not too bad, but the pregnancy was terrible."

"So was mine; my labor was awful too, it was my first child," confided Khadija. "Fourteen hours."

Abdul Nasr, a wiry baby with bright eyes, wore a short cotton *gullabiya* and a sweater; he tottered barefoot about the court on sturdy legs. But Davy, full of vitamins and antibiotics and cortisone, shielded from drafts by pants, sweater, shirt, socks and shoes, could not even crawl after Abdul Nasr. He tried, but in a moment, wheezing and out of breath, he settled for sitting instead.

"My boy hardly ever gets colds," said Khadija, "but when he does, I give him date honey. Would you like some? We make it from our own dates."

"Thank you, Khadija, I'll try it."

Naima had finished washing all the breakfast dishes, including ours, and had laid them out to dry on a bare wooden bedstead set in the sun; she was now sweeping the bedrooms. Dahiba was squatting some distance away, rinsing clothes in a large flat pan of water. Hanim Ali, on the mat with us, was packing Saleh's water pipe with honey, tobacco and *kamanja*, the local species of hemp or marijuana, tamping the fragrant mixture down into the narrow-necked glass bottle, its sides painted with flowers.

"The pinch of *kamanja* with the honey gives a pleasant smoke," said Hanim Ali, smiling under hennaed hair, which she had arranged in two coquettish wings on her forehead below her black head scarf. As was proper for a woman past the age of childbearing she wore no gold necklaces and bracelets, but on her brown fingers, twisted with work and age, were a number of curious rings, dull silver, brass, set with rough-cut stones of turquoise, carnelian, onyx. I asked about them, but she pretended she had not heard me. Many weeks later Khadija told me they were sacred rings, magic rings, and Hanim Ali never discussed them, for fear of dispelling their occult powers.

Khadija sewed while chatting with me and keeping an eye on her son's perambulations around the court, here for a bit of bread from Naima, there for a kiss from Dahiba, back to sit with Davy and play with a duck pull toy. She was making a dress for herself, a flower-printed cotton to wear under the sheer black *gargara*, or overdress, that was standard southern Nubian garb.

"They say the sleeves will be shorter this year," remarked Khadija. "The fullness will be taken up by more tucking here," and she demonstrated on a sleeve of her own *gargara*, a garment which seemed to me highly impractical for life in Erd-Moz, a wide, full dress with a train that gathered dust and bits of straw when one walked in the sand, and sleeves so wide they had to be folded back when one cooked over an open fire.

"It is lovely, the *gargara*," went on Khadija, "but hard to keep clean."

The garment, if impractical, was exceedingly feminine.

I had already noticed men turning to watch the way a woman walked down the village street, a shining kerosene can of water balanced on her graceful head, the *gargara* trailing behind her like a black peignoir upon the golden sand.

The train, we were told, erased the women's footprints as they walked and thus kept secret their indiscretions.

"Your vegetables are going to burn," said Dahiba pointedly from her laundry position near the stove.

I pulled myself up off the mat, took the pot off the stove and sat down again with the pureer. Every meal which Davy ate had to be prepared immediately beforehand, since our kerosene refrigerator, imported and shipped to Nubia at so much trouble and expense, worked only erratically. I was not very efficient with the pureer, and I could tell by the side glances from Saleh's women that they thought so, too. I'm sure I presented a wan, incomprehensible picture to them. After all, what was the matter with me except pregnancy? And did I not have Saleh to cook most of my meals, Naima to bring water from the river, a woman to wash clothes for me?

Fortunately, the ladies seemed inclined to take a charitable view.

"You're tired, I think," said Hanim Ali. She propped her hand covered with those odd rings under her chin and gave me a look.

"Yes," I answered, "the trip, the pregnancy." I did not add, squatting, sitting, bending, walking in sand, trying to impose our own routines, our ways of living upon this new and strange environment. Baths, electricity, running hot water, a pharmacy around the corner, a doctor at the other end of the telephone, how long had I taken these things for granted? I knew rationally that they were not vital; the children would survive without a daily bath, we had plenty of medicine, there was a doctor about an hour away by boat (if the motors were working), boiling the drinking water purified it, obviously, and a little diarrhea was not a disaster. It did not seem to me that during our years in Iraq, either Bob or I had been so fussy about the details of our daily lives, but then, the children's presence changed things. The rational point of view faded before the awful "If."

"Pray to God," Hanim Ali was saying to me, glancing at Davy involuntarily as she spoke. She inserted Saleh's pipe into the painted glass bottle full of honey and tobacco, turning it and straightening it with a good wifely gesture, then placing the pipe at the edge of the reed mat where Saleh would sit and smoke after lunch. "Pray to God," she repeated. "God knows best."

She rose, lightly and easily though she must have been fifty, while I stumbled up from my squatting position, feeling a clumsy fool; the women watched without comment.

"Pray to God you carry a stronger child within you," concluded Hanim Ali and went into the kitchen to start a fire for the daily bread baking.

At lunch, Bob told me to visit elsewhere.

"Saleh's family is not typical," he said, "and our relationship with them is complicated."

"Why?"

"We are renting part of their house. The women perform services for us, bringing water and so on. You know the women don't like that, they aren't supposed to work for other people, they don't want other people to know."

"What about the woman who washes our clothes?"

"Saleh says her husband is the descendant of a slave, and that family has never had much pride. But, anyhow, it's better to make friends outside. Dahiba is already annoyed to be jolted out of her house, you can see that. Go to Abdulla's house. His mother is the midwife."

"The midwife?" My voice came out higher than intended, and Bob's face tightened.

"A professional visit you have in mind yet?" said Susan lightly.

Bob laughed, and I silently thanked Susan. She had decided, I realized, and rightly, that her role in Erd-Moz was not only to help me with the children but to ease, with wit, the atmosphere of worry and fear within which Bob and I were operating. Defusing a potentially explosive conversation was one way, and she was very good at it.

"Not exactly," he answered, with an amused glance at me. "That is, it might be interesting, but I doubt that B.J. would agree. Anyhow . . . oh, I don't care. Go to the schoolteacher's, Abdul Majid's, or to Mohammed's. He's our best friend here, and he'll be very hurt if you don't appear soon at his house so his wife can say you've come. I don't know much about his womenfolk, though I feel quite close to Mohammed, curious."

"You didn't know much about the women in Iraq either," I pointed out, "at least from their men."

"It's a bit different here, I think," mused Bob, "but I don't really know. That's why I want you to visit and see."

"The women are more independent than I expected," put in Karim, "maybe because the men are often away and then they have to take charge of the farming, even. They certainly seem to control the purse strings."

"Susan, you choose. Where shall we go this afternoon?"

"Well," confessed Susan, "when Laura Ann and I were looking at the sheep this morning, a woman invited us to tea. Her name is Sherifa and she lives down the hill a bit."

"The schoolteacher," prompted Karim. "Abdul Majid."

Six ladies had assembled in Abdul Majid's spotless and well-furnished guest room (sofa, table covered with an embroidered cloth, chairs, cushion, photos and calendars lining the mud-brick walls). They had come to get a look at us, and they sat comfortably, cross-legged on a mat, all in proper black *gargaras* over printed cotton, their long, sheer head scarves wound about their heads and shoulders, trailing yards behind. It was Susan and Laura Ann and me, David in arms and sniveling and wheezing, who sat stiffly upright on the sofa with Sherifa's sister, Sitta. Sherifa, after greeting us at the door, had departed, presumably to make the tea and to satisfy the needs of her three toddlers, which were more immediate than ours.

Six pairs of adult eyes and those of several uncounted children, in arms or on laps, stared at us; the eyes were bright with interest and the throats and ears and wrists and ankles were bright with the gleam of gold and silver. Gold earrings at the tops and bottoms of the ears, long necklaces of round gold pieces, of agate and silver beads, silver or bright plastic bracelets, a few heavy silver ankle bracelets. Against the somber black gowns, the shapes and colors of the varied jewelry looked, as the fashion magazines say, exactly right.

The women's brown feet were bare, for were they not sitting on a mat inside a clean house? Beside the door stood a row of plastic shoes, like shower shoes, in glorious shades of orange, turquoise, pink and green. I smiled in a patronizing way at the plastic shoes that first day, but I lived to regret that smile. Plastic shoes were excellent for walking in the sand (and so easy to empty out); they wore like iron and all they needed was a dip in water to look as bright and clean as the day they'd been bought. I would have liked a pair myself.

"You have come to Nubia for your son's health?" inquired a middle-aged lady. Scarification marks, like the traceries of a fine pencil, ran high up her brown cheekbones.

Startled by the question, I mumbled something about the dry climate.

"Far better than Cairo, certainly," said another. She held a tiny baby, swaddled in flannelette. "There you breathe dirt from the factories and dirt from so many people. Here the air is clean. . . . I am so glad I came back to deliver my baby *at home*."

"When I think of Cairo—"

"That awful city—"

"It's not awful, they have cinemas, electricity—"

"Electricity!" sniffed the woman with the scarification marks. "What is that? They charge for it, don't they? And you pay for every date, every grain of sand. You have to buy sand little by little, like fruit. Here *some* things are free."

The speed of the conversation made it hard to follow. The women spoke in Arabic and in their own dialect alternately, translating back and forth for each other, and it was soon apparent that unless we entered in, the conversation would go on without us.

"You've been to Cairo?" Susan broke in.

The young woman with the baby laughed. "Have I been to Cairo?" she asked the group mockingly. "Yes," she said to Susan, "five times I have been and five times my husband has tried to persuade me to stay and live there. But I said no. Those apartments in Bab el Loukh! Phew!" She held her nose. "You can scrub and scrub those toilets, they never get clean. Where do you and your cousin live in Cairo?"

"Garden City."

The middle-aged lady with the scarification marks, the widow Fatooma, nodded her head. "Well, that's a pleasant enough quarter. I lived there when I was a child. My father was a *boab*. Is the *ganeena* as clean as it used to be?"

At this juncture, Sherifa rustled in with the tea tray, and Sitta served us, from rose-sprigged bone china cups, the best tea I had tasted for months.

"Where did you get the tea?" Susan asked. "It's excellent."

"It's English tea from the Sudan."

"Sudan? But how do you get it through the Egyptian customs?"

The women laughed and nudged each other, white teeth flashing in the dark faces, gold and silver clinking and gleaming against the black *gargaras*.

"We have ways," said Sitta, one of those bandbox women

who always look as if their clothes had been freshly pressed five minutes before, "ways and means."

"She means smugglers," I said to Susan in English. "There's quite a bit of border trade in consumer goods, Bob says."

At the sound of the English, a slight hush fell, and I could tell from the dark eyes that they realized we had understood.

"Ali should be here next week to take orders," said the widow.

"We'll let you know when he comes."

"He also has good needles and German paring knives and very light, warm English blankets."

Laura Ann was playing in the court with Sherifa's children, but Davy still sat on my lap, reaching for this, reaching for that, whining a little, wheezing a little. The poor child was constantly uncomfortable, hence never content.

"Why don't you let your children drink tea?" our hostess Sherifa asked. "Tea would be good for your son's cough."

How did they know I didn't give the children tea?

"Give him some now, it will calm him."

Sitta, without waiting for my answer, half filled a cup with tea, stirred in milk, sugar, blew on the mixture to cool it and offered it to Davy, who, with her gentle, efficient help, slurped it up eagerly, down to the last drop.

The ladies were delighted.

"You see?" said Sherifa. "He likes it."

"What did we tell you?"

"It will help him, you'll see."

I looked around the friendly group, for they were friendly, informal, kind ladies, all of them.

"What else should I do to help him?" I asked.

They all broke into speech at once.

"Give him cumin seed tea."

"Mastica will stop the cough."

"Rub his chest with oil and put newspaper on his back and chest when he sleeps."

"Keep his head wrapped up at night."

"Dress him all in flannelette or all wool, but not half and half, like he is now."

I looked startled at the wool sweater, the corduroy overalls. Maybe they thought the corduroy was flannelette?

"Otherwise he will chill," they finished.

But in this rush of suggestions, Sitta had remained watchful and silent.

"I am surprised that you ask us," she said. "After all, you can take him to doctors in Cairo and get him good medicine."

"I have, but it hasn't helped."

And feeling suddenly that I was not up to a question-and-answer session on Davy's condition and prospects, I stood up, making excuses about the small tasks that had to be done before darkness came.

Sitta and Sherifa saw us to the door, Sherifa apologizing for the untidy courtyard, her children rushing about with Laura Ann, chickens scratching in the sand, lines of laundry drying, fuel half stacked into several piles, tea dishes to be washed.

"There is no one here but me," she said. "Sitta lives near the temple of Abu Simbel. She is here to help me today because you came."

"Your husband works at the temple?" Susan asked Sitta.

"No, he is in London."

"LONDON?" repeated Susan in astonishment.

"Yes," said Sitta, and drew herself up, a bit proudly, in those pristine ironed-looking clothes. "He is a chauffeur for the Egyptian Embassy in England. I went with him to Tunis and Damascus, but London was too far. Besides, I wanted the children to go to school here in Nubia, with their own people."

"Didn't you like Damascus and Tunis?" I asked.

Sitta sighed. "Oh yes, Damascus is beautiful, and I made many friends in Tunis. But—well," she turned to me, "don't you ever miss your family and your country of America?"

"Yes, I do."

"That is how I felt. London might be nice, but here I have my own house, my own date trees; my husband will come in summer. He sent us some English books for the children. Perhaps you and your cousin could come to my house one day and read the English to us? The children will study English in school when we go to Kom Ombo."

"Thank you, Sitta. I would love to," I answered.

The distance between London and the tiny village beside the temple of Abu Simbel seemed immeasurably great by almost any standard, distance, culture, technology, language, yet Sitta found it quite natural that her husband should be there now but would return in the summer, bringing, no doubt, a tin of good Darjeeling tea and British woolens from Marks and Spencer for all the family. She was secure in her knowledge of her place in the world, secure like my friends in a small Iraqi village had been. But she had traveled, as they had not, and she had met and observed many kinds of people, as they had not.

Yet, exposure to other ways does not always change one's view of the world. Often it serves to strengthen one's views. Sitta was a perfect example of something Bob had noted about the Nubians in the few months he had lived among them. They, like Sitta, had been observant in new surroundings and had adopted some things they liked, but had maintained their own values.

Susan interrupted my dune-climbing reverie home. "What did Sherifa press into your hand?"

"Tea," I replied. "I protested, but she said it was English tea for Davy."

"Very nice of her. They were all very nice, I thought. Sitta was quite remarkable, don't you agree?"

"I agree."

"What else did Sherifa say? You talked for quite a time at the door. I could hardly keep Laura Ann from rolling down the hill in the sand. That child is strong!"

"Sherifa's pregnant again, and has bad backaches the way I do."

"Really? Poor thing."

"She didn't seem to feel that way," I answered. "She lost a baby last spring, but she has three sons and perhaps another on the way. She said she was luckier than I."

"Well, perhaps the English tea will help us all feel better," Susan said gently.

Each morning, the women swept the rooms and the walkways of their houses and once a week, at least, they changed the sand in the central courts. The old sand was carried out and thrown over the hill, and with the debris from the houses, and the dried goat and sheep droppings everywhere, it was surprising that the outside sand retained such a bronzed, clean look, a golden sand, still only a shade or two lighter than the rectangular flat-roofed houses set upon it.

"Oh, we have lots of sand, sand everywhere, it cleans itself as it goes down," explained Fatima airily.

She was that kind of person, breezy, good-natured, anticipating little but taking from life what it offered to her, eagerly and with thanks. I had expected someone quite different, though what I had expected I could not have said. True, she was the wife of Abdulla, a man of some status in the village, for he was not only the barber, the circumciser and the official registrar of births and deaths, he was universally respected as a lay religious dignitary. He offered the call to prayer during Ramadan and he was regularly asked to lead the Friday morning services in the village mosque. Further, Bob had told me, he was much in demand as a mediator in family quarrels. Perhaps I had thought Fatima would be a lady who rests on her dignity. She was not.

"*Mascagna!*" she called out to us cheerfully the first time we went to tea. "*Mascagna!*" greeting us in Nubian and waving at us from down that sandy street that cleaned itself.

"*Mascagna!*" we echoed, a bit self-consciously.

"*Na!*" repeated Laura Ann, jumping about on her fat legs.

"Rrrrrrr!" Fatima nuzzled Laura Ann in the cheek with her fist, and Laura Ann smiled with pleasure. It was not often people in Erd-Moz paid that much attention to her. "Ah! Your children will learn to speak our language. You learn, too! Good! Come and have tea!"

Sailing gracefully down the street, Fatima made me ashamed of my plodding. Today I did not even have Davy as an excuse, for Susan was carrying him, but Fatima held a small sickly baby in one arm and had a toddler hanging on her long black skirts, pulling on her trailing black head scarf which she was constantly readjusting and patting back to place. He tripped over her train and bawled in anguish after her. Fatima would set him on his feet again, placate him with a kiss, then turn and greet the women standing at their doors to watch us pass.

"Well!" shouted Fatima gaily. "Can't you speak to our guests? They don't care whether you talk Arabic or English, they're going to learn our good Nubian language, *aren't* you, Beeja?" with a quick glance at me.

I nodded, but Fatima had already turned back to another neighbor.

"Come on!" she called. "Cheerful greetings, please! It's a beautiful day!"

Every day we had been in Erd-Moz had seemed a beautiful day, but Khadija warned me darkly that I had seen nothing yet. Bad sandstorms in spring, unbearable heat in the summer more than made up for these mild sunny days of winter, she said.

However, Fatima was a different sort of person. Khadija, for all her dusky beauty, was not happy; she was known in the village as one who looked on the dark side.

"It's her husband, she's lucky he's away in the Sudan," the women said. "He drinks, and when he drinks, he beats her. She hopes he will not come back."

"Fatima on the other hand," our informant had said, "has a good, steady, loving man. She enjoys what there is to enjoy in life."

She did seem to, Fatima.

"*Yallah!* Gamal!" she called to a small boy, perhaps five or six, with a goat in tow. He had white teeth and a neatly shaved head and obediently joined our parade, the fuzzy brown goat trailing behind.

"*Mascagna!*" The women raised their hands to us and chuckled behind their head scarves.

Down the sandy street that cleaned itself we marched, the strong clear sunlight warming us all, Laura Ann with her yellow hair wisping out of its pony tail, Fatima with her necklace of massive gold coins, Gamal with his white shining teeth, Davy with his white face, too white against Susan's Shetland sweater.

"*Mascagna!*" The greeting followed us to a green door where Fatima shifted her baby around, slapped the goat out of the way and worked her long-pegged key into the carved wooden lock.

"*Ya,* Gamal!" The boy sprang to hold the door open for us, and when Laura Ann skipped through, he touched her hair gently, as one touches a strange bird or an unusually colored butterfly.

Fatima caught my eye above the heads of the children, one so dark, one so light, and she smiled. In the pointed face, her deep-set eyes flashed black; her front teeth pro-

truded slightly in an appealing way; even in repose, Fatima
looked on the verge of a giggle.

"Let Lor-Ann play with my boy Gamal in the court,"
she suggested. "We'll go in to Aisha."

After the bright glare, I blinked in the dark and smoky
room. A tiny fire burned fitfully in the traditional hearth,
a three-legged clay griddle fashioned by the Nubian housewives themselves, and so cleverly designed it concentrated
the heat of the smallest fire.

Around the hearth mats were laid, and from a pillow
close to the fire an old woman raised her head and stared
at us with sightless eyes.

"Must be Aisha," whispered Susan. "The midwife, Abdulla's mother."

Aisha cocked her head. She had heard that whisper.

"*Mascagna! Ahlan!* Welcome to our house!" she called out
in a deep, imperious voice.

She was in black, without jewelry; from a scarf of bright
orange satin tied tightly around her head, two thin braids
of gray hair fell onto her sloping shoulders. Raising her
arms in their full black sleeves, she commanded us, with
grand sibylline gestures, to be seated.

Aisha smiled with nearly toothless gums. She bore no
facial tattoo marks, only the usual scarification lines, which
seemed, in her aged face, simply wrinkles, a special set of
wrinkles cutting across the grain of her brown skin.

"Ah!" she expelled her breath. "So this is the Amerikiya,
wife of the doctor, come at last! Aha! And her cousin
Susan, too."

She smiled and stroked my arm, smiled and peered at
the floor as though she could see the forest-green wool of
my sweater projected upon a screen in her innermost eye.

"Fatima!" She spoke to her daughter-in-law in Nubian,
quickly, commandingly.

Fatima did not seem to be offended by her tone.

"Aisha wants me to tell her everything you have on, you

and your cousin, every single thing and its color," she translated.

Halfway through Fatima's catalogue of our clothes, Davy began to whimper, and Aisha stopped her daughter-in-law and said to me, "I am sorry for your trouble with this boy, I have heard about him. Tell me his symptoms more carefully. Perhaps I can help. I used to be able to cure with herbs and cupping or burning, if it were bad. But children are difficult."

"Why?" asked Susan.

"Because sometimes it is God's will that they are not strong enough to live. Then there is nothing we can do."

I saw the expression on Susan's face—pure, clear distaste for the old woman. I gulped and impelled myself to say, "Look, Aisha, he is not so weak, it is only that he wheezes and coughs. He has the asthma."

Aisha raised a hand. "Don't tell me. I may not see, but I can hear well enough to know that. He is a year?"

"More. Thirteen and a half months."

"He walks?"

"No."

"He has been circumcised?"

"Yes."

Aisha ruminated, clearing her throat loudly and looking at the floor. I watched Fatima's movements about the room, putting the blue enamel teakettle on the hearth to boil, feeding the fire with tiny sticks, taking pots from hollowed niches in the walls, cups from neatly arranged shelves, shelves edged with strips of newspaper, hand-cut into lace, an attractive border against the gray mud wall. Beneath one shelf, a woven reed plate hung, and two dish swings, the Nubian method of keeping food out of the reach of mice. In the *diwanis*, or brides' rooms, of the houses the dish swings were merely decorative, but in Fatima's kitchen, beside the hearth, they were put to use.

"Give me your boy for a moment."

Pretending not to notice Susan's unwillingness to let go of Davy, I pushed him forward. Aisha groped for him, found his hand, ran her strong brown fingers up his arm, across his chest and back. He drew back, wheezing softly.

"Yes, yes," muttered Aisha and let him go.

She looked down at the mat again. "Cupping, no, not cupping, that would not help," she said to herself.

The door burst open. "Careful, children, careful!" called a younger version of Fatima, balancing in her hands a large platter of dates and popcorn, the traditional Nubian offering to visitors, and trying to push ahead of her into the room Laura Ann, Gamal and several other children.

"My oldest daughter, Wahiba," Fatima introduced the girl, who resembled her mother but lacked the deep eyes and the slightly jutting teeth that gave Fatima her individuality.

Susan said, "Fatima, I can't believe you're old enough to have a daughter this age."

"Really?" Fatima grinned broadly. "You think I look young? Well, thank God, I have a strong constitution or I'd never have lived through it all—eight children, five living and three dead."

Aisha's head jerked up at a giggle from Laura Ann. "That is your other child," she said to me. "I want to see her. Come here, girl!"

Laura Ann, recognizing the tone of authority, came, Gamal with her. "It's my grandma," he was saying, "she can't see you so she wants to touch you."

Aisha began feeling Laura Ann carefully all over, legs, arms, stomach, Laura Ann standing quietly enough until those sensitive hands of Aisha reached her head.

"Now! Now!" chided Aisha. "You're a girl, aren't you? A nice girl, and you must learn to be still."

To my surprise, Laura Ann did stand still, staring at the long wrinkled face beneath the orange scarf, the deep caverns of the eye sockets where the dead eyes were buried.

"Strange, it is so smooth, her head, what color is her hair?"

"White, Grandmamma," responded Gamal with a smile, kneeling beside Laura Ann to support her during this thorough investigation of her personality. Daughter Wahiba looked on silently, Fatima's sickly baby cradled in her lap.

"Your daughter has been circumcised, of course."

I ignored the question. I knew the Nubian custom of circumcising girls as well as boys, "for reasons of health," but I did not want to engage in an ideological battle on the subject with old Aisha. She, herself, as a midwife, performed such operations. Only the clitorectomy was done here now, said the women, not the more radical operation known as Pharaonic circumcision, which had been forbidden by the government as well as the Islamic religious authorities. The men had told Bob circumcision was good for emotional as well as physical health; it calmed a woman's sexual desires and made it easier for her to remain faithful if her husband had to go away and work in Cairo, for example. The women themselves believed circumcision made them healthier, but more important, made them more feminine, more truly a woman. I disagreed, but there seemed little point in arguing about it.

"Aisha," said Fatima, "let the child go now."

"All right, all right," the old woman answered pettishly. "Go then," and with a last pat on Laura Ann's head. "You don't need me, thank the good God for that. Here," and reaching forward to the platter of dates and popcorn which Khadija had placed before me, she burrowed into it with sure fingers and came up with a large date. "Here, take this."

Laura Ann took it and laughed, leaned down and picked out another date for Gamal.

He looked at his mother. "Take it, the guest gives it to you," she said. "Now go!"

"Let the other children have some," said Susan.

"No," said Fatima. "They must learn what it is to respect guests and to wait their turn. You have to begin early with children or they stay animals all their lives."

And although three small children sat on the other side of the fire, in full sight of that fulsome platter of dates and popcorn, not one moved, not one asked for food.

Fatima served us tea from a painted wooden tray and poured a cup for Aisha.

"Here, Um Abdulla!"

"No! No!" Aisha waved a hand impatiently. "Not till the guests have drunk. I'm not that old!"

But I could see the corner of her mouth twitching. She needed that tea and was sorely tempted to help herself.

"Come, Um Abdulla," I said, "you'd honor us, since you are older than we, and wiser, by drinking with us."

Aisha, making mock protest, took the cup which Fatima placed carefully in her hands, and sipped the hot tea loudly and appreciatively. It did taste good, that tea, I felt it all the way to my bones, tired and cramping from the hour of sitting cross-legged on the mat.

"Fix *me* some tea, Wahiba," Fatima said, and to me, "I need the milk. I give this baby the breast all the time, but she is never satisfied."

"How old is the baby?" I asked. With sticklike arms and legs, an overlarge head, she looked at best perhaps two months.

"Oh, nine months, ten months," said Fatima lightly. "She was born after the last big feast, I can't remember exactly how old she is."

"God's will be done!" pronounced Aisha in a ringing voice.

"God's will be done!" assented Fatima, trying to cradle

the pitiful lolling head in the crook of her arm so the baby could hold onto the nipple more easily.

"But about the boy," Aisha began, thwacking my knee with a long strong finger. "We will think together and we will pray."

"Yes, Aisha, thank you," I stretched my legs in preparation for departure but crafty Aisha was before me.

"Uh—uh—uh, don't go yet," she ordered, that thwacking finger on my knee again. "I want to talk to you about your pregnancy."

She cleared her throat professionally and I sat back automatically, like a patient responding to the voice of a familiar doctor. Aisha had that effect on everyone, I was to find.

"The child moved when?"

"Four months, about."

"Good. You carry the child high or low?"

"High."

"How does she look, Fatima, her eyes, her skin?"

"Terrible," laughed Fatima, truthfully.

"Mmm, that complicates things," mused Aisha. "Carrying the baby high, probably a girl, looks terrible, probably a boy."

"We must go," I said and rose from the mat, breaking the spell Aisha was beginning to cast.

"No, no!" cried the old woman. "You have come a long way to get to Erd-Moz, and we are only beginning to know each other."

"Yes, Aisha, but soon it will be dark and the children will be asking for their supper, and my husband is waiting for me. Another day I'll sit with you for a long time. Because I want to know you also. I hear you are the best midwife in the whole Abu Simbel area."

Aisha reached up and pulled me down again with those iron hands.

"Ha, ha!" She gave a cracked, pleased laugh. "She's

heard of me, has she? Well, I *am* a good midwife. See my hands?"

She held the long, seamed brown hands close to my face. "They are strong, you see, but they are also gentle, from years and years they know the way the baby comes and they bring it easily, at exactly the right moment! Why go back to Cairo to have your baby when I'm here?"

"I'm sure you are very good, Aisha," I said politely, "but—"

Aisha scoffed. "I know what you're thinking. You think I can't see, eh? Who needs to see? I'm a better midwife without sight than most of the new ones who have both eyes and no skill. Skill is what it takes, and strength and kindness. Believe me, my girl, I don't leave my patients alone with their pain the way those modern men doctors in Cairo do."

I stood up and moved out of range of Aisha's hand. We *had* to go. We were shaking hands with Wahiba, with Fatima, but Aisha was not to be ignored.

"You listen to me, you Amerikiya!" she cried, reaching out with those hands, raising her sightless eyes under the orange scarf. "I'll wash my hands in hot water, I'll make a good strong knot in the cord, so—" she snapped the long fingers to punctuate her offer. "My son Abdulla can do the circumcision, if it's a boy. I'll do it if it's a girl, and all for nothing. Doesn't that sound good? What else do you want?"

"Yes, yes, thank you, thank you, we'll talk about it," I temporized.

Fatima's eyes were bright with mischief. I could see she had enjoyed the exchange between Aisha and me.

"She's strong, isn't she, my mother-in-law? Well, women have to be strong or they don't live long in *this* world. Gamal!" she hollered after her son, running with Laura Ann, dodging in and out of the long shadows cast by the houses on the darkening sand of the street.

"Let him come home with us. I'll send him back," I promised.

"All right, but don't let him stay and bother you," insisted Fatima. "Good night! Good night! God go with you!"

She was gone in a trail of black dress and veil, a whiff of sandalwood perfume in the acrid dust our footsteps raised in the street.

"That old woman!" said Susan crisply. "Cupping, burning," she shifted Davy to the other shoulder. "She'll wash her hands in hot water, will she?"

The sun was poised, a flattened orange disk, on the very rim of the mountains. Twenty more minutes before total darkness fell, I calculated, and the women in their long black dresses hurrying home with loads of fuel and cans of water, the children driving goats and sheep toward shelter, seemed to share my view.

"B.J.?" It was Susan.

"I can always say my husband won't allow it," I answered.

"Well, why didn't you?" Susan was quite indignant. "Circumcising, too. My God!"

"Laura Ann! Laura Ann!" Karim called.

Time for the nightly ritual of play before supper that warmhearted Karim had introduced into the family routine. In her joy, Laura Ann ran to him and to her father, her new friend Gamal forgotten.

The women of Erd-Moz were proving to be far more independent and far more knowledgeable in the ways of the world outside their tiny village than any of us had expected. Bob had discovered that most Nubian adult men had spent some time working in the cities of Egypt, and therefore he was not too surprised to find the men showing a great deal of sophistication in dealing with him. What was surprising was that the women, theoretically more secluded and isolated, should also demonstrate a certain worldliness, a certain awareness of other values.

Sitta, whose husband worked in London and who had herself lived in Damascus and Tunis, was not unique, we found. Every woman in Erd-Moz had been at least to Aswan more than once; most had lived for extended periods of time in Cairo, Alexandria or Khartoum. Many women echoed ideas about health and child care which I thought they must have heard from Western-trained doctors or from their own husbands.

Bob had told me about the forward-looking ideas of Mohammed, the handsome tambura player who was becoming his best friend in the village. Mohammed moved easily in many kinds of worlds—among his own relatives and friends, with Egyptian archeologists at the temple whom he took duck hunting, with transient European tourists whom he often invited to stay in his house.

I suppose, after the example of Sitta and others, that I rather expected Mohammed's women to follow his lead. His wife, Nezla, and his mother, Shemessa, were very proud of their beautiful double cradle, made to order after a European model, for Mohammed's youngest children, twin baby boys. It was true that when we went to tea at Mohammed's house, tins of lard and folded clothes reposed in the cradle, and the twins were cuddled in the arms of their grandmother Shemessa. But I had not really given the situation much thought, except to note that the twins were whisked out of sight as soon as I arrived and inquiries about their health were met with an abruptness bordering on rudeness. Why?

Nezla was timid and sweet, with a frail beauty gradually being eroded by hard work and childbearing. Shemessa, her mother-in-law, was a tall, commanding person, who ordered Nezla about in an especially unmerciful way, even in a setting where brides can expect little quarter from their husband's mothers. Neither woman appealed to me

particularly, yet suddenly and involuntarily I found myself in the middle in a struggle between old and new which
was being waged, quietly but fiercely, in the house of
modernist Mohammed.

It began one day at lunch.

"Mohammed has asked me if you'll show his women how
to take better care of the twins," announced Bob.

"What? You can't be serious."

"Well, Mohammed is."

"Bob," I said, "Shemessa has raised five children, Nezla
has three others besides the twins."

"Mohammed really wants you to help."

I frowned. "No," I replied. I could not think of anything
worse than becoming identified with the men of Erd-Moz
in some kind of struggle against their women, women
whom I liked and admired (though it was true I did not
much like Shemessa).

"No," I repeated.

"But those twins are constantly sick, eye infections, ear
infections, cough, dysentery," observed Bob. "Why not
help Mohammed out and give the women a few suggestions."

"If Mohammed is as progressive as you say, why does
he need me? He can take the babies to the doctor in Benha."

"He has," said Karim, "but the women forget to put the
medicine in or they give too much or too little."

"Let the doctor explain to the women," I argued.

"They wouldn't listen to the doctor, they tune him out.
He's a man and not their relative. Mohammed thinks they
might listen to you, since you're a woman and have children
too. You should be flattered!"

"Ha!" I laughed hollowly. "Nezla and Shemessa listen to
me? They're suspicious of foreign medicine to begin with
and they can see it doesn't help."

"What do you mean? They haven't given the medicine a
fair chance."

Susan intervened. "That's not what B.J. has in mind. Everywhere we go the women look at Davy and say, 'Don't you give him expensive medicine, how come he's still sick?'"

"They begin muttering in dialect," I said, "and they mean, why should we bother? We hardly present a shining example of what Western miracle medicine can do!"

The subject was dropped. I visited Mohammed's house again, but I felt more uncomfortable than before; it was hard to explain why. Then the twins, with dysentery, began passing blood and mucus. "Would I please come?" Mohammed asked.

"You'd rather not meddle in local customs but let the twins die instead," said Bob to provoke me.

This I could not take. "I'll try, I'll try," I said, "but Nezla and Shemessa don't want me messing with the twins; just ask Susan."

"B.J.'s right in a way," said Susan. "It's not the same as at Abdul Majid's or even Saleh's."

"Hmph," retorted Bob. "Feelings. Impressions. Give me some concrete evidence."

I reminded Bob and Karim of all the Nubian beliefs about twins; they were really cats; one twin could not live without the other; they flew out at night; beliefs which Bob thought had developed to explain multiple births and the inevitable death of one or both babies, since it was unlikely, in a subsistence economy, that more than one baby could survive. The Evil Eye figured in all this, too, and I could see it in Nezla's and Shemessa's treatment of the twins. Though they were boys, they wore girls' dresses and frilled sunbonnets, their necks were hung with charms to ward off the Evil Eye.

Bob heard me out and said, "What does all that have to do with you?"

"They think I'm bad luck, too."

"Oh, B.J., don't exaggerate."

"I'm not exaggerating, you should see the way they *look* at me."

"They seem to be *watching* B.J. all the time," put in Susan.

"What imagination!" expostulated Bob.

I said nothing, but I felt Shemessa's nearly open hostility and I also felt, from the bottom of my heart, the same uneasiness and distraction in Nezla, the same sense of inadequacy about those sickly twins that I felt about Davy. I knew enough, I hoped, not to be driven to tie beads around Davy's neck or put hot nails on his forehead to drive out the evil spirits, but I was worried all the time. Nezla knew less about the causes of illness than I; she was worried, too, and an unknown quantity like me only added to her burden. But I agreed to go down the next morning and administer the medicine Mohammed would bring from Benha that afternoon.

I set off alone after breakfast, down the wide street of sand, not relishing the prospect of my mission at all.

"*Mascagna!*" called the women on their way to the mountains to gather fuel.

"*Mascagna!*" called the old widow Fatooma, sitting alone before her door, weaving a small reed plate. "You're going to Mohammed's, hey, to see the sick babies?"

"Yes," I answered.

"Leave them be," she advised. "They're twins!" And she jabbed her long needle between the rows and brought out the free end of palm fiber. "Twins!"

"Yes, I know!"

At the open gate of the primary school, the doorkeeper sat, rolling himself a long, thin, brown cigarette. He nodded to me as I passed. "Off to see Shemessa, eh?" he remarked.

Did everyone know my destination this morning? I could hear the drone of the morning lessons, boys and girls together, reciting.

"What is the capital of America?"

"Washington!"

"What is the capital of Egypt?"

"Aswan!"

"Idiot! No, it is not Aswan. What is the capital of Egypt, children?"

"Cairo."

"Right. Now repeat after me . . . the capital of Egypt is Cairo."

Cairo. I had a full moment of homesickness, not for America, but for Cairo, crowded streets, cinemas, coffee shops, the entire restless urban bustle of my adopted home. I knocked and knocked on Mohammed's door. Finally it gave a crack, and the narrowed eyes of Shemessa met mine.

"*Ahlan wusahlan!*" she said in a falsely bright voice and threw open the door.

"How are the twins?"

"Fine, thank you, just fine."

I was in the court now and Shemessa, winding and unwinding her head scarf, was pacing back and forth and darting glances at me from narrowed eyes while she called, in that falsely bright voice, "Look, Nezla! It is Beeja, come to drink tea with us."

"No, thank you, Shemessa, no tea. I have only come to help you give the babies their medicine. Mohammed, your son, asked me."

Shemessa stopped in her nervous pacing.

"Medicine? What medicine? The twins are fine, just fine. A bit tired this morning is all."

"I'm glad," I answered.

What to do now? I could not tell Shemessa that I knew she was lying, for Mohammed had stopped last night at our house and shown me the bottle of antibiotic he had brought back.

"Well," I said cheerfully, "then you don't need me. I must be getting back to my children."

"Oh, no," cried Shemessa, "you must have tea first. You will shame our household."

She blocked the door. "That we would let a guest come in through our door and not offer them something?" Her voice shook. "My son Mohammed will not forgive you."

I stood irresolute, realizing only too well that it was Nezla and Shemessa that Mohammed would not forgive, and in that moment Nezla emerged from the kitchen, a twin baby whining on each arm and her face twisted with worry.

Do your duty, I thought to myself, and get out. "I only stopped to inquire after the twins and help you put in the medicine, Nezla," I said.

"I can't *find* the medicine!" wailed Nezla, "and Mohammed made me promise to have you give it to them, and he will be so angry."

"Shhhhhh!" hissed Shemessa and swept the twins out of Nezla's arms, disappearing into one of the bedrooms.

"How are they?"

"Not good," said Nezla, and bit her lip, for in her distress she had done a bad thing. She had admitted to me that the babies were ill. One never admitted in this society that *anyone* was ever ill. He might be a little tired, very tired, might not eat, might be able to take a little tea only, but he was never, never ill.

Suffra, Mohammed's sister, banged open the door, her year-and-a-half-old son on her hip. "How are the twins? Have you come to give them their medicine," she asked me, "like Mohammed said?"

I nodded.

"Well, get it, Nezla," said Suffra. "It's in the *mendara,* I saw my mother, Shemessa, hide it there this morning, after Mohammed had gone."

We sat in the court while the medicine was produced and measured out, Shemessa blustering, "Why do they need this, they are all right, a little tea, it will help, that's all they can take."

Nezla looked from me to Suffra to her mother-in-law, no doubt feeling, as I did, the disapproval in the older woman. Poor Nezla. She seemed torn between her distrust of what I represented and her own beliefs, yet she obviously wanted to do something for her babies. They were so thin and small, their faces so pinched under the frilled bonnets.

"Don't forget the ears are infected, too," reminded Suffra, in a matter-of-fact way. "Mohammed made you promise."

The bonnets were untied, Shemessa hardly able to contain herself, and I bent close over those running, suppurating ears, hardly able to contain *myself*, but for different reasons. The twins were so weak they did not even cry out when the ear drops, warmed briefly as per instructions, went in. They simply closed their eyes, and I saw that the thin eyelashes were matted together with pus.

"Oh, that!" said Nezla. "All the children have eye infections, that is easy to cure; I put the medicine in myself."

"My children have them, too," I said, and in a strained voice I added, "let's put some medicine in now."

This was difficult, but finally accomplished, Suffra again officiating, holding the babies' eyes open until the drops and the ointment went in, Nezla and Shemessa looking at each other wordlessly above us. It was like a pressure, a drift of air, so intense was that silent struggle, and Suffra must have felt it, too, for she said something in dialect and Nezla got up and left the court.

"Put some in my boy Elias' eyes too," Suffra said unexpectedly when we were finished and the pathetic babies had been bundled off by Shemessa, presumably to be put right after my ministrations.

"Now you must have tea, I have already made it," Nezla said, looking exhausted.

We sat together in the sunny court, quietly, while the water jar in its wooden frame gently dripped into its pan and the pigeons in their cotes high on the courtyard wall sounded their low throaty calls.

The atmosphere gradually softened, portents and presences fading, with the departure of their object of concentration.

"Ah, Beeja," said Suffra, half jokingly, "what will we do for him?" picking up her Elias, wiping his runny nose, hugging him and setting him on his unsteady legs to walk again. "He's too old to be satisfied with my milk but too young to eat meat. Here we don't have any food between the milk and the meat that children can grow strong on."

Shemessa had come back just in time for this last complaint. She drew herself up. "Nonsense! We have mashed potatoes, rice, you can soak some bread in milk for him. Babies that are meant to live, live. It is God's will."

"Why is it only God's will in the country?" Suffra asked scornfully. "In Cairo the babies don't die for lack of food. They have beans and bananas and eggs. By God, I will be glad to leave this place and move to Kom Ombo."

"Suffra!" remonstrated her mother. "Don't speak like that of our blessed land. We have enough. We should be content!"

"Enough for old people, yes," agreed Suffra.

I remembered she had recently lost a baby, so perhaps Shemessa was being lenient with her; it was not acceptable to contradict one's elders.

"The city is not perfect either, my girl," and with a glance at me, Shemessa lapsed into dialect.

I knew what they were saying, look at Beeja's baby, expensive medicines, doctors, warm woolen clothes and still . . . the morning had come full circle. It was time to go.

Shemessa rose, almost friendly again after having satisfied herself once more that what will be, will be, despite the efforts of modern upstarts to change anything.

"You should not leave your son alone," she cautioned me. "He needs your protection all the time."

When I smiled and thanked her for her advice, however, she pushed her face close to mine, all the muscles working and the eyes narrowed to slits, and whispered hoarsely, "Who knows where the Evil Eye hides, hey?"

I shivered in the sunshine, and the peaceful courtyard seemed once more to be filled with portents of unknown, unexplained evil. The shudder was involuntary, but Nezla had seen it, for she said quickly, "When one is pregnant, it is hard to keep the other children always with you."

I looked at her. Something in the face . . .

"You're pregnant, Nezla?"

"Yes, I think so. Two or three months."

The sun was hot, the street was empty. Bob and Karim and Susan were in the *mendara* with the children.

"Well?" said Bob meaningfully.

I told the story of the morning, leaving out my own reactions to Shemessa for I felt embarrassed and could not explain them even to myself. But when I thought of Nezla at the end, that sad, tired face, I felt angry. All the tumultuous emotions of the morning crystallized in anger, and I found myself shouting, "Nezla is pregnant again."

"Really?" echoed Bob. "Well, you don't have to yell at us. I'm surprised. Mohammed hasn't said anything."

"Probably doesn't consider it worth mentioning," I burst out. "Mohammed and his modern, progressive ideas!"

Since Bob and Karim said nothing, I raced ahead. "I am sure," I said, feeling like the seer of the mountains after my skirmish with mother-in-laws, folk medicine and the Evil Eye, "that when Nezla delivers this child, the twins will die. The poor woman can hardly produce milk enough for one baby, let alone three!"

"Don't get so excited," said Bob mildly. "You can't do anything about it, so why don't you write down what happened or rest or something while Karim and I finish our morning notes."

What *could* I do? Nothing. I did not feel like writing about it, so I reached for Davy and went outside with Susan and Laura Ann to sit in the sun until lunchtime.

The afternoon had been set aside for our official visit to the *omda*, chief of Nubia's Ballana district. "A pleasant outing," Bob promised, "but be sure to put on your best clothes and clean up the kids. The *omda* is a distinguished man!"

I laughed hollowly to myself. Two weeks of bucket baths, hand-washed clothes, straight hair, sunburned face, swollen ankles and front, it seemed unlikely that I would make even a mildly favorable impression on the *omda!*

But the visit to the *omda*'s did turn out to be a pleasant change. We buzzed upriver in the *Susan,* one of the three motorboats Bob had ordered for the project's field camps. Motors had come from Europe, but the boats had been built in Cairo, and Bob had originally thought of them as communicating links between the camps, emergency transport in case of illness. He and Karim did use the *Susan* to do surveys and interviews in villages around Abu Simbel, to go to Benha for supplies, to the temple for mail brought by the post or express boat. He had planned to use them more than he really did, for the problems of shipping gasoline south of Aswan were great and one or the other motor was always out of order.

Today, though, the *Susan* was purring along on both motors. I breathed the clear soft air; a flock of birds rose winging south to Africa, calling across the river to each other, the river which seemed so wide and vast from our position in the tiny boat. I watched Laura Ann trailing her hand in the water, clutched from the rear by ever watchful Susan, and I held Davy tighter and cast off the mood of depression that the morning had produced. Bob and Karim too forgot, for a moment, their concerns with land tenure and irrigation and cow ownership, and actu-

ally laughed at a new joke about the government cooperatives, which had found its way to us, even in this remote
place.

I found I responded almost gaily to the *omda's* formal
welcome and even his silent perusal of sniffly Davy and his
single comment, "and this is your *only* son?" did not dis-
turb me as much as usual.

We sat on the *omda's* freshly scrubbed white porch
overlooking the river and the ruins of the Islamic fort of
Jebel Ada and had a curiously urbane conversation with
Suliman Ali Mahmoud Haj, *omda* of Ballana province,
descended on his mother's side from the Kashefs, Turkish
overlords in Nubia until Mohammed Ali's reign, and descended on his father's side from the Nubian family of
Rashwan, a family who had lived in Ballana, it was said,
as long as anyone could remember. The *omdas* had once
ruled the districts of Nubia, under a broad grant of power
from the central government. Since 1952, the government
had taken a more direct interest in Nubian affairs, but the
omdas still remained figures of some importance.

"Do you prefer plane or boat travel, madame?" asked
the *omda*. He lounged, a slight elderly figure, in one of
his cretonne-covered porch chairs. He had offered us English cigarettes, which he smoked in a long ivory holder.
Ivory to match the rest of him; except for the pale coffee-
colored leather of his face and hands, he was white, spotless
gullabiya and turban, white beard and mustache, even im-
maculate white shoes.

I said that I preferred boats, especially on warm winter
days like this, when the breeze was not too strong.

The *omda* agreed. Feluccas, he found, were by far the
best mode of travel when the object was pleasure. "But I am
glad they have invented airplanes," he said, "so that unpleasant trips may be over quickly."

"You have a beautiful view," offered Susan.

"Yes, I like it," responded the *omda*, and after a magnificent tea had been served, with biscuits and pound cake and raisin cookies, he instructed his servant to bring dates.

"These are our best dates," he admitted when we oohed and aahed about their sweetness, their flavor. "We pack them in fat to keep them soft. Let the boy have more," and with that, he excused himself, he had other urgent business.

"He's a shrewd old bird, that *omda*," mused Bob, as we putt-putted back down the river toward Erd-Moz. "He's still a force to be reckoned with, despite the fact that he's not supposed to have any power at all."

"How can he be a force?" asked Susan. "The Egyptian government is in close control of everything now, I thought."

Karim, at the wheel, his wrinkled white sun hat pulled down over his curly black hair to the rim of his sunglasses, smiled. He would never laugh at our innocence, but he quite often smiled that smile.

"Americans sometimes do not understand," he said gently, "about power. There are lots of ways of keeping it, once you have it."

We were nearing the palm groves that marked the boundary between Dekhla and Erd-Moz. Davy and Laura Ann were unusually quiet, lulled by the purr of the motor and the piles of the *omda*'s best dates which they had consumed.

"He's most impressive," I said.

"Impressive, but perhaps a bit out-of-date," said Bob.

I remembered the sitting room of the guest house where I had gone to change Davy midway through tea. Chintz sofas and chairs, a table beneath a window through which was framed, and not by chance, I thought, the broken towers of the old Jebel Ada fort. Was it the silver inkwell and pen tray, the wooden shutters over glassless windows, the pound cake for tea that gave the *omda*'s riverside house an air of the colonial past, of a time finished and completed elsewhere but still persisting here?

Bob cleared his throat. "I don't want to bring up the business with Mohammed's babies again," he said, "but aside from that, how do things seem to be going with the women?"

"Well enough. Everyone is kind and friendly."

"No problems of rapport, no awkward pauses and so on?"

Susan laughed. "Awkward pauses?" she hooted. "Come along some day and watch us try to keep the children's little hands out of the food."

She went on to recount our disaster of yesterday afternoon when Laura Ann, after admiringly watching a small girl strutting about the court with an empty plate on her head, was suddenly moved to action. I saw her small hands fold around the huge plate of popcorn and dates laid out for us; Susan and I both moved, but too late. Laura Ann raised the plate on high and popcorn and dates rained onto the fine sand of the court, a shocking thing to happen in a society where food is considered sacred, and even dirty or spoiled bits of food are blessed before being given to the animals.

"Never mind," our hostess had muttered automatically but made no move to help as Susan and I picked out of the sand, one by one, the grains of popcorn and the flat dried dates. When the plate was refilled, one of the women took it away, and general conversation was resumed.

We tied up at the dock, Bob took Davy from Susan and hoisted him to his shoulder for the climb to the top of the dunes. Laura Ann clutched Karim's hand happily and I dropped behind, taking the safe, slow way upward, greeting the women with their evening water cans. Fatima's son Gamal, his brother by the hand, was skipping stones into the muddy water of the shallow canal. In some shelter nearby a cow bellowed to be milked. One week more and Susan would return to Cairo. Beryl would come

to help me with the children, but I scarcely knew Beryl.
Mona would come from the American University as a research assistant, to work with the women, and I didn't know
her at all. One day at a time.

"Bob has promised to take me to the temple tomorrow,"
called Susan from above, where Bob sat with the men ad-
miring the sunset. From the west, the fading golden light
slanted across the veranda, giving the mud-brick pillars a
look of monumental stone. Bob's face was lost in shadow,
but the turbans of Mohammed and Saleh and the china
plates above the door gleamed white against the gray mud
wall.

"How could I ever explain to my relatives in New York
that I lived beside Abu Simbel for three weeks and never
got inside it? You and Karim are my witnesses. He has
promised!"

Karim waved his white sun hat. "Okay, Susan," he answered.

The women resting before the houses, Khadija, I thought,
and Hanim Ali, were laughing at our long-distance inter-
change. Susan turned and laughed too and sank down on
the sand with them.

Abdul Nasr crawled into her lap beside Davy.

CHAPTER 10

NUBIAN HOUSEKEEPING

When I was a child, I was fascinated by those pale images of the roadside reflected in the window of our moving automobile. One image unrolled at eye level, like an over-exposed filmstrip—fields of corn, red barns, blue silos, children waving and running past white farmhouses on the gentle slopes of rolling hills. But the reflection of the opposite side of the road seemed to have been threaded wrongly into the projector. The landscape whipped past at an unpredictable angle, lop-sided farmhouses, crazy half hills, oddly suspended children disappearing diagonally into an unknown sky. I would find myself glancing quickly, furtively, across the highway to check on the second half of the landscape, to make certain that this odd imprint which I watched was an illusion.

In Nubia my fears for Laura Ann and Davy were like that distorted reflection, an unreal image I tried not to face directly, while the field work moved along reasonably easily, like the eye-level landscape of my childhood travels. Beryl, who had come with Susan's departure, was not only helping me with the children; like Susan, she entered spontaneously into our work. The new research assistant, Mona, had also been quickly absorbed into the life of Erd-Moz, rather to everyone's pleased surprise, including her own. Mona's comfortable upper middle-class Cairo home, staffed by many servants, could hardly have prepared her for the difficult life in the village, one would have thought, but Mona re-

minded us that she had spent her summers on the family
farm estate in the Delta.

"I feel at home in the country," she said.

"And the Nubians are a very appealing people," added
Beryl.

Both girls were intelligent, but it was their warm hearts,
I thought, which contributed more to their obvious enjoyment and appreciation of life in Nubia.

At first together and then often separately, as we developed our individual friendships, we visited the women
of Erd-Moz and they visited us. We sat together in the
courtyards or on the tawny, sun-drenched dunes before
the houses, listening, talking, trying to understand the people among whom we were living, to record the techniques
and skills that the women had developed to deal success-
fully with home life on the Upper Nile. This was a life
far from the lives we had led and known, a life which
made different demands upon wives and mothers and
daughters than any we had experienced before.

Mona, challenged one day by laughing and teasing
friends, had attempted to imitate that deft movement of
both arms for which Hanim Ali was famous. With only a
flat reed plate as a sifter, Hanim Ali could separate, we
were told, a bushel of wheat from its chaff without losing
a single valuable edible grain. Mona tried valiantly, but
stifled giggles from the audience soon erupted into loud
laughter, and Fatima, her eyes streaming with tears of
mirth, finally took the plate away.

"You don't want to waste all my grain, do you?" said
Fatima, and at Mona's stricken guilty look (several scores
of grains of wheat had disappeared into the sand during the
experiment) she patted her on the shoulder. "Never mind,
Mona," she said, "it takes years of practice, and even
though I've been doing it since I was a little girl, I'm still
not as good as Hanim Ali."

"You can do other things we can't do," reminded Wahiba.

"Like what?" pressed Beryl.

"Well, er . . ." Wahiba looked around her, "read, things like that," she gestured, widely in the hot cloudless air.

Reading, I thought, could be learned by Hanim Ali more easily than I could ever learn that rhythmic sifting movement. A bushel of wheat without losing a grain? Incredible.

Sherifa was drying mint when we went to tea, sorting the leaves and laying them in the sun upon the woven leather "spring" of the classic *angareeb*, the Nubian bedstead with feet carved like the feet of Pharaonic furniture. One of these bedframes stood in almost every bare courtyard, used to keep the freshly washed dishes as well as the drying vegetables off the ground.

"My children have coughs all winter long," Sherifa said. "Mint tea settles their stomachs and soothes their throats and Abdul Majid likes it, too."

The mint was tied into bundles with shreds of palm fiber before being hung with the strings of okra and green beans from the rafters of the warm summer kitchen.

Mona walked to the mountains with Wahiba and Fatima to graze the goats and gather dead branches and shrubs for fuel. Beryl, taking Laura Ann by the hand, walked to the river with Naima, Khadija's young sister, to watch the nomad camel caravan pass. I listened to Hanim Ali's tale of woe as she lay in her bedroom, ill with stomach trouble, dosing herself with a purging brew and clenching her fists, covered with those magic rings, to keep herself from crying out with pain.

The women had long ago learned to take advantage of every single resource available to them in their limited environment. Empty kerosene cans, for example, were not thrown away; they were used as water cans, or, hung high on the walls of the courtyards and with door holes cut in the sides, they became pigeon lofts. In the mud-brick walls of the kitchens, niches had been carefully hollowed out to serve as special built-in cupboards, a small niche (high up and away from children) for the matches, a long flat deep hollow for fuel, shorter ones for the primus stove, the cooking pots. A place for everything and everything in its place was the neat Nubian housewife's motto.

It was in the care of their floors, however, that they seemed to me to exercise the most ingenuity. Cleaning and changing the sand in the courtyards every week was not enough; the walkways and doorways had not only to be swept, they had to be renewed regularly. Each year, before the two principal feasts in the Moslem religious calendar, the women gathered together and pooled their energies in a final orgy of spring cleaning and house refurbishing. Not a quilting bee nor a roof raising, but a complete floor replastering took place in each household.

Khadija came in the day our house was to be done, carrying great flat pans which she had filled with a mud and water mixture.

"Who's coming to plaster?" asked Beryl.

"Almost everybody, except Nezla, who isn't feeling well —the twins again," she threw out offhandedly, "but Suffra will take her place. After all, the floors are a big job. Everybody must help. Whoever doesn't come here, well, we won't go to *her* replastering."

Using their hands, the women spread the mud and water plaster over the walks and doorways, smoothing it and edging it carefully with a knife. The new coat of mud baked in the sun to a hard smooth gloss by the end of the afternoon. A final swipe with the broom and presto, chango, shiny new mud floors, thresholds and doorjambs, a surface which would have degenerated quickly under the impact of leather shoes, but lasted a long time with the barefoot tread of our friends (who carefully left their shoes outside when they entered a house).

One day Karim and Bob reported that a strange leafless tree had been carried with some ceremony into Mohammed's house. What, they wanted to know, would they be

using that oddly shaped tree for, if not for fuel? We waited
an hour and then "visited" to find Nezla and Shemessa
and Suffra mixing a kind of spaghetti to be used in a
special sweet for the feast coming at the end of Ramadan.
The dough went into a meat grinder and came out in
strings. And the tree? It had been carefully chosen by
Shemessa herself as a special drying rack, since for this
task the bedstead would simply not do, she said. The
spread between the branches and twigs allowed each string
of spaghetti to be draped separately and dried individually
in the sun.

Mona shared *iftar* with Fatima, the breaking of the fast
during Ramadan, and was treated to *gargabida,* paper-thin
slices of crisp bread soaked in lime water and served as
the first light refreshing taste of food and drink after the
long day of fasting.

After the joyous *iftar* meals, Beryl practiced traditional
dance steps with Wahiba and Naima and the other unmarried girls. In the cold winter moonlight, which cast
their vague girlish shadows on the darkened walls of the
houses, they danced to a drumbeat punctuating their own
singing.

> "Now that I've seen you," they chanted
> "O my love,
> How can I live without you
> O my love!"

It was Beryl perhaps who came closest to actually taking
part in the life around us. She was younger than Mona,
without the traditional attitudes of Egyptians toward their
less fortunate fellow countrymen; she was younger than I
and unmarried, more open to new impressions, not bound
up in the wife-mother sets as I had become. She danced
and sang and learned the steps, and years later, in Cambridge, she sang my children those old Nubian songs.

But wherever I went, whatever I did, my fears for David and Laura Ann were with me, irrational fears, that at night before sleep or in unexpected moments during the day would unwind before me and flash like that other nightmarish landscape reflection of my childhood, diagonally into the unknown sky. In my dreams the figure of my own mother, the white farmhouses of Wisconsin childhood summers appeared confusedly in company with blind Aisha, with Shemessa hissing about the Evil Eye.

Davy's asthma, contrary to our hopes, had not improved, but on the other hand, it had not worsened. His fungus infections seemed to be slowly drying up, but he was plagued by new irritations and illnesses; ear infections, eye infections, dysentery (like the twins, the dreams whispered). Laura Ann had several eye infections and developed a hacking cough. We dosed them both with antibiotics from the first-aid suitcase which Karim had prepared so meticulously in Cairo more than a year ago. The infections, the cough, the dysentery got better, only to recur.

"That's the way children are, Beeja," Fatima said. "One day they're sick, one day they're well," and she gestured to her sniffling three-year-old. "What else do you expect?"

I was silent. Should I ask Fatima about the other problem that had risen to haunt me, Laura Ann's relationship to the village children? Abruptly I burst out, "What about Laura Ann?"

"Our children don't mean any harm," said Fatima.

Perhaps they didn't. Probably they didn't. But Laura Ann, our once happy daughter, was miserable. We had thought that since Laura Ann had, practically since birth, played in the *ganeena* with children of all sizes and colors, her attitude toward the Nubian children would be a perfectly natural and friendly one. We were right. What we had not reckoned with was the attitude of the Nubian children toward Laura Ann.

"Mama! Mama! Play!" Laura Ann had insisted excitedly

those first mornings in our new home, entranced at the thought of all that sand, all those children, all those donkeys and goats and geese and chickens. Dressed and breakfasted, she would race out and head for the nearest cluster of Nubian children, drawing pictures in the sand with pointed sticks, playing jacks with small stones or practicing the ancient jumping game depicted on the walls of Pharaonic tombs. One hand high, two hands high, three, four and six hands high the little boys would jump.

As Laura Ann approached, however, the children would stop their play, still their chatter and their gay, high-pitched laughter. I would watch through the cracks in the shutters, praying that today things might go differently.

"Play?" Laura Ann would go up to a child. "Play?" she would repeat, trying it in English and Arabic, in a piercing little voice I could hear all the way to the house. The Nubian child would back away, good-humoredly enough, but still back away, and in a moment, blonde-haired and white-skinned Laura Ann would find herself the center of a tight ring of dark children, with flashing eyes, skullcaps and *gullabiyas*, tight little pigtails under their red shawls.

"Play?" she would say once more, for at first she had thought this was a new kind of game. But it was not "Farmer in the Dell" or "Drop the Handkerchief." After a brief silent pause the teasing would begin. One child would rush forward and pull on Laura Ann's red sweater. She would turn, to find someone yanking her hair from behind. Another child would lean forward and pinch her leg. By this time, a number of dark mothers would have emerged from doorways to admonish their children and the circle would break.

The Nubian children would laugh and run away, and Laura Ann, left alone, would burst into tears and run for home. After about ten days of this treatment, the poor child refused to leave the house without Susan or Beryl or me.

When I saw her on the porch, rocking back and forth with her dolly, her little face tight with unhappiness, I would ask myself, what am I doing? Why am I allowing her to go through this? Is it really necessary for me to stay here? To whom do I owe my first responsibility? Bob? But what about the children? Don't I owe something to them, too?

Fatima pointed out that her son Gamal was very fond of Laura Ann. "You see how nicely they play together here," she said.

True. Alone, Gamal was very kind and gentle with Laura Ann and she would follow him devotedly, carrying a stick when he carried one, sipping water from the water jar when he did. But in a crowd, Gamal would not stand alone against all of his friends and relatives.

"They just want to make sure she's real," Khadija laughed. "Watch how Abdul Nasr, even, touches her hair and feels it, he's never seen hair like that before."

I thought she had probably come closer to the truth than anyone, but it was difficult to explain this refinement to two-and-a-half-year-old Laura Ann.

Every few days Bob and I would discuss the current problems with the children, and I would decide to leave; I had done my duty, it seemed, by demonstrating that my husband was a respectable family man who could be trusted to supervise properly these unmarried research assistants. Bob would make reservations on the express boat. But before the boat arrived, Davy would improve or worsen, Laura Ann would be uncomfortable with another eye infection or would seem momentarily happier, and the long, arduous trip to Cairo would be postponed again.

So the winter days passed, warm and sunny, with windy nights and freezing mornings. Before sunup I would hear

Davy wailing and, struggling up from sleep, I would throw
my clothes on in the icy cold, rush across the court and
get Davy quickly before he woke Laura Ann and Beryl.
Bundled in sleeper and blankets, he would stop crying
when we came out of the dark bedroom into the predawn
light of the court.

Even in my cold, blurred sleepy state, I could see why
the child quieted and looked. From the porch the dark
mountains on the opposite shore seemed gilded with an
edge of radiant gold; the sun was rising. Khadija, a heavy
shawl over her head, would emerge and nod before heading
down the hill to feed the cows bawling with hunger in the
cold.

A dog woke and barked.

The sky was red, the palms a dusky green beside the
dark river. Saleh would come out, his head shrouded in
white; in his hand the primus stove blazing and ready
for me to cook Davy's early breakfast in the *mendara*.

"Good morning!" he would say between chattering teeth.

Davy, pointing upward into the lightening sky, would
answer, "Bird" (wheeze), "bird!"

Saleh would laugh in the cold and nod at Davy, yes,
there were always birds flying over the village toward the
river, the flapping of their wings unnaturally loud in the
early morning quiet.

The sky lost its redness while I knocked at the door of
the *mendara* where Karim was asleep on a cot; Saleh
would leave the primus stove hissing beside me.

"Karim!" I'd call again, banging on the shutter to get in;
he would answer sleepily he'd be dressed in a moment.

The sky was now clear and limpid, the enormous round
red sun showed above the mountains and slowly, as it rose
in the sky, seemed to diminish in size, while the palms, the
river, the mountains and the sand dunes beside me took
color from its light.

Cocks crowed. More dogs barked.

The primus stove hissed yellow, blue, red and back to blue.

Just at the moment when I felt on the point of desperation, jumping up and down to keep warm, Davy struggling to get out of his nest of blankets, the primus stove threatening to die in the morning wind, always at that point, it seemed, Karim would unbolt the door with a loud thonk.

"Good morning!" he would say briskly, rubbing his eyes and adjusting his glasses. "Excuse me, please." Huddled in his sweater and coat in one of the two folding plastic armchairs, he would tune the transistor radio, searching for the morning news from Radio Cairo.

Light filtered through the cracks in the wooden shutters, closed against the cold and Davy, momentarily fascinated, fingered carefully those strips of light on the aluminum surface of the table, before becoming bored and banging insistently for breakfast.

"Coming, coming!" I would promise, stirring up the cereal on the primus.

"*Sabeh el-Khayr*, good morning, ladies and gentlemen," the radio spouted between bits of static.

President Sukarno of Indonesia was in Cairo on a state visit; John F. Kennedy was giving a speech in Baltimore, *Merry*-land, the newscaster pronounced it; Queen Elizabeth and her children were spending St. Valentine's Day at Balmoral Castle; two Russian technicians—it all seemed light years away from our sand dune village, where I spooned cereal into Davy's protesting mouth, then cleared off the primus and the previous evening's notes and papers and set the table with jam and silverware, dried milk and Nescafé.

"Good morning! Good morning! Good morning!" Bob came in, Mona, and Beryl with Laura Ann by the hand, still in her sleepers and bathrobe. When Saleh brought in the scrambled eggs and brown flat bread, a pot of hot water for the coffee and tea, we would wolf the food,

sitting there in our coats, and gird ourselves for the long
day ahead.

"Interviews at the school?" Bob would ask.

Karim would nod over the coffee.

Ah, that coffee! Years later, in my centrally heated
house, with its electric coffee pot, I can still taste that
stale Nescafé (courtesy of Ali from the Sudan). It was
superb! The temptation was to sit outside on our porch,
warming in the morning sun and have a second cup. This
was fatal, for by the time the second cup of coffee was
finished, the children's sleepers would be covered with dust
and sand and by the time we had cleaned that—well, it
was simply not worth it.

We dressed the children, Laura Ann crying, "Cold!
cold! cold!" Beryl and I worked as quickly as our numbed
fingers would allow. Faces were washed (no fun when the
water is icy), but I remembered Naima who had carried
the five gallons of water up the hill that morning and tried
to be cheerful. Brrrrrr!

Beryl would take the children off for a morning turn to
look at the goats' new kids. Bob and Karim and Mona
would set out on interviews, and Saleh would come in to
plan meals and do accounts.

This was a more complicated process than it sounds.
Erd-Moz had no markets. Everything that was eaten was
grown and stored in the village itself, brought by boat from
Aswan or on donkeyback from the county seat of Benha,
three miles south along the Nile. Saleh's one-legged brother,
Abdou, went to Benha by donkey each day, and shopped
for us. So careful planning at this particular moment was
necessary to assure that we would have enough to eat for
the rest of the day, and, hopefully, something reasonably
good.

My friends in Erd-Moz planned their meals according
to the amounts of dried dates, flour and beans remaining
in their clay storage jars. I had to keep reminding myself

how lucky I was to have access to the market; it was not always easy.

"Meat stew?" I would suggest to Saleh.

"Probably all the meat will be gone when Abdou gets there," Saleh would reply gloomily. He had once been an excellent chef in the house of Sir William Willcocks, the British irrigation engineer, but that was many years ago. Saleh was getting old, he was getting lazy, he did not obviously care for cooking on primus stoves with limited supplies.

"Well, fish?"

"Fish. Your husband doesn't like fish."

That was true. But it was also true that Saleh did not like to prepare this pulpy river fish, mostly carp, in fact. It was not very good fish, but it was a change in our monotonous diet.

"Tuna? Don't they have canned tuna in Benha?"

Saleh would shrug. "Who knows?"

"Well," I would finally give in. "What do *you* think, Saleh?"

"Abdou can bring some bones, perhaps, for soup, maybe there'll be a *little* meat we could eat on the bones, though I doubt it. And lentils for the soup."

"Take the little meat off the bones and make a curry."

"We have no rice."

"Abdou can buy rice."

"If there is any."

"Vegetables? Fruit?"

Saleh would look disgruntled. "Maybe some wilted spinach, maybe not. And I know there's no fruit."

"No fruit? Not even dates?"

"Well, we have dates here."

"We need sugar."

"Humph," from Saleh. "No sugar till Friday when the boat comes."

I knew Saleh had few resources to work with, but I knew

he could do better than he was doing. His soups were always excellent, so we did not starve. Why wasn't the rest of the meal as good as the soup? He refused to make desserts and on this point we struggled long and bitterly.

"Cake? You certainly can make cake," I had said, after my suggestions of custards and puddings had all been pronounced impossible.

"No cake. It takes eggs. All those things take eggs."

"There must be eggs," I insisted stubbornly.

"Where?" from Saleh.

"Where there are chickens there are eggs," I had replied, half laughing and proud of the way that sentence had come out in Arabic, like a proverb.

"And where do you see chickens who will lay the eggs?" Saleh had returned, triumphantly. That sentence had sounded like a proverb too, a proverb of poverty.

Where indeed? I remembered Saleh's nephew spent all afternoon, every afternoon, searching the village for enough eggs to provide us with breakfast.

The phrase "subsistence economy," which I had come across many times in my reading, began to have reality for me.

"Here I am, ready to go if you are ready," boomed Abdou at the door, knocking with his wooden leg. His standard morning joke followed and a laugh, the same laugh every morning. I would give him money and approximately the same shopping order I had given him yesterday.

I made one last attempt. "Abdou, Saleh says there is no fruit, but we must have fruit. Aren't there even oranges in Benha?"

Abdou thumped his wooden leg thoughtfully with his fist. He was an odd man, always laughing loudly and raucously, in spite of or perhaps to belie the basic bitterness of his nature. He had lost his leg in a Cairo trolley-car accident. The government-owned company paid his medical expenses and he was entitled to a new wooden leg each time the shape of his stump altered (not more than one per year). Abdou had so far collected seven wooden legs, on the theory that the government, or somebody, owed him something for his loss. He kept the macabre collection in his guest room and was delighted to show off the various models to visitors. It was poor Abdou's only distinction, Karim had suggested.

"Maybe we could get some fruit from Khartoum," Abdou was saying. "The post boat comes tomorrow."

"Khartoum?" My voice rose. The children needed fresh fruit, we all needed fresh fruit. Khartoum was a thousand miles away.

"They might have some in Halfa," said Abdou. "How much do you want? Might take a while to get it."

I calculated quickly, Bob and Karim and Beryl and Mona and me, David and Laura Ann, plus extra for guests, say, ten pieces of fruit per day for ten days. No, more, the oranges would keep.

"A hundred oranges and a hundred guavas," I announced.

Saleh and Abdou regarded me as though I had become suddenly raving mad.

Abdou laughed gleefully. "A hundred oranges and a hundred guavas, let's see, that would be about three pounds, plus tip to Mohammed's cousin, the waiter on the boat who will buy them, three and a half Egyptian pounds! A *lot* of money! Ha!" He cast a side glance at Saleh.

Saleh muttered to Abdou in Nubian; I heard Bob's name spoken. Aha, this large outlay of money must be cleared with a responsible person, i.e., a man.

We had been meal-planning for more than an hour. Now another half hour to track down Bob in the middle of an interview and ask him if he would allow his wife to throw three and a half pounds foolishly to the winds on a hundred guavas and a hundred oranges. Meanwhile, all the good meat in the market would have been purchased and we would dine on stringy leftovers. Annoyance was breaking over me like an allergic reaction and I fought it down.

"Here's the money!" I repeated my order. "If you want to check with my husband, please do so."

"Oh, madame, but a *hundred* oranges?" Abdou limped out, giggling, and shaking his head at the vagaries of the weaker sex. I discovered that evening he did actually check with Bob before setting out. Five days later, a hundred oranges and a hundred guavas came through the palm groves and up the dunes, tied on the back of Abdou's donkey in a bundle of sacking.

Mekki, the boatman, was a traveling peddler, one of several who worked up and down the Nile from Aswan to Wadi Halfa. He would put in to the dock slightly north of the village about once a month, and the word "Mekki's here" would pass quickly from one house to another. Soon a troop of ladies would wind down the path, baskets of dates on their heads, for Mekki did not barter for money, he bartered for dates. Women who did not have dates on hand but who owned shares in the palm trees could still shop with Mekki, and he would write in a black notebook with a stub of pencil how many dates would be owed him at harvest time in exchange for the beans, the cloth, the sugar that he measured into sacks and baskets.

"Mekki sometimes has good *mish*," said Karim one day. "Why don't we go down and see?"

Mish was the strong, aged cheese of goat's milk, probably an early ancestor of roquefort, I thought. Why not? It would be a good change.

Mekki cut us a sliver from a great hunk of white cheese reposing in a barrel of salt water on the deck of his felucca.

"This isn't *mish*," said Karim, wrinkling up his nose.

Mekki smiled. He was a Sayyidi, not a Nubian, and had the strong arms and barrel chest of the Upper Egyptian peasant. "No, it's white cheese," he said.

"Doesn't taste like white cheese, either," Karim complained.

"It is though," Mekki asserted and we bought a large slab. I decided it was simply very old white cheese, unlike the soft fresh cakes of goat cheese we bought each day in Cairo, and had accumulated unto itself various and sundry flavors during its long river journey in that cask of salt water. However, cheese was cheese.

We bought some olives, as many as he would sell us. "I have to keep some for my clients upstream," Mekki explained, with another smile. And I bought Laura Ann a plastic bracelet from the tray of trinkets and mirrors, which Mekki left out temptingly beside the sacks of beans and lentils and macaroni, displayed on deck for the two-day stand in Erd-Moz.

"We don't have any dates, sad to say," said Karim, but Mekki took our money and waved us on. We had long ago learned that dates were the real sign of wealth and prestige in Erd-Moz. Date products were used for innumerable things: Fronds were cut down and burned for fuel, the branches were cut into strips for building the walls and roofs of animal shelters; smaller strips were used to weave baskets and mats; women scoured pots and pans with balls of palm fiber, and Bob had even reported seeing woven palm frond bandages on a man's leg.

Dates meant date trees; date trees meant property; and property meant, as it does in every village and city of the world, status, solidity and respectability.

Saleh's chefly soul must have been reminded of past culinary glories in Cairo by the arrival of Mekki, for that day he concocted for lunch an excellent cold Greek-style salad of marinated kidney beans, squash and potatoes, all made more tasty by the wrinkled black olives and the slices of that old white cheese.

Occasionally small peddlers passed by, a man on a donkey who made the round trip from Benha to Abu Simbel

with a load of onions or tomatoes, lured by the prospective
customers on the antiquities boat at Abu Simbel Temple.

Women peddlers came, too, on foot over the sand, a
bundle on their backs, a basket on their heads. One was
a Sayyidi fortuneteller, and she wore, not the long trailing
gowns of the Nubian ladies, but the shorter, homespun,
black garments of Upper Egypt and the Delta. Middle-aged,
blue tattoo marks in her chin, eyes narrowed from years
of adjusting to the glare of sun on sand, she had a strong
face, a face full of life observed and rejected, life embraced
and lived, a shrewd face. She measured carefully, she bargained well and she read palms with dramatic lifts of her
head toward heaven and casting of her arms to the skies.

We gathered around her on the sand in front of Saleh's
house, as she laid out her wares on a length of rough
cloth: combs, head scarves, thread, safety pins, small needles mounted on a bit of hammered tin to clean the
burners of primus stoves.

Khadija was there, with Abdul Nasr, and Dahiba and
Naima, Hanim Ali, old widow Fatooma, Beryl, Mona, the
children.

The woman refused to read my palm.

"I know nothing of this lady and her people," she announced flatly, and gazing upward, intoned, "Allah the
most Merciful, the most Compassionate," passing off her
refusal very sensibly, I thought, as though it were decreed
by high powers.

Beryl bought a packet of needles from her and Mona
pressed closer and asked for a fortune.

"Hmmm," remarked the woman, her eyes slowly taking
in the quixotic presence of Mona in this village which she
must have known well, she had been coming, the women
said, for many years. Mona—wool skirt, good foreign shoes,
a green sweater, a Nubian head scarf (we all wore them to
be polite), an open intelligent face. What was she doing
here?

"Hmmm," she repeated, gazing not at Mona's hand but at her face.

Khadija teased the woman. "*Ya Amina,* here we thought you were a great fortuneteller, but maybe you can only read our Nubian fortunes," she said. "Beeja, all right, she's a foreigner, but Mona is a Moslem like us and an Egyptian."

"She is a Moslem?" asked the old woman.

"I am a Moslem," repeated Mona. "Yes, I certainly am," trying to banter with the woman, who suddenly straightened Mona's hand with a jerk and a nod which silenced us.

"Sickness, death, I see. That is what the fates decree," she droned.

"That's all?" quipped Mona.

"Sickness, death, yes," repeated the woman doggedly.

I could not bear the look on Mona's face. "She's already been sick this week," I said lightly. "Give us some new news."

"Yes, yes," chattered the women.

The fortuneteller dropped Mona's hand. "You will marry for love," she announced, but not pleasantly, and began to tie up her bundle of wares.

"Wonderful!" Mona's face broke into a smile. "I shall marry for love."

"Stay for tea, *ya Amina,*" Khadija said.

"No, not today, I have some cloth to take to Kemak." She stood up, shading with her hand the narrow eyes deep-buried in wrinkles, and stared at the river and the sun. "It will be dark soon," and she trudged off across the sand, her bundle under her arm, her basket on her head, alone.

"Sickness, death, marriage for love, some mixture." Mona was trying to dispel with words the mood that had settled on us from the abruptness of the fortuneteller's departure.

"Where will she sleep tonight?" I asked Khadija.

"Maybe somebody in Kemak will invite her," said Khadija, not much concerned.

"Nobody troubles her alone like that?"

"Troubles her?" It was Dahiba. "Who would trouble an old woman in our blessed land, where everyone is honest? In Cairo, yes, in Cairo you let a chicken out of your sight for two minutes and someone has stolen it and cooked it and eaten it, but here . . . here you could leave money in the street, it would sit there until it rotted, because no one would take it."

This was a familiar theme, the Nubians' pride in their proverbial honesty. Khadija chimed in with a story about a shoe that had been lost for three weeks and found; and old widow Fatooma told her version of the five-pounds-in-the-street story.

"If everyone is so honest, why do you lock your doors?" asked Mona, half laughing. The long, pegged wooden house keys went everywhere with the women.

"Me?" asked old widow Fatooma. "Because I can't see the door of my house from here, that's why."

"But if you aren't worried about people being dishonest, why does it matter?"

The women looked at us. "We always carry our keys," said Dahiba. "It's the best way to take care of our houses."

"But—"

"Look, Mona," said the widow Fatooma, "my door's open, my bracelet is gone. I might even think my old friend Dahiba has it."

Dahiba snickered behind her buck teeth, though her eyes were watchful.

"But," continued Fatooma, "if I've locked my door, then I can't blame anybody but myself."

In the afternoons when the children wakened from naps, we had tea. Originally this had been a kind of conference, a time when our group could assemble and discuss interesting problems that had arisen during the day, what might be useful to do tomorrow. But the longer we stayed in Erd-Moz with the friendly Nubians, the more the tea hour became a social occasion rather than a conference. This particular afternoon of the fortuneteller we had not thought of tea until it was too late. Bob and Karim had drunk their tea, and our share had gone to Mohammed, Abdulla and Abdul Majid, who just happened to be visiting. The stove and the primuses were all occupied with dinner, so we nibbled a few dry dates to stave off hunger till evening.

It had been a reasonably good day, I thought, as I fed Davy and Laura Ann mashed beans, dabs of pureed meat and rice. We had had some interesting conversation. Karim had cleaned the water filters; no one had been sick; Bob had gotten the refrigerator working; I had remembered to boil water and mix milk, and Naima had brought the lanterns before darkness fell.

"Let's bundle the children up and let them look at the stars before they sleep," suggested Beryl, and she whispered, "I think Saleh is making something special for Bob's birthday. He got a jar of strawberry jam from me."

The day had been so long and full I had almost forgotten my morning conference with Saleh, if not a cake for Bob's birthday (no eggs), surely he could produce something. Saleh's eyes had flickered, but he had not indicated what, if anything, he could or would do.

At the end of the meal, which was undistinguished, to put it mildly, Saleh banged at the door and Karim stood up.

"Happy birthday!" he cried. "To Bob!"

Saleh brought in a huge flaming platter.

Bob opened his eyes in surprise.

"Happy birthday!" we shouted.

Saleh had made crepes suzette!

"How did he get them to flame?" asked Bob, in between mouthfuls of the crepes filled with Beryl's jar of strawberry jam.

Karim and Beryl looked at each other.

"Karim gave him a jigger of whiskey," she said, "and started to tell him what to do, but he already knew. Apparently Sir William whoever-he-was liked crepes suzette. These are wonderful!"

That evening, we sat around the tape recorder, the faint Bach competing with the hissing of the Coleman lantern. We discussed our own life histories, we talked about politics and music. But we returned always to Nubian life histories, to Abdou and his seven wooden legs, Mohammed with his modern cradle and his superstitious mother-in-law, Sitta and her husband far away in London, that strange mixture of sophistication and simplicity of one culture and several others which we had all observed in our friends.

"Sometimes I feel as though Mohammed is guiding me along when I'm supposed to be interviewing *him*," said Karim, "suggesting a question, and so on."

"Yes, yes," agreed Mona, "it's an odd feeling, as though they were managing us, helping us."

I described our visit to Sitta's house, on the dune behind Abu Simbel, where we were served tea from fine Bavarian demitasse cups and offered cigarettes from a beautifully carved old Damascene wooden box.

"Sitta even told us the milk had been boiled so it was safe for Laura Ann and Davy to drink," put in Beryl. "You should have seen B.J.'s face!"

This was typical of our friends. They anticipated our customs before we had a chance to allow for theirs, a measure of real sophistication.

"And yet," mused Bob, "whatever talent they may have for assimilating other ways of doing things, it doesn't affect their own sense of identity. They are always Nubian, at least those who find their way back here."

Bob was right. No matter how well traveled or how well acquainted with urban life, the Nubians retained pride in themselves and their own traditions, not confusing a higher standard of living with a better way of life.

Mona insisted on making us a cup of Turkish coffee, and Karim told us the latest jokes from Cairo that had been relayed via Mekki. That evening, when I crawled into my sleeping bag by lantern light, I realized that for nearly four hours my mental landscape had been calm and level. I had forgotten for the moment the social isolation of my daughter, the painful wheezing of my little son.

CHAPTER 11

THE BEGUM AGHA KHAN'S
WEDDING PRESENT

The Begum Agha Khan, tall, statuesque and kindhearted, drifted in and out of our lives that year in Nubia. I never did meet her, but Bob did and communicated with her secretary for months about gasoline for our motorboats. The Begum's houseboat was often at Abu Simbel with guests who had come from Paris to visit the Begum at her winter home in Aswan, near the tomb of the late Agha Khan. Then, quite unwittingly, she became the catalyst in a drama that was to involve all of us in Erd-Moz. It had all begun some time before with a wedding present.

The family budget of each household in Erd-Moz was, of necessity, carefully and minutely calculated to take advantage of every possible resource, to plan for every possible expense. Only in this way could a family survive. The bushels of grain expected from each foot of arable land, the fruit from every date palm, the number of pieces of dead wood which might fall from the trees to be used for fuel, the number of pounds or piasters which might arrive from relatives in Cairo or Khartoum—all were estimated long in advance. Wedding presents, contributions to help pay for wakes after a death in the family, hours of labor given to help a neighbor replaster a floor, these were noted in real or imaginary ledgers. One good turn required another; reciprocity was a standing rule.

In such a tightly organized situation, any serious loss or any unexpected gain upset the delicate balance and created serious problems. How could the Begum Agha Khan have known this? On a visit to Abu Simbel, she had simply expressed a desire to see a Nubian wedding.

Mohammed and Saleh, who were in the crowd of Nubians gathered to formally welcome the Begum, had stepped forward.

"We are having a wedding in Erd-Moz this week," Saleh had said. "My niece Naima. Her fiance Jalal is here from Cairo."

The Begum said she would be delighted to come and a date was set. Saleh and Mohammed were then faced with the problem of providing a wedding. Saleh's statement that a wedding was scheduled was only partly true. The wedding he had in mind, that of his niece Naima to Jalal, son of Saleh's dead sister, had been in the discussion stages for years, but negotiations had recently struck a snag. Jalal's father, remarried to a woman in Cairo, opposed the match. It was Saleh who continued to push, and very cannily he had seized on the Begum's request as an ideal way to force Jalal to the altar. Since the code of hospitality is sacred in Nubia, Saleh had a strong weapon. Besides, it was correctly assumed that the Begum would be a generous guest.

Jalal, however, said no. He would not marry Naima, he vowed, unless his father agreed.

Relenting a little, Saleh suggested that the contract be written, the feasting and dancing and the singing of the bridegroom to the *diwani* take place, but the marriage not be consummated, the contract not signed until Jalal's father had given his consent.

Jalal was still doubtful.

"We have promised the Begum," Mohammed had said. "She is the widow of a great leader of Islam. Can we tell her that our word as Nubians is not to be honored?"

Faced with a phalanx of his relatives and friends, Jalal

could not hold out. He reluctantly agreed to go through a mock ceremony. After all, honor—and money—were at stake.

On a beautiful sunny winter afternoon, the Begum, accompanied by her party from Paris and three archeologists (one of them a French acquaintance of ours), stepped out of a white launch onto the same stone wall where we were later to land with the children.

She was escorted to a little roofed pavilion of palm fronds which had been erected on the dune below Saleh's house, facing the river, in order to receive properly such an honored guest.

The bride Naima, in borrowed finery and gold jewelry, was properly shy (and confused); Jalal, the groom, handsome and brooding in a suitably romantic way (he was very angry). The dancing to the beat of the big flat drums was spectacular, our friend told us later, the music on the flutes and tamburas of the best.

At dusk, when the sun dropped behind the mountains, suffusing the sky with gold and crimson, the happy couple was escorted to their nuptial chamber near the *diwani,* which had been decorated with a magnificent collection of reed plates (gleaned from all the houses in the village). Pleased with the proceedings, the Begum provided a wedding gift of one hundred and fifty Egyptian pounds (about $400) before traveling back to the temple by moonlight.

Jalal returned to his job in a Cairo textile factory. Naima resumed her household duties in her uncle Saleh's house. And the hundred and fifty pounds? The Begum's chance generosity inadvertently caused long-buried trouble to erupt between the family of Saleh and the family of Jalal.

As the eldest, Saleh became the guardian of the money. Abdul Majid, the groom's brother, was the first to object. The money should be left with a neutral party, he said, to purchase household belongings when Jalal and Naima were properly married. Had the money not been given to the couple? Saleh, after all, was the brother of the bride's father and could be expected to take her side if any dispute should arise.

Naima's mother suggested that half the money should be given to her daughter now, to buy jewelry and clothing. For what if the real marriage never took place? Jalal had left too abruptly, people were saying. Was Naima to be shamed before her relatives and friends, her reputation marred for going through a mock wedding ceremony? She should at least have some of the money.

Saleh, enraged, pointed out that the bride was living in his house. Was he likely to cheat a beloved niece by blood on his father's side? Furthermore, he had also raised the groom Jalal and his brother Abdul Majid as his own sons when their mother died and their father had gone to Cairo. Had he, Saleh, and his wife, Hanim Ali, not worked for this marriage for years, believing it to be the best thing for the children they loved?

Abdulla was called in as mediator. His solution was to keep the money intact until Jalal could be consulted. To this, all parties agreed. Saleh said he would give the money into Abdulla's safekeeping until Jalal decided definitely what he wanted to do about the marriage. But Saleh did not give up the money to Abdulla, as promised.

"It's his wife, Hanim Ali!" whispered someone. "She won't let him give it up."

To avoid an open clash, the mediator suggested the matter be dropped momentarily, in view of Saleh's and Hanim Ali's years of devotion to the young couple in question. The men sympathized with Saleh, who had always had difficulty keeping Hanim Ali in a proper wifely position of subservience. Perhaps the women may have sympathized a little with Hanim Ali in her effort to bring Jalal back into the community. It was getting harder and harder, the people said, to persuade the young men who went away to work to return to Erd-Moz and wed their cousins, the proper and expected Nubian marriage.

By the time I arrived in Erd-Moz, the Begum's present and the controversy over the marriage had been sources of fascinating conversation for more than a year.

Jalal gave one excuse after another for not coming. His most recent was that he could not get a three-week leave from his job.

"He needs three weeks to get married?" Bob asked.

"It is the custom," explained Mohammed. "People would not approve otherwise."

But it was easier for Jalal, far away in Cairo. He did not have to listen, day by day, to the gossip. With only seventy households in Erd-Moz, each household knew everyone else's business intimately and had plenty of time to talk. The fact that two of the oldest and largest of the village families were involved only added spice to the discussion.

Further, this marriage raised many basic questions. To whom did Abdul Majid and Jalal owe first loyalty—to their absent father with another family in Cairo? Or to Saleh, who had raised and supported them in the years after their mother died? This was a theme that touched many houses in Erd-Moz, for Abdul Majid's father was not the only migrant laborer who had gone to the city to work and had left a wife and children behind. Some sent money regularly to support their families. Some did not. What about inheritance, palm trees, parts of plots of land, shares in a donkey, a water wheel?

Talking out Jalal's and Naima's quandary in every possible variation was a good way of lightening one's own burden of sadness, guilt, uncertainty about the future.

"Why is your father so opposed to the marriage?" Bob asked Abdul Majid.

"He hates Hanim Ali," responded Abdul Majid promptly.

"Didn't she treat you well as children?"

"Oh, yes," said Abdul Majid. "She was very good to us,

but we respected her, we never loved her. Believe me, Bob, with all my schooling, I haven't the wits to think like Hanim Ali."

Karim pressed on. What was the source, then, of this violent feeling between Jalal's father and Hanim Ali? Hanim Ali was hated simply because she was intelligent? It did not seem logical, said Karim.

Abdul Majid was a tall man, a handsome man, but his short neat beard hid a weak chin. He hesitated before answering.

"My father thinks women like Hanim Ali are bad for men." He smiled, a bit sheepishly. "They take a man's strength, he says, like a scorpion sucks your blood. Well," and he lit a cigarette, inhaling deeply before going on, "and is he wrong? Look at the way she runs Saleh now! You must have women like that in America."

"Oh, yes," Bob answered, "in English we would say it's the woman who wears the pants in that family."

Bob's remark puzzled Abdul Majid, but only for a moment (in Nubia both men *and* women wear long full underpants and long, full overgarments). Suddenly he guffawed delightedly at this new twist which Bob had contributed to the discussion.

The little joke, rephrased suitably to fit its Nubian context, went all over Erd-Moz in the next two days.

"Have you heard that in Saleh's house, it's Hanim Ali who wears the turban?" giggled the staid old widow Fatooma to a teatime ladies' group, and the audience had dissolved in laughter.

What was Jalal going to do?

Abdul Majid went to Cairo and visited his brother. "I don't know," he reported gloomily. "Jalal is spending half his salary on whiskey! He never drank before. My father's hammering him on one side, Saleh on the other, he's so depressed he can't take it much longer. He says he doesn't want to marry anybody, ever."

And what of Naima, the bride? Throughout the months of gossip, she went about her housework unconcernedly. Only once had she spoken of the situation, to Mona and me while we sat together one afternoon in our courtyard, peeling and eating, with pinches of coarse salt, sweet lemons that had ripened on Saleh's tree. "I've known for years I was to marry Jalal," she said calmly. "My aunt Hanim Ali wants it, and she runs the house. Why should I worry about it? It is not my decision."

Saleh's cow calved; old Aisha, the midwife, went to Cairo for a cataract operation; Ramadan, Moslem month of fasting, was in progress. Each evening before sunset, Abdulla would walk to the veranda of Saleh's house and stand quietly while a few people gathered. He would raise a hand before him while the sun disappeared behind the black mountains, and then he would call, in a strong, full voice:

> "Allah! There is no God but Allah!
> And Mohammed is his Prophet!"

The prayer signaled the end of the daily fast, the beginning of the *iftar* meal, the dancing, the feasting, the music and the talking which followed late into the night.

Saleh kept the Begum's wedding gift and Jalal did not come.

An Egyptian psychiatrist, trained at the Sorbonne, once declared to me that he longed to live the life of his peasant countrymen, the fellaheen.

"Their life is so simple," he said.

I raised an eyebrow. "Simple? I think it must be very difficult," remembering the crowded Delta villages, the dawn-to-dark toiling in the fields.

The psychiatrist considered. "Physically difficult, perhaps, but emotionally simple. The sun, the moon, the earth, the flooding of the Nile." He sighed. "Just think of it, madame!

A wife, a child, a loaf of country bread, some beans, tea, a few peasant customs, of course. What a marvelously uncomplicated life." His dark intelligent eyes in the worldly face were troubled. "No neuroses," he added.

"None at all?"

He shook his handsome head. "They have no real problems, you see. They are swept along inexorably by the rhythm of their magnificently natural routine."

Now, in Erd-Moz, as I watched the maneuvering, the scheming of Hanim Ali as she strove to drive on her husband, threaten her nephew and deceive everyone else, in a mighty effort to reach a single goal—the marriage of Naima and Jalal—I wondered what my psychiatrist friend might say. The sun rose a little earlier as spring approached, it waxed hotter over the plots of millet and wheat, ripening the dates, the mangoes, the pomegranates, bringing the acacias to bloom. Hanim Ali could do nothing about the sun or the moon, either. It rose gloriously, pouring silvery light on the villages behind the temple of Abu Simbel, and during its brief period of ascendancy, dulling the thick stars that filled the wide sky.

The flooding of the Nile? Someone had already begun to change that, without Hanim Ali's help, as the Aswan Dam rose higher and higher north of the first cataract.

But between the rise of the sun and the rise of the moon, while the fields were flooding, Hanim Ali worked hard. She persuaded Saleh to go to Cairo himself to see Jalal.

The women of Abdul Majid's house whispered nastily that Saleh was "doing Hanim Ali's business."

Because we came upon her one day in the back court with the wooden lids off her storage jars, her scales in the center of the room, we knew that Hanim Ali was remeasuring her hoard of dates, figuring out again just how much currency she had to trade at Mekki's boat for the extra sugar, extra tea, extra butter needed for the wedding and the seven days of feasting.

"Hanim Ali has to buy things for Naima's household," explained Khadija, seeing my eye drop to those piles of dates.

But even Fatima, the most kindhearted and easygoing of women, hinted that Hanim Ali, at the prospect of spending the Begum's generous gift, was getting rather inflated ideas.

"She wants Naima to have new pots, new dishes, all right, but a kerosene stove?"

"What if they don't marry after all?" asked Mona.

Fatima explained that the money would have to be divided some way between the two families.

"If the wedding does take place, Naima will get it all?"

"Yes," said Fatima. "For the bride price, the household, and so on, it's the custom for most of the money to go to the bride's family. But who in Erd-Moz has ever had a kerosene stove, I ask you? Primuses were always good enough for us before."

When we visited Abdul Majid's house, Sherifa could barely suppress her rage against Hanim Ali.

"Who cares about kerosene stoves?" she cried when Mona mentioned this rumor. "Hanim Ali" (she fairly spat the two short words), "Hanim Ali is ruining poor Jalal's life. Everyone knows he wants to marry my sister and not that nitwit Naima. Isn't that true, Mona? Haven't you heard that, Beeja? Beryl?"

Mona and Beryl and I said nothing. These were the occasions when I was glad for the inevitable interruptions provided by the children. But Laura Ann had disappeared into an inner room and Davy was calmly juggling a few date pits.

"I mean, my sister is no genius either," Sherifa hastened to add, filling the silence which she wrongly assumed meant we were politely not mentioning the fact that her sister was considered not quite bright. "At least my sister is prettier. Naima is so awfully *plain*. Don't you think so?"

"Uh—er . . ." stammered Mona.

"Owwwww! Oooooh! Mama! Mama!"

I could scarcely restrain a smile at that howl from Laura Ann. She had saved us again. Beryl and Mona quickly jumped to their feet.

"What is it?"

"What is it, Laura Ann dear?"

Laura Ann was carried out to me with so much fanfare she was undecided whether to stop crying or continue her howling so that more attention would be forthcoming.

It was not serious. She ran back to play. Meanwhile the awkward moment had passed when we should have made some specific response to Sherifa's angry remarks.

"Who knows what is destined to happen in this world?" asked Mona noncommittally.

"Who knows?" repeated Sherifa. She laughed harshly. "Hanim Ali knows. She *makes* it happen."

What about the magnificent natural routine theory in this case, I thought.

"Jalal is coming soon," Hanim Ali announced brightly, when she went with the women to gather fuel and fodder in the mountains behind the village houses.

"Oh, no, he isn't," said the widow Fatooma. "His father won't let him, Sherifa says so."

Hanim Ali pretended not to hear this kind of remark.

"We will have a wedding when Ramadan is finished," she said, when she went down the hill to feed the cow.

People began to believe her. Hanim Ali, I saw, was one of those vital forces in the social mechanism. Bearer of tradition and sometime manipulator of tradition, it was she, more intelligent and forceful than average, who dimly perceived the reasons and uses for the "peasant customs" which were actually a far more complicated web than my Egyptian psychiatrist friend with his good French education would have guessed.

It was not easy to keep the fabric of tradition and order

intact, as the marriage in question demonstrated. Familial ties were loosening with the migrations of men away from home; it was hard for children when their fathers were away for years, it was hard for women to be without their husbands. Naima and Jalal were both products of such disrupted families. Jalal's father had gone to Cairo, married there and had not returned; Naima's father had "gone bad" in the Sudan and had never come home again.

"Why," Hanim Ali explained to Mona, "none of this trouble between our families would have happened if the men hadn't stayed away from the blessed land so long and learned the evil ways of the city."

I admired Hanim Ali's determination, but I saw, too, that in the manner of her mending of the family rupture, her doing what she felt had to be done, she was becoming heartily hated by everyone.

It depended whose side you were on, whether you viewed Hanim Ali as a conserver of tradition or, as Jalal's father had said, a scorpion of a greedy, overbearing woman. The munificent gift of the Begum gave her activities an ambiguous motivation, to say the least.

"Naima and Jalal will have a *proper* wedding," said Hanim Ali proudly, as she bargained with the merchant Mekki for a pile of powdered henna leaves to complete the traditional bridal baths. "Someone has to show people so they will remember, in Kom Ombo, how to give *their* daughters proper Nubian weddings."

Understandably, the other ladies on Mekki's deck, waiting their turn to be served, sniffed at this overweening statement. Abdul Majid's wife, Sherifa, even tried a giggle, but Hanim Ali paid no attention. She counted out her dates into Mekki's scales, set the basket of green henna powder on her head and sailed grandly past Sherifa without a glance.

At dinner, Bob and Karim reported that among the men they had found the same air of suppressed excitement: "Will Hanim Ali win? Will Jalal come?" That night the nearly wornout Bach tape, which Karim faithfully rewound each evening by hand, was superseded by Saleh's announcement with the coffee.

"Jalal is arriving tomorrow on the express boat!"

"Wonderful!" we chorused, but we were not too impressed. For the last five days the word had been that Jalal would be here "tomorrow."

"*Enshallah* he will come!" offered Karim.

"He will," asserted Saleh. "He has never broken his word to me."

"Would you like me to take you to Abu Simbel in the *Susan* motorboat and bring him back in style?" asked Bob.

"No, thank you," said Saleh.

In the morning we discovered he had left by donkey for Benha, the boat's first stop in Ballana province. Saleh was not giving his nephew any opportunity to get off the boat early and shirk his duty at the last moment by disappearing into the desert.

"What will they do *now* if he doesn't come?" asked Beryl.

We all wondered. If, after all this advance publicity, the day of the marriage announcement set and even the henna purchased, Jalal should fail to appear, relations between the two families would be severely strained. Saleh would be humiliated and Hanim Ali's reputation ruined forever. A major squabble was sure to erupt if the Begum's gift would, in the end, have to be divided. Many people in Erd-Moz would not be too unhappy to see proud Hanim Ali brought low and even Saleh, but a serious break between two large families would take years to mend and would be bad for the peace of the entire village.

At teatime Saleh had not returned.

"The boat may be late," said Karim.

But he still had not returned at dusk, and I could feel the tension in Naima herself when she brought the lanterns. After a makeshift dinner, served by Khadija (we did not dare to ask whether Saleh had returned), Mona announced she would go into Saleh's kitchen and make us some decent coffee.

She was back more quickly than it would have taken to light the fire, much less boil the water.

"He's come! He's come!" she cried. "You should have seen! There was Jalal, Hanim Ali with both arms around him, weeping. Saleh was crying too."

"Saleh did bring them both up, after all," pointed out Karim.

"Yes, and obviously they care for him," said Mona. "We pick away at their motives, but think how much this marriage must mean to them, childless as they are."

In the flush of her triumph, Hanim Ali gave in on one point: The *samma*, or marriage announcement, and the cleaning of the grain for the marriage bread would take place, not in her house, but in the house of Jalal's brother, Abdul Majid. This was considered a gesture on Saleh's part, to give Abdul Majid some sense of having participated, in place of their father, in the wedding of his brother.

Three hundred-pound sacks of grain were brought from Saleh's house to that of Abdul Majid. Sherifa, now that all had been definitely settled, swallowed her pride, her dislike of Hanim Ali's bossing, and supervised the ceremony.

In the court lay yellow heaps of grain, shades lighter than the sand. The women and girls in their black garments picked out the big pieces of mud, they tossed the grain on the orange and purple and beige plates, and while they worked, they sang, trilling happily in anticipation of the coming marriage.

"All the married women in the village came except four; two were sick, one was away, and one is very old," said Hanim Ali, pleased.

At lunch Bob asked, "How is the bride-to-be taking all this?"

Mona and Beryl and I glanced at each other. We did not

know. No one had asked her. Naima had sat in a corner of the court while the women cleaned the grain, and we had heard Hanim Ali speaking sharply to her.

"She was telling her to be quiet, and not to laugh so loud," said Khadija. "Hanim Ali," and she smiled a bit, "is determined that my sister Naima shall be the politest, quietest, most proper bride ever seen in Erd-Moz!"

"What about the bride's own mother? Doesn't she resent Hanim Ali?" Karim wanted to know.

We had asked about that, for it was well known that the real celebrators and enjoyers of a Nubian wedding were the mother of the bride and the mother of the groom. To cement the always tenuous ties of the family in the ceremony of a good marriage was the mothers' triumph, product of years of child raising and hard work. This was the moment when they were congratulated on their efforts by other members of the community, who brought food for the feast, small presents for the married couple. The mothers had done their duties, helped work to provide gifts for daughters, bride prices for sons, provided some future for children and grandchildren and at the same time assured themselves of a refuge in old age.

"Naima's mother is luckier than Hanim Ali," pointed out Mona. "She has already married two daughters. She's letting Hanim Ali have the pleasure of this one wedding. It will be all she has."

Crack! The shotguns being fired outside meant that the prayers, the promises before the official (the *mazoom*) were finished and the marriage contract was actually signed. The air was filled with the women's ululations and we went next door to congratulate Naima.

"Stay and have sherbet," urged Dahiba.

Saleh brought into the court the suitcase of gifts which Jalal was presenting to his bride and her family. What had he brought? A gift of $100 and two gold necklaces; two black *gargaras*, three cotton dresses, a black woolen shawl, plastic shoes, three head scarves, two bottles of perfume and two new sets of underwear (ruffled pantalettes and slips, blue and green). Presents for Hanim Ali, her co-wife Dahiba, for Naima's sister Khadija, for his uncle Saleh. The pièce de résistance (admired loudly, *"Allah! Allah!"* by everyone) was a tea service: twelve teacups and saucers, a teapot, milk jug and sugar bowl of beautiful white, gold-rimmed china!

At the end of the first day of celebrations, nine and a half pounds of tea and fifty-five pounds of sugar had been consumed, to say nothing of the dates and the sherbet.

"We borrowed every cup and glass in Erd-Moz," Hanim Ali told me jubilantly. "The girls were here washing dishes till almost midnight."

Her head scarf was a bit bedraggled from the long day's work, but her eyes were shining with pleasure and the two coquettish wings of dyed hair were still in place on her forehead, held firmly by the paste of henna.

In the morning, wedding bread was baked in both the bride's and the groom's house, the sisters and cousins bending over the clay hearths, cooking hundreds of flat loaves from the grain that had been cleaned and then ground at the mill in the village across the river. When had they had time to do that? Between afternoon and late evening, it seemed, Saleh had gone over to the mill in a felucca. This was the bread that would be used for the wedding feast and, on the seventh day after the marriage, sent folded to every house in the village.

Mona and Beryl and I walked with the children between the houses.

In the *diwani* Fatima and Dahiba were giving Naima a ritual henna bath, the first of three. Wearing old clothes, Naima sat quietly while the henna powder, mixed into a greenish paste with herbs and oil of clove, was applied like a mud pack to her arms, legs, back, chest, face. Little chips of sandalwood burning in a tiny earthen bowl scented the room.

Laura Ann looked on with curiosity.

"Laura Ann," buck-toothed Dahiba actually smiled, infected with the nuptial excitement. "We will wash it off tomorrow and make her pretty."

"Let's go to Jalal's house and see *his* henna bath," said Mona.

Jalal, slim and dark in his spotless white *gullabiya* and skullcap, was seated on a new mat in his aunt Hanim Ali's house, flanked by his brother, Abdul Majid, his friends Mohammed and Abdulla. A cigarette jiggled between his fingers; between puffs, he joked with the young girls and women crowding into the court to watch this long-awaited henna ceremony.

> "Take up your golden knife
> And cut down the fronds
> Of your grandfather's green palm trees."

His sister-in-law Sherifa had begun, in a low, sweet voice, the very ancient song of the bridegroom, prince of the village for the days of his wedding. The women responded, humming, and Sherifa sang,

> "Mount your white donkey, oh, bridegroom, oh, prince,
> And all of your relatives will follow you with singing."

Hanim Ali stepped forward, the pot of henna in her hand, ready to officiate for Jalal in place of his dead mother. A thumbprint of perfumed green paste on his forehead, a dot under his skullcap.

> "You bask in golden light," sang Sherifa,
> "The bright light of honor,
> The honor of your family. . . ."

> "Your great-grandfather Hamza," chanted the women,
> "Your grandfather Ali Daoud,
> Your father Mohammed. . . ."

Hanim Ali bent and placed a handful of henna in each of Jalal's slender hands, and with her gnarled brown ones she closed his fingers over the paste. It would harden quickly. He would hold luck and richness in his hands.

> "Go take your golden knife
> And cut down the fronds
> Of your grandfather's green palm trees."

Jalal smiled nervously, his fists clenched over the henna, nodding at Abdul Majid, Mohammed and Abdulla, the prince bridegroom's courtiers for the wedding.

"Oh, my son!" began Hanim Ali, her brown weathered face puckered with emotion, her voice breaking as she placed a print of henna on the soles of Jalal's feet.

"Oh, my son!" she straightened up and her high, thin old voice emerged,

> "Oh, my son, you are nobler than pashas,
> Oh, my son, you are first among men."

Sherifa scattered grain over anointed Jalal, the good millet fruit of the Nile silt soil. She scattered the grain over the heads of the unmarried girls gathered round, waiting for a bit of the bridegroom's handfuls of henna paste, a bit for good luck, to harden in their hands and bring a fruitful marriage to them also.

In her bedroom, Naima slept in henna, and was bathed in fresh water early in the morning.

This was her wedding day. After the second application of the henna, a small stick dipped in the hot blood of the calf, slaughtered at dawn for the wedding feast, was shown to her.

"From this moment she is a real bride," quoted Hanim Ali with satisfaction, placing a black shawl over Naima's head, as though the sight of the fresh blood was something so foreign to a young girl's eyes that from now on until the consummation of her marriage she would not be allowed to look upon anything else.

This was Naima's wedding day. Her face veiled by the black shawl, her body covered with thick henna paste under her old clothes, she sat in the closed bridal bedroom off the *diwani*. People came all day to congratulate her and to bring presents, which Hanim Ali and Sherifa carefully recorded in their notebooks, but Naima did not look at the gifts: a goat, a chicken, sacks of dates, small gifts of money.

The butchered calf was cooking in brass pots over many fires. The wedding feast was served.

But Naima sat veiled in the bridal bedroom in her henna, after seeing the blood of the slaughtered calf. Only in the evening when the feast was finished, and people had set off for the dancing in the wide plain of sand below the village, when the boom! boom! boom! of the giant flat drums could be heard in every corner of Erd-Moz, it was then, and only then that Naima was brought into the lime-light once more.

Old widow Fatooma, one of the few women in Erd-Moz who had made the pilgrimage to Mecca, was brought into the closed bridal bedroom to take the cover from a great copper pot of water. That morning after the slaughter of the calf, the water had been brought from the river by Fatima and Nezla, two respectable women whose first children were still alive. (Hanim Ali was determined that each detail of the ritual be observed!)

Old widow Fatooma first sprinkled Naima with the river water, she poured the pot of water over the bride. Naima's body hair was removed ceremonially, with a sugar and water and lemon solution. She was bathed once more, her skin carefully dried and massaged.

"Henna is the best cleanser in the world!" pronounced Hanim Ali.

Naima's skin glowed with a lovely red cast.

"Henna is good for our brownness," agreed Khadija.

New clothes were placed on Naima, the groom's offer-
ings, green ruffled pantalettes and slip, a flowered cotton
dress, a black silk *gargara,* a black head scarf, gold necklaces, plastic shoes. A clean white veil and then a black
one were placed over her head.

Boom! Boom! Boom!

The drumbeats were louder, the stars winking, the lanterns flickering red in the sand, the brush fires lighted and
held up in handfuls to tighten with heat the skin of the
great drums. Every night since the cleaning of the grain
and the signing of the marriage contract there had been
dancing, but this, the wedding night, was the most important, the climax of the ceremony. Every able-bodied man
in Erd-Moz moved in the huge circle on the sand. They
clapped for the measured line dance, a shuffle back and
forth, the circle of men weaving back and forth on the
sand, singing as they moved.

The women danced behind, in groups of four and five,
in twos and threes, their hands locked together at their
sides, red-and-gold-striped silk scarves tossed over their
black veiled heads. So measured and controlled was their
dance that the loose silk scarves never slipped, but only
moved as they moved, to the drumbeat and the singing.
Gold gleamed in the firelight, with the fine-boned brown
faces, the white teeth, the white drums held high, boom,
boom, boom above the white turbans, the white *gullabiyas,*
the brilliant silk scarves floating. The people of Erd-Moz
were dancing, dancing on the sand.

> "Go take your golden knife
> And cut down the fronds
> Of your grandfather's green palm trees."

Older women moved through the line, without losing a
beat, to dance within the circle of men. The circle broke;

rows of girls and young married women formed; they danced toward and away from the singing men.

> "Oh, my son, I would keep you beside me
> Tie you with my necklaces of gold
> Keep you like the red-gold shawl
> I wear upon my head."

Hanim Ali, I noticed, was dancing by herself.

"She is not from Erd-Moz," explained Fatima. "Hanim's from the other bank of the Nile, she didn't dance with the girls here when she was young, so she has no partner."

Hanim Ali was all alone.

The song, the flares, the dancing, the stars. The moon had risen and set.

Hanim Ali danced on, facing the drums and the light of the flares. She was old; she complained of headache and racking stomach pain; she would probably not dance at many more weddings.

> "Go take your golden knife. . . ."

Naima sat in the bridal bedroom off the *diwani*, the white veil and the black over her head, the women taking turns sitting with her so she should not be completely alone.

Hanim Ali's face seemed calm in the firelight, without the jubilance I had noticed earlier in the day. The ideal for which she had worked so long was almost a reality.

Children slept on the sand. Fatima lay down to rest and I sat beside her.

"Oh, God, I'm tired," breathed Fatima.

"Why don't you go home?" I asked.

"Go home? Who wants to go home?"

"Sit then," said Mona, "and rest from the dancing."

"But if I don't dance at Naima's wedding, I can't expect Naima and Khadija to dance at Gamal's wedding," she explained.

"Gamal is only six!" exclaimed Beryl.

"I know, I know." Fatima wiped her sweating face, adjusted her veil, and rose to her feet. "But Naima will remember, and do you think Hanim Ali would ever forget?"

She giggled at us, took a deep breath and found her place in the dance line once more.

We went to bed late, the boom of the drums in our ears, but we were wakened again by the trilling cries of the women,

> "Go take your golden knife
> And cut down the fronds
> Of your ancestors' green palm trees."

The bridegroom was being danced to his bride. Ahead of him was Ahmed, the "forever man," who cried, at each step, the name of each member of the bride's family, the groom's family, alive and dead.

"Hamza," "Ali Daoud," "Daoud Mohammed."

The forever man chanted on and on, for Naima's and Jalal's family trees were long, ancient and well remembered.

To the drumbeat and the chanting the bridegroom was being danced to his bride.

And was it finished? Not at all. The Nubians do not hurry with important matters, Fatima had long ago explained to me.

"Everything has its time. Marriage is difficult for a girl, and for a man. Things go slowly. We give it time."

The bridegroom slept in the *diwani* with several of his relatives and friends. But the bride slept in the closed bridal bedroom in her wedding finery, her girl friends and relatives around her.

The bridal couple, Jalal and Naima, had not yet even glimpsed each other in all the four days of ceremonies.

Before breakfast, I heard Fatima and Wahiba passing our door. Beryl, Mona and I followed the girls to the *diwani* where they had come to dance for the bridegroom and his friends. This, too, was a ritual, but a gay one, to occupy the eager groom, keep his natural frustration within bounds while the third and final henna bath took place nearby in the bridal bedroom. Naima's dark hair was oiled and combed and perfumed, her smooth brown body was bathed in incense and another set of new clothes donned.

Formal noon prayers in the *diwani* were followed by lunch. The guests departed.

Old widow Fatooma took off Naima's dark black veil; she placed a white veil over the bride's head, raised the girl up. She opened the door and led the bride out of secluded darkness into the sunlight of noon on the threshold of the bridal *diwani* where her groom Jalal awaited her. The reed plates on the wall glowed orange and purple in the sunlight, the mock chandeliers swayed gently, the white shells clacked softly above the new bridal mat, where the groom Jalal sat intensely upright, staring at the threshold where shy Naima on the arm of Fatooma had stumbled and regained her balance.

Hanim Ali brought forward a plate of grain and sweets and handed it to Jalal. He filled his hands with the grain and emptied them into the white-veiled bride's hands, who sat with head bent, her hands over the plate. Seven times he filled his hands with grain and seven times she emptied them back into the plate.

"Grain is good," pronounced Hanim Ali with satisfaction. "It brings luck and sweetness and richness to the bride."

Jalal solemnly scattered sweets and a few coins about the room. Hanim Ali, the bride's mother, Khadija, her sister, Sherifa, her bridegroom's brother's wife, and old widow Fatooma accepted the sweets, congratulated the couple and withdrew. The door was shut, to remain shut until the following morning.

Naima and Jalal were alone.

"Will Jalal sleep with his bride immediately?" Mona asked Hanim Ali.

She looked shocked and pursed her lips.

"Some do, of course," she allowed, "but a good and decent bridegroom waits until night falls, and in the meantime tries to put his bride at ease. Our girls are modest; they are shy being alone with a man for the first time and they resist as long as possible. That is the way we bring them up, and a good thing, too."

In the morning, the bride and groom would take their ritual ablutions after intercourse and wash their faces and hands in river water before being served breakfast.

Hanim Ali and Sherifa took the wedding breakfast milk and butter in an earthen bowl, Khadija carried the fresh-baked bread.

Hanim Ali's face was drawn with tension and fatigue, but her eyes were still bright.

She bristled at me, "These young people! I tried to get Naima to go down to the river and wash as *we* used to do, but she wouldn't. That girl is so *lazy*.

"Of course, in the old days we lived closer to the river," she admitted. "I still remember. . . ."

Her eyes looked beyond us, her harsh face softened.

"On my wedding morning Saleh and I went to the river, it was still almost dark, only a little light in the sky."

Her face was open for a moment, open and young, and I saw how she might have been had their marriage been fruitful, not only a determined defender of tradition, but a more personally satisfied member of the community to which she was so devoted.

"Khadija!" She turned from Mona and me and called to Khadija crossing the court, "Don't forget the green palm fronds!"

An edge of irritation was in Khadija's voice. "Yes, *Amitii*, I haven't forgotten, I've already taken them in."

"And you let them burn on the threshold until the fire died by itself?"

"Yes, *Amitii*, yes."

"Why didn't you tell me?" Hanim Ali scolded. "I wanted to see Jalal and Naima step over the burning fronds seven times." She sounded pettish, old.

"It's done, *Amitii*, that is the most important thing," said Khadija in a kind voice.

It was done. More guests were coming to the door with presents for the bride, chickens, pigeons, sacks of flour, trays of dates.

"Where is my notebook?" wailed Hanim Ali. "I have to write down all these presents!"

She was gone.

Five days of ceremonies and feasting, and more to come, but the greater part of the ritual was finished. She, Hanim Ali, had done it, almost singlehandedly, although Saleh and the Begum Agha Khan had helped. Hanim Ali's incipient neurosis, as my Egyptian psychiatrist friend would have refused to define it (peasants have no problems), had been happily averted. Social harmony had been restored. Naima and Jalal were united in marriage. The magnificent natural routine had been re-established once more.

CHAPTER 12

AMULETS AND OMENS,
SIGNS AND WONDERS

"I don't think I should leave the children," I said.

"Mona and I'll stay," offered Beryl. "We've been to Abu Simbel. You haven't."

"Go, B.J.," urged Mona. "The temple should be wonderful tonight."

I hesitated. Laura Ann was coughing again, yet Davy's wheeze was no worse than usual, and neither child had fever. Tonight Abu Simbel was to be specially illuminated for UNESCO visitors who had arrived that afternoon by private steamer. Abdul Wahad, a famous Nubian singer, had come from Aswan to entertain the party; there would be Nubian dancing, and Mohammed, our friend Mohammed from Erd-Moz, was to play his new compositions on the tambura before the British and Egyptian television cameras.

"Come on, B.J.," said Bob. "This may be your last chance to see Abu Simbel in all its glory. I promised Dr. Zaki faithfully I'd have you back in Cairo a month before the baby's due. You'll have to go soon."

I did not want to leave Erd-Moz, but I had to go while I could still travel without worry. I did not feel as cumbersome as with David and Laura Ann, and for that I could thank the life in Erd-Moz. The minimal diet, the walking on sand, the sitting and squatting had not been easy, but it had been good for my lazy muscles, an excellent, if sometimes unwelcome, antidote to the lassitude of pregnancy. We had been so busy during my months in the village, that, although we had planned to go several times, we had never made the promised private visit to Abu Simbel.

Yes, I thought, I'll go.

Down the shadowy dunes, through the whispering palm groves, we threaded our way to the river. It was a moonless night. The outlines of the mountains on the opposite shore had long ago disappeared into the darkness, and the boundary between land and river was marked only by the vague movement of water against the quiet shore.

"I don't like it," said Mohammed, looking up at the sky where shifting clouds masked the stars. "Smells like a sandstorm, or some kind of storm."

"A sandstorm this time of year?" asked Bob. "That means choppy water, then. Maybe we shouldn't try it, Mohammed."

Mohammed was silent. He wore a newly wrapped white turban, a pale blob before me in the night, and he clutched his tambura under his arm, that five-stringed homemade instrument from which he could coax the most joyous or the most plaintive of music. I knew he wanted to go badly for it was he who had first suggested the trip to Bob; it was not often he had an opportunity to play for an audience such as was assembled tonight at Abu Simbel.

"What do you think, Abdulla?" he asked, passing on the responsibility for undertaking the trip.

Abdulla must have known how much Mohammed wanted to go; he knew, too, the vagaries and dangers of the river in storm.

"We can try, Bob," said Abdulla softly. "But I don't like the sky either," he added as we climbed into the Susan.

I said nothing, trying not to imagine how a sandstorm might affect allergic asthma. Mohammed had said earlier it would take at least an hour to reach the temple, three miles to the north. I huddled deeper into my coat, leaning away

from the wind which was pulling the waves up into miniature whitecaps and slapping the troubled water against the
sides of the *Susan.*

Bob was steering a straight course downstream toward a
glow in the sky, a line of light rimming the back of the
mountain within which the rock temples lay. While we
chugged steadily ahead, the glow gradually widened, the
sky seemed lighter, and fragments of music and bits of
conversations began to reach us across the tossing water.

"Oh! Look!"

The involuntary cry was Bob's. Rounding the lip of the
mountain unexpectedly, in one brief second we had been
catapulted from darkness into a blaze of incandescent day-
light.

Abdulla and Mohammed leaned forward in the boat and
stared at the splendor of the temple which they had lived
beside all their lives, but perhaps had never really seen thus
as itself before, so much was Abu Simbel a part of the
mountain, the colossi of Ramses a rest stop on the dune
paths to the river from the villages over the hill, the shaded
courtyard beside the acacia tree an oasis between the graz-
ing pastures of goats.

"*Yallah,* Bob!" cried Mohammed. "Let's *go!*"

Bob turned the boat westward toward the pool of light
and sound, the only such splendid man-made display in the
thousands of miles of darkness which stretched away on all
sides of us.

"This is the BBC," a voice kept saying as we docked.
"Over. Radio Cairo. This is the BBC. Roger."

Colored lights were strung along the masts and decks of
the moored feluccas; a row of lanterns on the sand outlined
the stage before the temple where deck chairs had been laid
out, where the cameras and sound equipment had been set
up.

"Now aren't you glad you came?" whispered Bob, taking
my hand, and I nodded.

We walked up on the bank. Sudden tongues of wind pushed at us, flickering the lanterns on the shore which, like buoys, marked boundaries against the unknown darkness. None of the guests strayed outside the border of artificial light. They sat in their deck chairs like school children to watch the spectacle they had been brought a thousand miles from Cairo to witness.

"Feel that wind? We mustn't stay too long," cautioned Abdulla.

The wind was colder, it was rising steadily and bringing sand. The audience clapped halfheartedly for Mohammed's new composition on the tambura, for Abdul Wahad, whose songs and tone patterns spoke more to the Nubians than to the foreign visitors.

"*Mesdames et messieurs*," the announcer's voice broke through the applause. "A slight wind has come up, and we therefore cut this delightful program short to allow us time to exercise a very great privilege. Thanks to the generosity of the Egyptian Ministry of Antiquities, we may now tour Abu Simbel, which has been lighted tonight both inside and outside in honor of our esteemed guests."

We stood up and moved obediently toward the temple. Around the narrow door, between the pairs of colossi (my head reached almost to Ramses' stone shin) the family of the Pharaoh Ramses stood out, lighted from behind. There was Tue, his old mother; Nefertari, his wife; the three princesses, the pharaoh-prince son, tiny statues beside the towering figures of the king. The guide pointed out on one of the colossi the famous graffiti of the Greek mercenaries. They had written their names, Archon and Pelekos, on the Pharaoh's stone leg while resting during the Egyptian campaign against the Nubian kingdom, in the sixth century before Christ. We passed into the lofty rock temple, into the mountain itself which had been hollowed out by man.

Eight square pillars rose thirty feet to the ceiling of the great hall, and against the pillars stood Osiris figures of the king, flat and dreamlike despite their height, even in that blazing electric light. The artists of the nineteenth dynasty had recorded on all the walls of the eight chambers the triumphs, the sacrifices, the battles in Ramses II's long reign of almost seventy years. It was a superb tapestry in stone. The king stood, before a lion-headed goddess; he dedicated incense to Ptah; the king knelt under the sacred tree of Heliopolis, in the presence of the god Re-Harakhte, humbling himself only before the deities of his ancestors.

In the corners of the smaller halls flakes of blue and washes of dull red could still be seen, fragments of the paint which once covered all of the inside of the temple when it had been dedicated three thousand years ago.

"It must have been very different then," I said to Bob. "More cheerful."

"Cheerful?"

"Color as opposed to black and white."

"A gayer majesty than this," Bob smiled, savoring his bon mot. "A gayer majesty."

I smiled, too. The flakes of ancient paint were rough to the touch, but patches of the surface still retained some of the former vividness of color.

"Here you see Ramses' campaign against the Hittites," explained the guide; he wore a soft hat, but his voice was loud.

The stone shields of the Egyptian soldiers were arranged around the carved camp in a kind of stockade. Now Ramses emerges from the royal tent, holds council of war with his officers. In his chariot, the king dashes against the enemy line; he aims a monumental stone sword against the Hittite chief. Prisoners are brought before him, roped together, pleading for mercy.

"In the sanctuary of the temple, the most holy part, at certain times of the year, the sun strikes its first rays at the very center of the altar," cried the soft-hatted guide. "The rays are red. It is very remarkable, a trick of the pharaoh's architect."

We stood on the threshold of the empty sanctuary, tiny and bare. A plain block of stone formed the altar where the sun's rays would strike red. That was all there was, except that the air was close, oppressive, and vaguely perfumed here (from thousand-year-old incense?), one hundred and eighty feet into the mountain from the narrow entrance.

I stirred a bit uneasily, remembering the story of the two veteran American filmmakers who, caught by a light failure here, at the entrance to the sanctuary, had been overwhelmed suddenly, they said, by such great unexplainable fear that they had flung themselves to the floor and then bolted, screaming, for the door.

Bob was whispering with Abdulla. We had to leave now, before the storm worsened. It would take more than two hours to get back to Erd-Moz as it was, for we would be returning upstream and fighting the current and the cross wind all the way.

"He thinks it would be dangerous to wait any longer," murmured Bob, taking my arm.

A last quick passing look at the battle reliefs and up to the ceiling, with its carved border of flying vultures. I peered into a side aisle, and there the stone ceiling was still bright with golden stars painted upon a blue sky.

Outside the wind struck us, whipping my coat against my legs. While Mohammed, Bob and Abdulla struggled to get the boat off, someone threw the switch and Abu Simbel lay in shadow. A few lanterns still flickered like fireflies on the sand, the tourist boat sent out weak beams of light from all the cabin windows where presumably the UNESCO guests were preparing for bed in their warm cabins.

Nothing lay ahead of us but fields upon fields of black water. How could Bob find his way back in utter darkness? Larger waves struck us, the boat pitched up and down, backward and forward; the *Susan* turned crazily for a few moments, like a matchstick tossed into an underground pool, and I clung to the sides of the boat, frightened but afraid to cry out. We are surely lost! I wanted to shout.

Yet Bob, with Mohammed's help, steadied the boat and turned us straight south, and then for a long time we heard only the wind, the angry slapping of the water, the feeble mechanical chug of our motors. I closed my eyes and prayed I would not be seasick.

"It seems hours since we left the temple," said Bob. "Aren't we getting near Erd-Moz, Mohammed? Shouldn't I begin to cut over?"

Mohammed shaded his eyes (against what, I wondered), stared into the darkness and conferred with Abdulla.

"A little farther," he answered.

The two Nubians obviously had much better eyesight than I, for I could see nothing anywhere except darkness and emptiness.

"Mohammed," called Bob, "don't forget we have to throw out the anchor behind before we get to shore, or the boat will smash against the stone wall."

I shivered. I stared ahead. It was an act of faith on Bob's part, I thought, to even head inland from the safer reaches of the river when there was nothing to guide him but a dim approaching horizon of the tops of palm trees. But then, we could not stay on the river all night. And what about the children?

"Now, Bob!" shouted Abdulla. "The anchor."

"No," contradicted Mohammed. "Not now. Where's the shore?"

"Now!" shouted Abdulla. "Throw it. We're going to hit!"

Mohammed tossed the anchor into the water, at the same moment the prow of the boat whammed against the unseen wall, and Bob, clambering quickly out to grab the prow before it cracked on the stone again, caught his leg between the wall and the banging side of the boat.

"Ow!" he hollered. "Damn it!" and it took all three of us,

pushing the boat away from the wall against the force of the wind, to free his leg. Thankfully, it was not broken, only badly bruised.

By the time we had climbed the dune, we were exhausted.

Beryl was waiting up for us by lantern light.

"Both children seem very hot," she said.

They had fevers of 103, 104. Davy, wheezing, cried out in his sleep. Laura Ann's cough had deepened and she rattled with each breath.

"I think I *must* go back to Cairo this time," I said. "The sandstorm will make everything worse."

We stood in the open court, shivering in the wind as the tourists had shivered outside the temple of Abu Simbel.

"We'll see," Bob said brusquely. His leg was paining him a great deal, I could tell. "I'll go for the doctor in the morning if we can get the boat off."

"But I must leave," I repeated. "I *must*. Don't you see?"

"Yes, yes." He limped into our room.

Through the wall of the children's bedroom, the wheeze reached us, one wheeze, Laura Ann, another wheeze, Davy.

Beryl said, "We better all go to bed, B.J."

Next morning, while we dressed the children, a great commotion arose outside. Women were hurrying past the house and Khadija, with Abdul Nasr on one arm, banged on our door.

"A child of Fatima's has just died," she cried. "I don't know which one. I must go to her. Are you coming with me?"

"Khadija, I can't now," I answered.

She looked at me briefly before joining the crowd of women who were emerging from the streets on the lower dunes, from doors all along our street, and with black head scarves hastily thrown over their heads, were heading for Fatima's house.

"B.J., you must go, too," said Bob. "Khadija is right."

I stared at him. I knew that in Erd-Moz the obligations after death were rigid; one must appear at the house of the deceased as soon as possible. Fatima was my friend, but this morning how could I go to her? I was needed here.

Bob said sensibly, "While you're condoling with Fatima, Beryl can watch the children, and I'll take the boat with Karim and get the doctor from Benha."

"I don't care what he says, I'm going anyway."

"Don't be silly, B.J. You might do the children greater harm by leaving."

"Really?" I cried bitterly. "Really, do you think they'd be better off here in these drafty rooms than in a cabin on the boat?"

"Shhh! People are staring."

"I don't care." My only instinct was to do something, anything.

"We'll abide by the doctor's decision," Bob said firmly.

To my surprise, I burst into tears.

"Go on!" Bob practically shouted at me. "Fatima lost a child this morning. Think of her instead of yourself for a change."

"Let the children sit on the sunny side, out of the wind," I said to Beryl, wiping my eyes on her proffered handkerchief, "although," I added, "I don't know why I'm telling you, Beryl, since you suggested it in the first place."

"Never mind, B.J., go on, they'll be all right."

Mona and I set off together, down the street to the familiar green door where Fatima was receiving mourners outside her house.

"Fatima!" Mona and then I embraced her, a ritual act after death.

I drew back. Fatima and I stared at each other. She was dry-eyed, that appealing, always laughing mouth firmly closed. It was the malformed baby with the lolling head that had died; already the three-year-old boy was pulling on his mother's hand again, whining to be picked up.

"I'm sorry we're outside," said Fatima matter-of-factly, "but Aisha is sick this morning, and the noise would be too much for her."

She took her little boy's head on her lap while she sat with the friends and relatives who had come to keep her company in her mourning. She did not cry, but patted the child on the back, slowly, rhythmically, until its eyes closed, its whining ceased.

The rows of women talked in low tones. They held their head scarves in place against the gusts of wind which stirred all the sand in the street except where the women's garments lay heavily upon it in black patterned whorls and circles. The wind had been blowing all morning, and a fine screen of sand veiled the sky and the sun.

"Where are your children, Beeja?"

It was old Shemessa, eyes narrowed. This morning those eyes seemed like malevolent slits to me, although I knew in another part of my mind that she was simply, like all of us, keeping her eyes nearly closed to protect them from the moving shifting grains of sand.

"Your children, they must be very ill," she went on. "You don't have to tell me. I know."

How did she know?

"The twins, on the other hand," continued Shemessa, "are fine this morning, thanks be to God."

"Ahhhhhh!" cried Wahiba, Fatima's daughter, sitting down beside us, and arranging her dress around her. "Ahhhhhh! Beeja! She died in her sleep, poor thing. Ahhhhhh! Shemessa! We didn't even hear her cry."

Shemessa was staring at me, I knew, but I kept my eyes on Wahiba, who seemed much more upset than the dead child's mother. Her weeping was perhaps pretty much form, I decided, since babies are not mourned as greatly as adults, but Wahiba's grief for her dead baby sister was not all assumed.

Her father and her uncle took her to the mountain this

morning to bury her," wailed Wahiba, covering her face with her black scarf.

"Ahhhhhh!" murmured the women.

Widow Fatooma's face crumpled, a tear rolled from her whitened sightless eye, she buried her head in her hands.

I could hear our motorboat on the river. It would take them a half hour to get to the doctor's, longer to get back against the wind.

Shemessa moved off down the row to speak to Nezla.

"Only a few stones to cover her, she was so small," cried Wahiba.

"Ahhhh!" murmured the women.

"Mona," I whispered, "Shemessa asked me about the children. How did she know?"

Mona shook her head.

Nezla came up. "Beeja!"

"The twins are well?" I murmured.

"Not bad."

I looked at her face, puffy with fatigue, and I knew they *were* bad. (Like Davy and Laura Ann, the dreams whispered.)

"This is for the boy," she said, slipped something small and smooth and round into my hand and was gone.

"She died in her sleep, poor thing, we didn't even hear her cry," began Wahiba again.

"Poor thing!" repeated Sherifa, who had sat down beside us.

"They took her to the mountain this morning," wailed Wahiba, "her father and her uncle."

"To the mountain," repeated Mona.

How long had the boat been gone? I had no idea.

"Only a few stones to bury her, she was so small," cried Wahiba.

"Ahhhhhh!" I replied.

Was that buzzing above the wind the boat?

"She died in her sleep, poor thing," said Wahiba, her voice cracking.

I heard the buzzing again, louder.

It *was* the boat.

"Ahhhhhh!" returned Mona. "B.J., when you hear the motor stop, get up," she hissed from behind her scarf. "I will stay for a while, and you can send Beryl in your place."

"We didn't even hear her cry!" wailed Wahiba.

But I had already risen, paid my respects to Fatima and was walking toward my house. Bob and Karim and the doctor were climbing the hill, the river behind them dark and pebbled with the roughnesses of the wind.

I opened my hand. There in the dusty sunlight lay a bright blue bead with a dirty string through it, a present from Nezla, a charm to ward off the Evil Eye.

The doctor said Laura Ann had pneumonia; Davy had only a particularly bad asthma attack. Only. He gave us antibiotics.

"Six times a day for the girl," he prescribed. "For the boy his regular dosage of cortisone. The antibiotic won't help."

"I'd like to leave on the express boat tomorrow for Aswan," I said quickly before Bob could stop me.

A glance passed between the men. It was obvious they had already discussed this.

"I do not advise it, madame," said the Egyptian doctor. He was middle-aged, with a tired face. "Getting away from the sand in this wind might help the boy, but any change will be dangerous for the girl. Keep them both warm and quiet, and give them lots of hot liquids."

"Is that all I can do?"

"If you build up the boy's bed with pillows so his head is lower than his feet, I think you will find it will help the mucus to drain out."

Lay him on a slant. Give him tea. Wrap his head. Medicine won't help. Nothing will help. Travel will make

Laura Ann worse. So there was nothing I could do, except pray.

Mona came in with Mohammed, who asked if the doctor would look at the twins. They were very bad, he said, the same look on his face that I felt must be on mine.

I shook hands with the doctor. He and Bob and Mohammed headed down the street where the women still sat in rows on the sand crying and marking themselves with dust.

The children lay quietly on their beds; they were too sick to fuss.

The blue bead was in my hand. Almost without realizing what I was doing, I took the string and tied it around one of Davy's bed posts. The glass bead knocked against the palm wood.

Beryl watched.

"Nezla gave it to me," I said lightly. "A present for Davy. What else can I do with it? I can't very well throw it away."

"What did you give her in return?" asked Beryl. "For the twins, I mean?"

What indeed?

"I, I haven't—yet, I mean I don't know what to send."

"The plastic ducks," returned Beryl promptly. "The ones you pull on a string."

Now it was my turn to stare at Beryl.

"Yes," she said. "That's the thing to do. Mohammed's children have always loved to play with that toy, and so even if the twins don't improve, the others will enjoy it. And Nezla will be pleased."

I still stood there with my hand on the blue bead string.

"Well, B.J.?"

"You're absolutely right, Beryl, why didn't I think of it myself?"

"It will be a good omen for them," Beryl smiled, and she set off down the street with the duck pull toy wrapped in a towel, holding her own black head scarf across her face to keep the sand out of her eyes.

In the morning, Laura Ann's fever had risen to 104.6. She was flushed and panting. Davy coughed and coughed, almost without pause. Beryl and I had taken turns holding him up at night, but discovered the doctor was right, he seemed more comfortable lying on a slant, his head down.

Hanim Ali came, Hanim Ali with her hard bright eyes, her magic odd rings. "I have written for your son a sura from the Koran," she said.

Khadija came, bringing cumin tea.

Cumin tea. Sugared black tea. *Kharkaday,* the red tea of the Sudan, brewed by Dahiba. Every hour we tried to get some hot liquids down those rasping little throats. The wind was still blowing the fine sand through the crack between the roof and wall and into the bedrooms.

A second sleepless night passed. Between turns with Davy and Laura Ann, I stood in the dark court and looked up at the stars, dimly visible through the film of sand. In our room, Bob was trying to get Laura Ann to sleep.

"Oh where, oh where has my little dog gone," he sang. His voice was hoarse.

The second morning Laura Ann's fever was down. The antibiotic was working. One-legged Abdou brought her a shriveled orange from the market. Our hundred oranges had disappeared long ago.

"The boy?"

"Worse."

I dared not look at Bob directly. I was not too certain what he might do, but I was afraid that I might, at any moment, weep. Laura Ann's crisis had passed, but Davy still struggled for every breath.

"You take Laura Ann into our room tonight," Bob suggested to Beryl. "Maybe you can both sleep. B.J. and I will stay with Davy in here, and spell each other."

At dinnertime the wind blew harder, and Saleh predicted a storm.

"But isn't *this* a storm?" I said. "It's been blowing for four days."

"I don't know what to think," said Saleh. "It should have stopped by now. Maybe a big sandstorm is coming from the western desert." He furrowed his brow and seemed to listen to the wind.

"A big sandstorm?" Bob's voice rose. He tried to clear his throat.

Beryl, Karim and Mona looked into their coffee cups.

"Many children are sick in the settlement," said Saleh sternly. "God sends us only what we can bear. God knows best."

I felt dried and drawn, like one of the desiccated okras that hung from strings in Saleh's summer kitchen.

Later, I tried to stay awake on one bed while Bob dozed on the other. The wind banged a shutter, and Davy wheezed in, out, in, out. Bob, in his sleep, held a muffled conversation with himself. Bang, went the shutter. BANG!

In the ceiling above me, pinpoints of light winked in the roof beams, the eyes of tiny mice, crouching there, staring down.

Davy wheezed in, out, in, out. The shutter banged.

I shook myself awake. I must have fallen asleep, I realized, for though it was still dark, the wind had dropped. Inside the room it was quiet and peaceful. But something was wrong. Something was different. It was—no, no! There was no wheeze, no cough, nothing.

"Davy!" I shouted, springing up. "It's Davy! Oh, no!"

I found myself standing beside his crib and shouting, convinced that my son had died in his sleep while I, his negligent mother, had dozed nearby.

"What's the matter with him?" Bob, his hair standing up all over his head, had lifted Davy up and the child cried at being wakened so precipitously.

Beryl banged in, in her robe. Mona was behind her with a lantern.

"Is he—?" she began.

"He's just fine," said Bob as firmly as he could. "He's breathing perfectly normally."

And then we all looked at each other in that fitful yellow light as the full force of what Bob had just said came over us. *That* was what was different. Davy was breathing perfectly normally. He had not breathed like that for six months!

"B-but," I stammered, "just a few hours ago, when I put him down . . ."

We listened again, and in the quiet, Davy calmed in Bob's arms, his eyes drooped, he was asleep. He breathed regularly, in and out. The wheeze was simply not there.

"Well," remarked Bob profoundly, "let's all get some sleep."

He laid David in the crib, and caught the blue bead string on his elbow.

"What's this?"

"Oh," I said hastily, "Nezla gave it to me. Maybe she was trying to say thank you for the medicine I gave the twins, or something. She said it was to protect him from the Evil Eye."

Bob looked at me. "And you tied it on his crib," he said.

"Yes, well, I didn't want to hurt Nezla's feelings, I mean, we gave her something in exchange."

"You gave her something in exchange," Bob repeated slowly.

"Yes," said Beryl, "the duck pull toy. They liked it always. It seemed like a good omen."

"A good omen," Bob repeated, still more slowly.

"It wouldn't have been proper to throw the blue bead away, would it?" put in Mona. "I mean, it's a sign of affection, to give someone else a blue bead, it means you feel the person's worth protecting."

"And Nezla will feel the same way about the duck, I'm sure," added Beryl earnestly.

Bob seemed speechless. For a moment I thought he might cry, and then I thought he might be close to uproarious laughter. He bent his head, so as not to look at us directly, three women clustered around his son's bed, and he turned the blue bead over and over in his hand.

"A plastic duck on a string," he murmured. "Even exchange, you think, Western magic for Eastern magic?"

The three of us stared at each other, at him. We smiled, a little uncertainly.

"Well, that's a bit of an exaggeration, Bob," said Mona.

"We were only trying to return Nezla's good will," said I.

"We just had to," said Beryl positively.

A little voice at the door interrupted. "Mama! Mama!"

Laura Ann stood there in her sleeper, rubbing her eyes. "Why everybody up?" she demanded. "Up in the dark? I'm *hungry*."

As the news of my son's apparently miraculous recovery spread, we were besieged by visitors.

"You see," said Khadija, "the date honey helped."

"It was the *kharkaday*," pronounced Dahiba. "We should have thought to give it to him before."

"Wrapping his head," said the widow Fatooma. "I told you so."

"Newspapers on his chest," Sherifa reminded me.

Hanim Ali nodded wisely, and said that a sura from the Koran was the greatest help in distress she had ever found.

"I prayed, too, Hanim Ali," I pointed out to the old woman.

"We all pray," she allowed. "What else can we do?"

Fatima came, rather surprisingly, I thought, because I knew that ordinarily after a death one does not go out of one's house for forty days. But Mona said that the death of the malformed baby had in many ways proved a relief for

Fatima, who had nursed it faithfully for the ten months of its pitiful life, even while feeling hopeless. The entire community felt that in this case God had acted for the best; and it turned out the period of mourning for an adult was often not observed in the case of babies.

"I'm happy for you," said Fatima simply. "Aisha sends you her blessings, and says she couldn't have done a better job herself, although cupping might have helped." She almost giggled, but contained herself. The time had not yet come for laughing again.

Nezla arrived too. The twins were some better, she told us, and smiled meaningfully. For a fleeting moment, I wondered how she had used the duck pull toy.

"Shemessa had to stay with the babies," she added, "or she would have come to see you too."

I'll bet she would have, I thought venomously, but not as venomously as usual. Shemessa had her own ways of fighting evil and uncertainty and it was hardly her fault that I in some way seemed to personify the enemy.

When the doctor came, I asked him what could have cured Davy.

"Do not use the word 'cure,' madame," he cautioned. "The condition may recur when you go back to Cairo. Chronic allergic asthma is seldom *cured*, but it is relieved like this sometimes, suddenly, after a period in a dry climate. That is why I come to work at Abu Simbel every winter, so that my wife, who also suffers from asthma, may have some relief."

"But, Doctor," I persisted, "for the first time in more than six months the child is eating well. His fungus infections are actually drying up."

"That is a good sign. Even a temporary recession will give the child's system an opportunity to restore and strengthen itself."

I nodded. "And Laura Ann?"

"Much improved. The pneumonia is gone. The element

of allergy in her cough seems to have disappeared temporarily. But I repeat, do not expect miracles."

"Thank you, Doctor," said Bob. "We are very grateful for your trouble."

"I haven't done much," asserted the doctor. "The climate, the system, the improved weather, the hot tea, who knows what has caused this great improvement in both your children!"

Who, indeed?

Bob looked at the doctor for a second. "The women tell my wife it's the blue bead they brought her which has warded off the Evil Eye," he said matter-of-factly.

The doctor looked at me, but he did not smile. "It is amazing to think that an American would use a blue bead," he said. "Superstition is stronger than I would have thought!"

I felt myself bristling to the defense of my friends.

"They were trying to help," I insisted. "I think anyone, any mother anyway, would do anything she could, *anything* that offered even a possibility of help for her child. Don't you agree?"

"Even cauterizing with red-hot nails, scarification, circumcision, madame? They are all quite common home remedies in this area."

"I didn't quite mean . . ."

The doctor nodded at Bob. "Your wife's argument is all right, but one can go too far," he said. "Ignorance, how I fight it—every day."

"Ignorance!" I felt terribly angry suddenly, as the strain of the last days began to slip away into ordinary fatigue. "Isn't that just another word for helplessness? Do the Nubian women have antibiotics? Motorboats to fetch you when their babies are sick? They do what they can—which is a comfort to the living at least and hardly matters to those who die."

After the doctor had gone, Bob regarded me tolerantly.

"He does the best he can, too," Bob pointed out. "He's a stranger in Nubia, just like we are, yet this is his country, and he's reacting to the women's behavior partly in a way he thinks we'll find appropriate."

"Well . . ." I temporized.

"He didn't create the situation either, B.J.," went on Bob. "He can't change it all by himself."

Nor can we, I thought, though I had to admit that my mind had been more on my own children these past weeks than on anything or anybody else.

"And," Bob added, smiling a bit, "the poor doctor didn't count on how similarly *all* women react when their children are in danger."

He was teasing me again, I knew, the first time in months, a sign of his own sense of relief at Davy's unexpected improvement.

A few days later we made our second official visit to the *omda*, who suggested sweetly to Bob, in my hearing, that really I should remain in Erd-Moz now, even though my third delivery might be difficult.

"After all, Dr. Bob," he remarked pleasantly, between small puffs of his English cigarette (today in a silver holder), "you can easily find another wife, but remember this child is your first-born son. If he is doing so well here, why take him back to Cairo and risk making him sick again?"

I merely nibbled another nice, plump date and found I didn't care a fig (or a thistle or a date) what the *omda* thought. For these days I watched Laura Ann beginning to run with Gamal, shrieking down the sand dunes, accepted at last it seemed, by the Nubian boys and girls as just another child, not a strange plaything. I saw Davy pulling himself up and standing alone, the discontented frown on his face replaced, quite often now, by a smile of genuine pleasure.

CHAPTER 13

A FAREWELL PICNIC

The river was calm for our last trip in the *Susan,* a pleasure excursion to visit Mohammed's brother. Ali Daoud taught school in Zingahoor, a small village several miles north of Erd-Moz. Because the day was so beautiful and it was nearly my last in Nubia, we went a few kilometers out of our way to look once more at the temple.

Around the knees of the colossi, clusters of khaki tents, like gardens of giant flowers, were pitched on the sand near the acacia tree, to house the engineering consultants from Italy and Germany. These technicians were busy laying ropes, measuring, preparing plans to save Abu Simbel.

"What do you think, Bob?" asked Karim. "Can they really raise the temple above the level of the lake?"

"Who knows?" Bob was at the wheel today, wearing a wrinkled white sun hat like Karim's.

Mohammed sniffed. "It's ridiculous," he said. "No man can raise the temple. It must go when our land goes, it is part of it. If they raise the temple, why not raise the land and the palm trees?"

The people in Erd-Moz discussed their coming move as though it were centuries rather than a single year away. Yet only last week government agricultural extension agents had registered the small date trees that could be moved, had dug them out of Nubia's ancient soil and wrapped them in damp cloths to send to new settlements in Kom Ombo.

When the barges pushed off from shore with their

cargoes of trees swaddled in white, some women had run along the banks of the river, wailing as they had at the death of Fatima's child.

"Dates are the basis of Erd-Moz' wealth," pointed out Karim. "When they go, the people know their change is near."

But today the move to Kom Ombo seemed centuries away to me also.

"It will be a pick-nick," Mohammed had explained, using the English word.

So in our picnic clothes we had set off, except for me, still wearing the trusty maternity jumper, bulging now in its final innings, that button threatening to pop again. Let it hold together till we get to Cairo, I thought.

Davy wiggled with joy rather than discomfort and climbed vigorously up and down Beryl's lap; mine wasn't of much use to him these days. We had Gamal along, Laura Ann's friend, and he sat solemnly beside Mohammed, deaf to the teasing of Laura Ann, trying constantly to escape from Mona's grasp.

It was early March, a beautiful Nubian spring day. The gentle sunlight fell on the dark mountains, stretching away in their basins of sand to the Red Sea. Along both banks of the river tiny squares and strips of ripening winter millet formed an irregular tracery of green in the miles of bronze sand.

"Isn't that Jebel Ada?" asked Karim.

"Yes," said Bob. "Where Nick's going to excavate next year, if his money comes through."

Near the white-pillared porch of the *omda*'s riverside guest house, women filling cans of water straightened up and shouted to us across the water.

Beryl waved. She sighed. "We should stay, B.J., it is so lovely, why must we go back to Cairo?"

She trailed her fingers in the wake of the boat and looked around her at the open sky, the imposing quiet of the

landscape. White foam rolled over the watery reflections of
the towers of Jebel Ada, the white houses, the black-garbed
women, the mountains, the patches of growing grain, turned
the reflections, blurred them; water broke over the reflections
in gleaming black ripples, golden-edged.

We spun on. The landscape gradually emptied of people
and houses, the mountains lowered, the river turned and
narrowed.

"There! We turn there!" cried Mohammed, indicating a
hillside, which looked at first like any other empty hillside
among the hundred we had passed in the last half hour, but
nearer, we could see it was distinguished by the marks of
man. An old-fashioned water lift, or *shadoof*, stood close to
the bank, its long-angled beam dangling a rope tied to a
bucket by which water was raised to irrigate the land above.

The hillside itself was an irregular rectangle of intensive
workmanship between the river and the sky, a cultivated
quilt thrown down on the floor of sand and rock. Terraces
were shored with rows of stone, so neatly and carefully
placed they might have been stitched into the hill. Green
shoots of young barley sprouted in the terraces, with vines
of peas, climbing runners of beans, froths of *kashrengegg*,
the Nubian alfalfa. A few whitewashed houses were spread
about on the angles of the hilltop, each open-shaded porch
placed to benefit from an unobstructed view.

"The last hill almost to climb, B.J.," whispered Beryl, the
only one who still remembered my doctor's strict orders not
to climb hills under any circumstances.

On the flagstone terrace we were greeted by the women
of Zingahoor, for this *was* Zingahoor, the one terraced hillside and the handful of houses. Laura Ann, enveloped in a
fulsome embrace by Ali Daoud's plump wife, Halima,
responded with fervor, touching and then fingering carefully
the hammered pieces of heavy gold which formed the
necklace of the laughing lady of the house.

"Pretty," said my daughter thoughtfully.

"It is yours, my girl, take it," smiled Halima, making the classic offer of an admired object to a guest, an offer she knew would be refused, but which was nevertheless perfectly sincere.

Mohammed clapped Bob on the back. "You've got to watch your daughter, Bob," he said. "She's learning about gold too young. How will you find a rich husband to satisfy her?"

Mohammed could joke and so could Ali Daoud, for they were happy in their marriages, they had children, they had enough land and trees to assure them and their families of a livelihood. When a man is satisfied with his life and does not look beyond to a second or third marriage, he buys his wife gold to show her his love and his appreciation. Hanim Ali had explained it so.

The children were fed in the court, rice and yogurt and an orange and put down for naps.

"Mohammed says you and Beryl and Mona are to have lunch with us," said Bob.

Mona and I looked at each other. "We should eat with the women," I said.

"Yes," agreed Mona.

"It will be easier for the women this way," Mohammed said. "They won't have to serve you separately. You're saving them work."

Mohammed had figured us out long ago.

On the shaded terrace a table had been set with a white cloth and thick white linen napkins. We waited and looked at the tranquil river.

What followed was a gourmet meal, one of the best I have ever eaten anywhere, an al fresco luncheon above the Nile, twenty miles from the nearest neighbor, one hundred miles from the nearest city.

We began with soup, clear broth seasoned with lemon and some delicate herb I did not recognize. The pasta course followed: buttered and spiced rice, served with a side dish of chopped livers and kidneys, in sauce with tiny new onions.

Hot flat bread came fresh from the hearth, wrapped in a spotless napkin, to be eaten with roast lamb, creamed spinach, potato puffs. Fresh mint sauce accompanied the lamb. Salad of thin cucumber slices and *gargeer*, the pungent Middle Eastern water cress, had been dressed with oil and vinegar.

"The food is certainly excellent," murmured Beryl.

"Mmmmm," answered Mona.

"They're amazing, the Nubians," said Bob. "The longer I know them, the more I admire them. Have you noticed, Karim, they are the true gourmands, picking and choosing among the motley cultural traditions of Cairo and Alexandria and bringing what they like back to Nubia."

Silence. Karim of the delicate stomach was enjoying his lunch.

"Don't you agree, Karim? It will be interesting to watch how they adjust to resettlement. Karim!"

"Yes, yes, certainly, you are right, Dr. Fernea," nodded Karim and helped himself to more salad.

Ali Daoud startled us by saying in English, "You like the food?"

"Delicious!" we chorused.

"Who cooked it?" I asked.

"My wife's uncle Sayyid," smiled Ali Daoud. "Sayyid is retired and lives here now, but he used to be a chef in a very important pasha's house."

"I wonder what he can produce for dessert," I muttered quietly, thinking of the egg shortage and my battles with Saleh.

We nibbled some more little bits of bread, wiped our mouths and waited, like greedy children, for another treat.

We were not disappointed. Persian cream arrived in a low bowl of antique Royal Doulton china—Persian cream served with mango slices. The mango was an inspiration, giving the dish an entirely new taste.

"Maybe Persian cream was originally served with mango, in some shadowy time in Isfahan," I murmured. "And Fanny Farmer had never heard of mango, or at least she couldn't get it in Boston, so guess what, she substituted canned fruit cocktail!"

No one was interested in my musings on the origins of Persian cream. They were all taking turns scraping the bowl, politely, but still scraping.

Oranges and ripe bananas from the trees on the hillside were placed on the table. And finger bowls.

"Couldn't we meet your uncle?" asked Bob, as we sat back in our chairs to rest from feasting. "We'd like to tell him how much we've enjoyed the lunch."

Ali Daoud smiled and nodded. In a moment Uncle Sayyid, an old man with a carefully trimmed gray mustache, came out on the terrace with a tray of Turkish coffee.

"Sit down, *Ammii*, I will serve the coffee," insisted Ali Daoud, and Uncle Sayyid did sit down, after shaking hands formally with each of us.

"*Ya* Doctor, welcome!"

"*Ustaz* Karim!"

"*Um* Daoud!" (that was me, mother of David).

"Mademoiselle Mona!"

"Miss Burl!" (that was Beryl).

Uncle Sayyid was a small man, but he carried his turban proudly and his eyes were clear and direct under gray brows, trimmed neatly like his mustache.

"It was nothing," he kept insisting while we praised the food. "Nothing," but he enjoyed the praise. "I'm out of practice, but if I had been in Cairo, I could have prepared something more suitable."

"The Persian cream with mangoes was excellent!" I said.

"You liked it?" Uncle Sayyid smiled and placed his hand on his heart to acknowledge the compliment. "I had hoped to offer you a chocolate soufflé, it used to be my specialty, but I could not find enough eggs. What the chickens can lay the children need."

We sipped our coffee.

"How long have you been away from Cairo?" asked Bob.

"Three and a half years."

"You don't miss it?" I asked.

"No," said the old man. "I lived in Cairo for thirty-six years, but my heart always remained here with my family, in the security of my own country."

We looked with him at his view. From our hilltop luncheon table the slight curve of the river was clear, the curve north to Aswan beyond the low mountains, and south toward Abu Simbel and Erd-Moz, the village I was soon to leave.

On the opposite shore lay low hills, the foothills of the old dark table-topped mountains I saw each day opposite our house in Erd-Moz.

"It is very beautiful," said Mona.

"Yes," agreed Uncle Sayyid.

"And how are your children, madame?" inquired the old man politely, turning to me. "I hear your son's asthma has improved greatly."

"Yes," I answered.

"I am not surprised at this miraculous recovery, are you, Ali Daoud, Mohammed?"

They shook their heads.

"Not surprised at all. You see the scene before us. Now smell the air."

We obliged.

"It is pure, my friends, no dirt, no germs."

I would have liked to agree with him, but I could not. Free of germs and dirt? Well, not entirely, I qualified to myself, thinking of the constant dysentery from which Mohammed's twins suffered, the eye and ear infections that plagued the children, the women who died in childbirth. Uncle Sayyid was right in a way though; people of comparable income were far worse off in the city than they were in Nubia. Perhaps the land *was* blessed for those who could survive its remoteness, its austerity, its rigors of climate. For us, fortunately, it had been blessed.

Karim, who loved Cairo, said, "You don't miss the city at all? I cannot understand that."

Uncle Sayyid considered. "No. You, *Ustaz*, who were born in the city and whose happy moments are associated with the city, you would miss it. But I was born here. Each night when I walked home from the bus in Boulaq, where the streets are so crowded and the children are crying, I thought of this scene before us, and promised myself I would come back. I did."

Bob seemed about to speak, and I had a terrible premonition that he was going to spoil our idyl and ask Uncle Sayyid how he felt about moving to Kom Ombo in the near future. . . . It hardly seemed the moment. But it was Mohammed who raised the issue.

"They say we must leave the blessed land, though, *Ammii*."

The old man sighed.

"Perhaps it will be better," said Ali Daoud, "at least for our children. They can go to secondary school there or to college in Aswan. Education is needed these days. Do you want your grandsons to work as cooks and servants?"

Uncle Sayyid shook his head. "I have heard that argument!" he said. "It is only partly true. Any work is good if the workman takes pride in it. Here we are our own masters. We have our own land and it is beautiful. What more can we want?"

"*Ammii*," Mohammed spoke now, urgently, "it is not good for families to be apart. You know that. It is not good for the women to be without men for years, the children without fathers. Did you enjoy living alone in a room in Boulaq? My father didn't. In Kom Ombo the families can live together again. We can be happy together, we can get better jobs."

"And there are doctors and a hospital," said Ali Daoud, who was known to suffer from liver trouble.

"Let us not talk of it." The old man waved his hand. "*Ustaz* Karim, there is only one thing I miss about Cairo." He smiled. "I am sure you can guess what it is."

Karim smiled back. "The coffee shops," he answered without a moment's hesitation.

Beryl, Mona and I joined the women of the house for tea when Laura Ann and Davy wakened from naps.

"I hear," said Ali Daoud's wife, Halima, "that Saleh and Hanim Ali spent nearly two hundred pounds on Naima's wedding. Is that true?"

"I think so," answered Mona.

"It must have been some wedding! Was the dancing good? And the food?"

"Oh, yes," said Beryl. "The dancing went on for days. It was a marvelous wedding."

"And now there's no living with Hanim Ali, I'll bet," said a shriveled old woman in black, without gold, without a single ornament, not even a ring, who was introduced as Uncle Sayyid's wife, Sekina.

"You know Hanim Ali well?" from Mona.

Sekina sniffed. "I knew her. Grew up on this bank. I remember her well. Stubborn, hard-headed, too proud of her family name, she was. I knew her all right."

"She took on airs," put in a second old woman, Sekina's widowed sister Radiya. "Sounds like she's still doing it. Wedding presents from the Begum Agha Khan! Hmph!"

"Oh, I don't know," said Mona. "Most of the Begum's present they spent on the wedding. And Hanim Ali isn't well, she has bad stomach pains all the time."

"Who doesn't?" retorted Sekina, resting her chin on knobbed and work-worn hands. Deep lines of discontent and worry ran from her nose down past her set mouth.

"You stayed here all the time your husband worked in Cairo?" I asked. I was almost certain of the answer, I found, from the bitterness in her dark old face. After all, I thought, while Uncle Sayyid cooked and tasted chocolate soufflés in the pasha's house, this woman had endured Zingahoor's burning hot summers and chilly winters for thirty-six years! Hadn't she been lonely, lost children in fever and childbirth, suffered unknown diseases and missed her husband?

Sekina narrowed her eyes at me, black and bright still, though nearly buried in the folds of her sorrowfully wrinkled face.

"Hmph," she answered rather rudely. "Hmph, and was silent.

"Oh, *Amitii*," fluttered Halima. "*Um* Daoud is our guest!"

What was going on? What had I done by asking what seemed a perfectly innocent question?

"I've been out, my girl," Sekina finally volunteered. "I could have left. I've been in Aswan a dozen times. I spent a winter in Cairo, a summer in Alexandria after my first son was born."

"A good change," offered Mona, looking around at the women, puzzled too, I could tell, by the turn of the conversation.

Sekina snorted. "Good change she says. Oh, yes, the climate was fine, but I couldn't stand the cities. Filthy places! Filthy people!" She spat the words. "I was glad to get back to my own house."

"And away from her husband," old Radiya put in slyly.

Mona looked carefully neutral. Beryl suddenly was very busy playing "peas porridge hot" quietly with Davy and Laura Ann.

Plump Halima laughed softly, showing several fine gold teeth. "You know how it is, madame," she said meaningfully, "how men get when they've been away from women too long. They can't have enough of their wives."

I nodded.

"You think it's better when they're around all the time, eh?" cackled Radiya, showing one or two broken teeth. "Eh, my pretty?"

Halima tossed her head, sending her head scarf flying and her gold necklace tinkling. Laura Ann drew near, attracted by the noise.

"Yes," she said shortly, "yes, it is, it's much more fun that way, and at least they don't spend their money on *Egyptian women,*" with a glance at bitter old Sekina.

The older women were silent. Halima leaned down to me.

"Ali Daoud and I have an arrangement," she said primly. "He always sleeps with me on Monday and Thursday nights. Of course, I don't let on that I enjoy it, or he might think I wasn't a good woman. How is it with you?"

I explained, rather feebly, that in the West perhaps some married couples had arrangements such as hers and Ali Daoud's, but others did not and tended to be more spontaneous.

"You mean your husband sleeps with you now?" Halima was visibly shocked.

"No, no, not just now." I was more than eight months pregnant.

The two old ladies looked at Halima and back at me.

"Of course," said old Sekina, "in America the women sleep with everyone, not only their husbands, and the men don't even mind, just like those *Egyptian women,*" she added venomously.

Had Uncle Sayyid enjoyed more of Cairo than just the coffee shops? Had he given Sekina short shrift on feast days, few presents, little attention? This might explain her bitterness.

"We-ell," I said, "what you say about America is not really true, Sekina."

In the breathless silence which followed, I had the curious feeling that Mona was waiting for my answer with nearly as much interest as Halima, Sekina and Radiya.

Beryl rushed in to help. What one saw of Western women was not what Western women really were, in their hearts, she said. "I mean in their appearance," she went on, "just because they don't wear the *milaya* doesn't mean they're not good women . . ." and she trailed off.

With all those eyes fixed upon me, Mona's and Beryl's as well as Halima's, Sekina's and Radiya's, I faltered a little in the speech I launched into. Beryl was right, I said, in explaining that Western women were not necessarily bad women just because they didn't wear the *milaya*. For most Western women, I said, family and husband were very important; Western husbands did indeed mind if their wives slept with someone else and though it was true that a few women might stray from the path of wifely virtue, in general I thought the average Western woman was probably as faithful to her husband as my Nubian friends.

Old Sekina cocked her head at Radiya. "You hear what she says, *some* women *might* stray."

"I heard," answered toothless Radiya shortly.

"And then they want to stop circumcising the girls," said Sekina, in the tone of voice which meant that this speech had been uttered often before. "Can't they see that circumcision is the only way we can help our girls behave themselves?"

"Does everyone behave themselves now?" asked Mona innocently. She and I had both noted that in Erd-Moz handsome Mohammed seemed to receive more greetings from women passing by on the street than did other men, and we had even heard he occasionally drank tea *alone* with a notorious young woman whose husband worked in Cairo.

"Of course," answered Sekina firmly.

"Naturally," averred Radiya, gazing out toward the Nile. Halima did not contradict the old ladies, and talk drifted to other subjects; Halima's new baby, as rosy-brown and plump as she was; Sekina's excruciating backaches; the Begum's wedding present again and its effect on Hanim Ali's character; and always Kom Ombo.

"I can hardly wait to get out of this godforsaken place and get there," cried Halima fervently.

The old women shook their heads. We were eating melon seeds now, roasted and salted, and Sekina spat out a husk before answering. "You think that now, my girl, but just wait! Those houses! Have you seen any of the houses the government is building for us, madame?"

I said I hadn't, but I has seen pictures of the plans.

"And it's true there are only three small rooms and a court, isn't it?"

"I think so," I temporized. "Some are bigger than others."

"And the animals are supposed to be in the same house with us. What a funny idea! Who thought of that?"

I said truthfully that I didn't know, and reflected that no doubt the architect had been born in the Delta, where the peasants were so afraid their precious animals might be stolen that they insisted on bringing them in at night.

"Yes, yes, *Amitii*," went on Halima, nursing her baby while Laura Ann watched solemnly, "but think of the wonderful markets in Aswan," her eyes took on a faraway look, "the cloth from Damascus, and the cinemas and the gold shops."

Sekina eyed her cynically. "And where will you get the money to buy the gold and the cloth from Damascus, my girl? Or I should say where will Ali Daoud get it? Here at least we can dream, eh, Radiya?"

The two old women chuckled at their good fortune and Halima's foolishness.

"We won't move," said Sekina, biting into a seed. "It's just talk. Men talk."

"Right," returned old Radiya. "We'll never move."

She had no teeth for the seeds, but she took one and

sucked it to be comradely, moving closer to her sister as she did so.

"How could they cover this house?" she asked me. "Look how far down the Nile is. It could never come this high."

Was it possible that before another spring came round, the terraced hillside, the whitewashed veranda, the palms and the banana tree would lie beneath the waters of the Nile? The plans being made in Cairo said that it was.

> "The world is charged with the grandeur of God.
> It will flame out, like shining from shook foil;
> It gathers to a greatness . . ."

Beryl was quoting to Karim as we chugged slowly home in the late afternoon light. The sky was strewn with streamers of pale rose-colored clouds, and the river was calm and golden.

"Poetry, eh?" interrupted Mohammed, who had recognized the cadence although he did not understand the language. He smiled brilliantly. "I bet you don't know this, though."

> "Shall I ever meet Buthayna alone again,
> Each of us full of love as a cloud of rain?"

Karim smiled back. "Oh, yes, I do, Mohammed," and he responded with the next couplet of Jamil. Rhythms in Arabic, then in French from Mona, in English from Beryl and me made a kind of counterpoint to the steady chugging of the motors, the soft breathing of the sleeping children as we retraced our course upriver and tied up in the growing dusk behind Erd-Moz.

Love for their beautiful hillside home was strong in the old women of Zingahoor, strong enough to compensate for other things they had missed in life, strong enough so that they could dismiss as obviously impossible any suggestion that it might ever change. For Uncle Sayyid, love for the blessed land of Nubia was strong also, strong enough to have conquered the temptations and delights which other ways of life may have offered to him. He had been restored in old age to his homeland, the reward to which his people traditionally looked throughout years of migrant labor. To what would future generations of Nubians look forward? Or would the Nubian men and women, without a homeland, quickly lose their special identity and disappear as surely as their fields and homes, their magnificent view of the Nile.

We went down the hill, through the palm groves, along the muddy footpath where the lemon and mango trees had bloomed, where the hard green fruit, the last for these trees, was ripening, to the stone wall, where Bob and Karim had the *Susan* waiting. Beryl carried David, Saleh and Mohammed had our bags, Laura Ann clutched to her stomach a small reed plate of purple and orange, a farewell present from Gamal. Khadija was at the bank with Abdul Nasr; Nezla, Sherifa; Fatima with Gamal, Wahiba, Suffra; even Dahiba and Hanim Ali had seen fit to come down the hill to see us off. Old Shemessa was not there; she was with the twins. I understood that perfectly well. And Naima, the new bride, had to stay in the house for a full forty days after the consummation of her marriage.

"I'll see you in Cairo, though, Beeja," she had told me, "when I come to visit my husband. He has bought me a kerosene stove," she confided.

When we pushed off from shore, the women in their trailing black gowns bent down to the river, dipped in their hands, and tossed after us handfuls of the shining Nile water.

"Come back!" they called. "Come back, *Um* Daoud! Come back, Beryl!"

At my feet was a sack of dates, hand sewn by Khadija,

the last crop from the blessed land, a present from our friends. We waved at the cluster of black figures until they had disappeared, become a part of the bank and the palms below the dunes.

The express boat did not arrive until midnight, and to save time the motors were kept running while the few passengers boarded. Beryl climbed up an iron ladder on the side, the children were passed to her, one by one, and I was hoisted up, with much difficulty, by four Nubian sailors, the black water churning below me and the goats bleating in fear in the hold.

"Good night!" called Bob. "Good night, Davy! Good night, Laura Ann!"

"Take care!" shouted Mona.

"Night night, Laura Ann! Night night, Davy!" It was Karim, bidding the children good night for the last time in Nubia. The bell on the bridge clanged its warning, the motors speeded up, the steamer churned toward mid-river.

Davy, who had dozed while we waited, only to be wakened again to board, sank onto my shoulder, asleep once more.

"Night night, Baba! Night night, Karim!" chirped Laura Ann, although Bob and Karim could not hear her. She, too, was nearly asleep, but the reed plate was still firmly clutched across her chest. "Night night, Gamal, night night, Abdul Nasr. Night night, Mona."

"Oh, B.J.," said Beryl. "It's over."

We looked at each other and found we had tears in our eyes as the white steamer of the Sudan Railways pushed down the Nile through the moonlight to Aswan.

Our third child, a daughter, was born in the Coptic Hospital the first week in April. Bob had come to Cairo to be with me and we named the baby Laila to commemorate her Egyptian origins. She had red hair and green eyes and Sister Angelina confided that Laila was prettier than newborn Davy, but perhaps not quite as pretty as Laura Ann. What did Matron Natalya think?

"She iss sound, thanks God, why does have to be pretty?" boomed Madame Natalya.

On the third morning of Laila's life, proud Roushdi bounced in with the telegrams from Nubia.

"Thank the good God you have a healthy child!" signed Fatima, Abdulla, Aisha.

"Congratulations!" Mohammed and family.

"Best wishes on the birth of your daughter!" from Saleh and family.

When Mona returned to Cairo from Erd-Moz, she brought a gift.

"The women want to make sure you're taking proper care of this child from the beginning," she said, "so I promised I would buy you a charm to keep away the Evil Eye."

It was a gold pin, inscribed with Laila's name and a blessing from the Koran.

"Oh, and B.J., something very exciting happened right after you left, did Bob tell you? On the seventh day after his wedding, Jalal got a telegram from his father in Cairo blessing the marriage to Naima."

"Really?"

"Yes, really! I think everyone was surprised, but Jalal was terribly pleased, too. I was in Saleh's court when the telegram came, and Hanim Ali nearly split my eardrum with the ululations of joy she managed to produce at that moment. Remarkable woman, Hanim Ali."

"Remarkable," I agreed. "What other news?"

"Old Aisha's eye operation was a success. She's to have the other cataract removed next fall and she says to tell you she'll be ready then to deliver your next child!"

Naima and Jalal were truly wed, with the blessing of Jalal's father; Hanim Ali must be content, I thought. My son, David, was walking, Laura Ann had hung her orange and purple reed plate on a nail above her bed and resumed her social life in the *ganeena*. I had borne Laila, Bob's work on the Nubian project was progressing according to plan. Three years had passed since our arrival in Egypt, and according to our agreement with the university, we were due for a summer's home leave with our families in America. The magnificent natural routine by which my Egyptian psychiatrist friend clocked the life of his peasant countrymen seemed to be working for all of us.

PART III

Egypt

CHAPTER 14

EAST AND WEST

September 12, 1962

Dear Mother,

We arrived back in Cairo safely last night. The children are fine. Our summer at home. . . .

Yes, what was it about our summer at home? The letter lay on my desk three days old. I could still see the anxious faces of our families as they waved good-by at the airport. When, if ever, will we see these foolish, wandering children again, they seemed to ask us sadly, and we did not answer.

I could not bring myself to write our families the truth, that we had sunk back into our life in Egypt with great relief. At last we were home from home.

Laura Ann, after flinging her arms about Abbas and Farida and Fawzia, had walked through the apartment, ceremonially sitting down in each chair and emitting sighs of satisfaction. Davy, whose asthma had not returned, despite Dr. Hanna's warning, had taken Farida and Fawzia by the hand and drawn them to the balcony, where they could see below the old familiar swings, Am Ashu at the gate with his basket of penny candy, Am Mohammed in his rumpled *gullabiya* sitting on his customary marble bench beneath the cottonwood tree, its leaves thick with the dust of summer.

To feel at home away from home and be homesick at

home is a reversal of life's expected order. The summer in America had dramatized rather sharply the fact that, without quite realizing it, we had become expatriates.

"Well," Bob's best friend had said, "you've been away five out of the last six years, when are you coming back for good?"

When indeed?

During the first days at home, Bob explained we would return to Egypt for three more years to finish the Nubian project. Our families did not refer to our defection directly. But the undercurrents of feeling were there, especially with the children.

Laura Ann had begun by bubbling about everything.

"Oh, Grandma, I think I like goat cheese better than this orange cheese!" or "Where is your *flat* bread?" and, finally, "But my nanny always lets me do that!"

Davy, caught peeing in the back yard one day, and excessively remonstrated, it seemed to me (after all, he was not even two), said with surprise, "Cairo, everybody do it!" Bob had laughed. He was the only one.

Eventually, the children lapsed into Arabic to converse privately, which further irritated noncomprehending cousins and aunts.

Our loving families did their best. They smiled, they said over the telephone to friends who invited us to picnics and lunches and teas how interesting it was to have "little Egyptians" in the house. But they were vaguely uncomfortable, and we sensed and shared their discomfort.

We had expected some problems with parents, but we were surprised and disappointed to have difficulty re-establishing contacts with our old friends. I reminded Bob that long ago we used to find nothing more boring than an acquaintance just returned from Norway or Pago Pago who was dying to show us colored slides and tell us all about it.

"Aren't we doing that, babbling on and on about Nubia and Egypt?"

"But they ask questions," insisted Bob. "Why do they bother, when they so obviously don't care what we say?"

Why should they? Egypt was far from the problems of American domestic politics, it was outside the perimeter of European travels within which most of our friends had journeyed and about which they would have been happy to swap slides and anecdotes.

When I sat with friends who were managing, without help, a big house and several preschool children, the conversation always edged around to my servants, Abbas who cooked and cleaned, Farida who slept in, Fawzia who had stayed on half time since her marriage to help with the laundry. In one breath my friends insisted they could never have borne servants in the house, but in the next they confessed their envy of my leisure to explore old Islamic houses and visit desert monasteries.

I finished the letter to my mother eventually, and the moments of doubt passed. Were we or were we not to remain expatriate? Beside the work to be done, the fact of our rich and busy lives in Egypt, the question lost its immediacy. We would think about that some other time, we told ourselves.

Yet a nagging little doubt hovered at the back of my mind. At home we had been exotica, travelers tossed up from the sea momentarily to talk about our experiences, soon to depart once more. We did not belong there. But we did not really belong here in Egypt either. Despite whatever intrinsic value Bob's work might have had, for Americans in Egypt at least, we had also become exotica, to be trotted out at dinner parties. Hadn't we "lived with the natives" but not become troublesomely odd in the process? If we were tame exotica at home and in our adopted home, how were we to know what we were?

Perhaps because of this, we found, during the next years,

that our circle of friends was changing. Susan had gone home to New York. Nick was leading an archeological expedition in Nubia. Omar had been posted to an East European embassy as cultural attaché, and Aziza was busy being engaged to an army officer from a prominent old Turkish family. Many of the Americans who had come to the university with us had departed. But we had remained to become members of a different society, Egyptians who had worked with us in Nubia, Egyptians married to foreigners or educated abroad, resident foreigners, English, French, Swiss, Indian, American. Like us, they were not transient foreigners or colonial representatives; they were teachers, writers, businessmen, artists, administrators, diplomats, long-time residents of Egypt.

We all had reasons for being in Cairo, we had a common interest in the Middle East. Although we complained about government bureaucracy, the troubles with the post office, occasional food shortages, we enjoyed the life we were living in Egypt and generally we would not have changed it if we had been able.

"Don't you feel oppressed by the political climate?" a newly arrived American journalist asked. He and his wife, fresh from Washington, had been introduced by departing friends, also journalists.

"Am I oppressed by the political climate?" Bob mused. "Well," he said, "I sometimes think I'd like to try being a citizen for a while instead of an expatriate, but oppressed, no. Are you?"

"No," answered the journalist, "but I've just arrived."

"I think you'll find most foreigners aren't directly affected by the political climate though it gets to you indirectly sometimes," said Bob. "My civil liberties aren't curtailed except by myself. And I'm not certain that many people's are. The fact is, the art of the possible is highly developed here—or perhaps I should say the art of the permissible."

The journalist looked at his wife and winked.

"Bob even thinks like a native," he said, with a laugh.

"If you mean I'm sympathetic to the problems of Egypt, then you are right," Bob answered, a little huffily. "But I try to be objective, most of the time anyway."

We were touring the bazaars of Khan el Khalili together. It was night and it was Ramadan. Colored lights were strung along the streets, and the doors of the shops were outlined with rows of blazing white bulbs. Tents had been set up in the square beside the Sayyidna Hussain Mosque. Here, against magnificent quilted linings of red and orange and blue appliqué, were displayed Egypt's new iron and steel products, the Ramses made-in-Egypt automobile, books from the major Egyptian publishing houses.

People surged through the narrow alleys, sat at outdoor tables eating kebab, spooning up yogurt, drinking tea in clinking glasses, watching the performers who filled the bazaar streets on these gay nights of revelry following the days of fasting. A man balanced a bicycle on the bridge of his nose, a blind dwarf sold Korans, a bare-chested man, not young, plunged down his throat a flaming torch.

"How," said the journalist, "how will these people ever get up in the morning and do a good day's work after fasting all day and carousing all night? You can't get any information from the press office during Ramadan."

"I agree," said Bob. "Ramadan is a problem in a country trying desperately to industrialize. I'm sure Nasser finds it a problem, too. But he can scarcely destroy, by fiat, a custom which is so dear to so many people."

"Why not? It slows down production. The economy is damaged in the long run."

"What about people's civil and religious liberties?" Bob asked slyly.

The journalist nodded. "You are saying that here some liberties are more important than others," he said earnestly.

"Absolutely."

"Bob," said the journalist's pretty wife, Amy, "you should go home for a while. You've been overseas too long."

From one of the closed tents we were passing came a deep rich woman's voice, singing.

> "Oh Oh Oh Oh Oh
> You say that you love me . . .
> And I know that I want you . . .
> Yet I tell you to leave me . . .
> And then I long for your return. . . ."

"Allah!" sounded the audience, in appreciation, and clapped as the voice perambulated a long, sustained scale of notes.

"These Ramadan tents are proving grounds for young, unknown singers," explained Bob. "Um Khalthoom started this way. Shall we take a look?"

The singer was young, sturdy and square. She wore a mid-calf brown wool coat (it was a cold night), and her head was wrapped in a white scarf. She gripped the microphone with both hands.

"Not exactly sexy," said the journalist.

"Don't be deceived by appearances," said Bob.

They both laughed.

"What about your children, though?" asked Amy, when we were once more on the narrow street; this one was dimmer and glowed with the flickering light of homemade Ramadan lanterns—candles shining through designs painstakingly cut out of tin.

"Do you really think the Port Suez Nursery School is adequate?"

"It seems all right. The teachers are loving, even if the crayons *are* awful."

"It's the environment that bothers me," said the journalist's wife.

"The environment?" I was surprised. "That seems the big advantage of the place. What do you mean?"

"What do *you* mean?"

"Well, Laura Ann and David have children of all nationalities in their classes, children from different cultural backgrounds, speaking different languages. Don't you think that diversity enriches the child's education, rather than vice versa? Careful!"

I pulled Amy away from the wall; she had nearly stepped on an old woman who sat upon a strip of cloth spread on the ground. Her fingers gripped a little low table, where reposed a strange machine. It looked like a thin slice of an old typewriter, a piece of a typewriter with five or six keys. A strip of paper inserted into the roller curled white onto the dingy street.

"Oh!" Amy shuddered. "How awful!" She shrank away and stared at the old woman, wrapped in a ragged *milaya*, her eyes lifted up and closed, the classic pose of the blind. But this one wore glassless eyeglasses over her blind eyes.

"It's a beggar," she cried. "Let's go! I can't stand them."

"But she's not a beggar," I said.

"Fortune, tell a fortune on the magic typewriter!" the old woman intoned, "the future is made known." Her hands were poised on the keys of the typewriter slice, her closed eyes behind those empty steel eyeglass frames raised upward to heaven. "Only two piasters. Two small piasters to read the future. Isn't that a bargain?"

"Amy," I said laughing, "don't you want to have your fortune told on the magic typewriter?"

"Oh, God, no," she wailed. "Let's go."

"Not today," I said to the old woman and pressed two piasters into her hand anyway. That slice of typewriter had fascinated me. Where was the rest of it? In the hands of four other fortunetellers in four other sections of Cairo tonight?

"Why did you give her money?" Amy whispered, after we had pushed ahead into the crowded alley, circumventing a line of college boys in their class blazers, snaking along gaily chanting the names of the current soccer heroes.

"Why not? She wasn't begging."

"Oh, B.J.," said Amy fervently, "don't you see that by giving her two piasters you are only salving your own conscience? You're not doing anything to basically change conditions, the terrible conditions that made the poor woman have to sit on the street there in rags in the first place."

"But—" I stopped. Her fervor surprised and almost amused me. Nothing she said seemed relevant. The woman had to eat tonight. Until the conditions were changed, and obviously this was something I could not accomplish all by myself, this particular evening, why not give her two piasters, why punish the poor woman?

"That is what I mean by the environment outside the Port Suez school. Do you see now?"

I shook my head.

"When I walk Caroline to school," she said, "we pass this pitiful family, a mother and three bare-legged children. They sit there on the cold street in the same place every day selling lottery tickets or something."

"Yes?"

"It upsets Caroline. She asks all kinds of questions."

"Amy," I said, "do you really think it's bad for children to know that some people are poor? After all, in this world, they're the rule and we're the exception."

Amy sighed. "You just don't understand," she said. "You have really changed, probably, in your years here. You should think about going home while your children are still young and can adjust easily to America. You don't want them to grow up *here*, do you?"

"Oh, I don't know."

"Amy," called her husband, "listen."

It was nearly midnight, and the revelers had hushed partially to listen to the high chant of the muezzins, sounding the call to prayers from every mosque in the quarter.

"What are they saying?" asked Amy.

"I have to confess I don't know," I said shamefacedly.

"But I do," said Bob. "Karim and I were talking about it today. It's a special call during Ramadan, 'Give food unto the poor and the orphan and the bondsman, saying we feed you for God's sake only, we desire no recompense from you, nor any thanks.'"

Amy did not speak.

While we walked silently along, into my mind crept a memory, a memory of an evening long ago outside the Anglo-Swiss Pension, the beggar on silent feet, hissing in my ear with the awful breath of despair. I had reacted much more strongly than Amy, it seemed to me. In the last six years I had changed, but was it for the better? Or was I merely beginning to become resigned to conditions which I could not stomach before? Years ago, I had voiced my anger to Dr. Laila: "How can you stand it, to live in comfort with all this misery around you?"

Laila had replied, "You don't stand it. You try to work for change as well as you can, or you go mad, or leave.

"And meanwhile," she continued, with some embarrassment, "I take care of people less fortunate than I, whom I know, servants and relatives. It's not a permanent solution, but it helps them and me."

We were doing this now. But we could not, as foreigners, despite all our lofty talk, have much effect on basic conditions. That was the responsibility of Egyptians in Egypt, as it was our own responsibility in America.

In the spring the flame trees burst suddenly into bloom. Below the Citadel, built by Saladin, the red-orange flowers blazed against the muted stones of the Sultan Hassan and the Rifai mosques. The single tree outside our apartment house seemed paler, but on the island of Gezira the row of resplendent trees cast a blurred yet fiery stain upon the water of the Nile. Hanim Ali and Saleh came to Cairo from Erd-Moz, bringing Naima to her husband, Jalal. They telephoned to say that they would pay us a call. I had a moment of misgiving. Abbas was a Nubian, too. Could I ask him to wait on his fellow Nubians?

I needn't have worried. As on other such occasions, the Nubians took charge and managed things so that I should be comfortable.

"Beeja!" cried Hanim Ali and Naima at my front door, enveloping me in embraces of black silk perfumed with sandalwood (they did not wear the trailing *gargaras* in the city, Naima explained).

Saleh was already in the kitchen, greeting Abbas and exchanging news about Nubia. Abu Simbel was to be saved, it seemed, raised to stand like a single island in the vastness of the new flood-lake.

"They'll never do it!" predicted Abbas, as he served tea. "How can they put that mountain of stone up?" (and he gestured to the ceiling with my best teapot).

"Well," said Hanim Ali with some asperity, "everyone said they'd never move us, either, but the people in the Kenuzi area have already gone. From the boat you can see the houses. They took the shutters along to Kom Ombo so the windows are empty. They look awful." She shuddered.

"If they can do that," put in Saleh, "I say they can lift the temple, too."

"Aren't you going to show me around your house?" asked Hanim Ali, after she had examined my teacups carefully from all angles. "You were always asking us to show you around our houses, Beeja. Now it's your turn!"

I nodded, there being really nothing I could say to *that*.

"Ah, you have a nice big bed, the doctor and you." She tested our mattress with the heel of her hand. "Seems comfortable, too. And where do the children sleep? Oh, my," she giggled and Naima echoed her. "You don't have a cradle like Mohammed, do you?" She ran her hand over the rails of the three children's cribs. "He said all foreigners had them. Hmph!" This discovery seemed to give her great satisfaction. "And where are the children?"

"In the park with their nanny." I led her to the balcony where a panorama of playing children, nannies in white and blue uniforms, Czech ladies in homemade spring prints, was spread out before us under the trees in the sunshine.

"A nice view," said Hanim Ali, leaning on the wall of the balcony. "Don't you think so, Naima? And that one flame tree there is pretty, just in front. Aren't you lucky to have a nanny? Hangs the wash out here, does she? Good idea, catches the sun and keeps the laundry out of the way at the same time." She passed through the french doors into the study in a rush of flowing veils, and paused under the round white Japanese lantern which hung from the ceiling.

"Is it made of paper?" she inquired.

"Yes."

"It makes the light of a small bulb seem stronger, doesn't it?"

"Yes, Hanim Ali."

She began to talk to Naima in the Nubian language, and I could almost see her mind working. I would not have been at all surprised to visit Kom Ombo later and find home-made paper lanterns around the electric lights in Hanim Ali's new house. Perhaps she was planning to experiment in Naima's Cairo apartment first. I marveled again as I remembered the Nubians' ability to see possibilities of beauty in the humblest objects, to make their surroundings attractive with a minimum of materials—a quality of mind they shared, after all, with the makers of our paper lantern.

"Have you got your kerosene stove?" I asked Naima.

She nodded. "It has four burners that work all at the same time," she said proudly. Remembering the work required to build one brush fire for tea or coax one primus stove into blazing flame, I appreciated again the luxury of automatic stoves.

"How about your apartment? Did Jalal get one from the company?"

"Yes, he did," interposed Hanim Ali before Naima had a chance to reply. "And it's a very good apartment."

I caught Naima's eye. She had covered the lower part of her face with her *milaya* suddenly, and I suspected strongly that she was smothering a giggle. Perhaps, in time, when she had the security of her own home and children, she, too, would develop the independence of Hanim Ali and insist on *her* daughters having proper Nubian weddings.

The fall of 1963 was the year of the onion fiasco. All along the road between Cairo and the suburb of Maadi, string bags of surplus onions stood on the street, and as the days passed, the smell of rotting onions filled the dusty air. What had happened? No one was quite certain, but two rumors circulated. A preliminary contract to export large quantities of onions to a new African republic had fallen through, or a mistake somewhere in the labyrinthine bureaucracy of economic planning had resulted in extra thousands rather than extra scores of acres being devoted to onion production.

At first, people came to take the onions and sell them, but the market was glutted. The onions were left on other corners to rot. Housewives in worn black *milayas* could sometimes be seen filling a basket from one of those curbside string bags. But hundreds of pounds still remained on the streets, unneeded, unused, mute testimony to the imperfection of human planning.

Rumors of trouble between Russian and Egyptian engineers working on the Aswan Dam were indirectly confirmed by two events: A new Russian construction chief arrived from Moscow, and a change in the top-level personnel of the High Dam Ministry took place. In the meeting of the National Assembly, televised and reported in the local press, people began to ask about occasional shortages of consumer goods.

"Sir!" began a joke which went the rounds that fall. "Yes, Abdulla *Effendi*?"

"My question, sir, which I wish to pose to the esteemed

members of the National Assembly, is this: Where is all the cooking oil, where are the tender chickens, where is the tea?"

"Thank you, Abdulla *Effendi,* we shall answer your question tomorrow."

The next day, "Sir!" said another voice.

"Yes, Mohammed *Effendi?*"

"The question which I wish to pose to the esteemed members of the National Assembly, is this: Where is the cooking oil, where are the tender chickens, where is the tea, and where is Abdulla *Effendi?*"

Nasser was reported to have laughed at this joke, as he supposedly laughed, like all other Egyptians, at jokes about themselves, their troubles, their failings, jokes which have been a feature of Egyptian life for many generations. "To be truly lighthearted, or *dem-khefeef,*" Omar had said when asked for a precise definition of that highly prized element of the Egyptian personality, "one must be able to laugh most loudly at one's own absurdities."

An Arab summit meeting was held in Cairo and tentative plans were announced for an Afro-Asian conference. Unrest was reported in Yemen and Aden. Hoda, President Nasser's eldest daughter, married, not Ben Bella, then president of Algeria, but an Egyptian engineer, the son of close family friends. His second daughter entered the American University.

By 1963, Egypt's population was increasing at a staggering annual rate of three percent. "When the Aswan Dam is finished," whispered economists, "the ratio between land and people will be just the same as when they started building it." The President made his famous speech endorsing birth control, and religious conservatives argued the subject in the press.

People had begun to be vocal in their complaints. The rich, reduced from three cars to one, unable to travel to Europe because of currency restrictions, complained loudly.

The middle class, teachers, clerks, whose expectations had risen far above the salary increases Nasser had been able to grant them, complained as they struggled to raise a family and save for an Egyptian car and an Egyptian refrigerator. The unskilled laborers, instead of being pleased that Nasser had raised the minimum wage from 25 to 75 cents a day for ten hours of unskilled labor, naturally wanted more than bare subsistence. And the very poor occasionally still threw themselves in front of moving trams in a desperate hope of maiming themselves sufficiently to receive the newly established insurance support for life. Price controls were clamped on rent, meat, oil and bread.

Despite national and international problems, however, no breath of corruption or gossip touched President Nasser himself, whose personal life continued to be exemplary. But he was discovering that he could not change everything in ten years—the social structure, with its remnants of several colonial rules, the heavy, unwieldy bureaucratic machinery, the unfavorable equation between land and population. It was becoming difficult for the most idealistic of his associates to retain their optimism and easy to relapse into a more selfish mood.

Bob and I, drinking our after-dinner coffee in the study one evening, heard Abbas' key in the lock. Abbas never came back after we had done the accounts and wished each other good night. Was he ill?

"The President has been shot!" he said.

"Nasser has been shot? When? Where?" Bob sat up.

"Not our president," he said. "Your president."

"Our President?" We both stood up. "President Kennedy?" How could he be? Things like that didn't happen in our country.

"We heard it on the radio downstairs," said Abbas.

"Well, the radio must have made a mistake," I said positively. "They sometimes get things wrong."

"I don't think so," answered Abbas. "It was the BBC."

Bob was already out in the hall, and I followed him upstairs to the apartment of our neighbor, a doctor with the American Naval Medical Research Unit.

"Kennedy's been shot," said Bob. "That's what Abbas says he heard on the radio downstairs. I'm sure he's mistaken, but could you try to get the overseas station on your shortwave, just to check?"

"Kennedy? Impossible!" Our neighbor clicked on the radio and for several exasperating moments, he played with the dials, getting jazz, blares of static, until a faint voice said, "In the Dallas hospital, Mrs. Kennedy and other members of the President's party are keeping a vigil of prayer for the President, who lies near death. . . ."

We looked at each other. It was true. President John Fitzgerald Kennedy and not President Nasser had been shot.

The phone rang.

In the next hours, while we sat beside the faint voice of the overseas radio, the phone continued to ring. All over Cairo, Americans were telephoning each other. "Was it true? Could it be true? How was it possible? What had we heard? What had happened? How could it happen? Here, yes, but in America. . . . Impossible! Was it true? Could it be true? . . ."

At 2:30 A.M. I went to bed, fell asleep immediately and had constant nightmares. Kennedy was in Egypt and had been shot. No. Nasser was in America and had been shot. No. My brother had been shot. No. He had been killed in the war. But . . .

At seven, Bob came down. "Kennedy is dead," he said, his face gray. "It is impossible and I have no sense of reality about it, but it must be so."

In the morning, Abbas, Farida and Fawzia greeted us with the condolences reserved for a death in the immediate family. We were considered to be officially in mourning.

Aziza's family and Mona's family sent flowers. In his

office, Bob spent most of the first week after the President's death receiving formal calls from his friends in the Ministry of Social Affairs, Cairo University, Ain Shams University. The *boabs,* Am Mohammed in the *ganeena,* Fadhil the nut vendor, all shook our hands formally and uttered those traditional words of condolences. People we did not know would stop us on the street to shake hands and express their grief.

We accepted the condolences without question, because we did indeed feel as though a member of the family had died, a member to whom we had given little thought before.

In the mosques, people prayed for President Kennedy and for his family. Bells tolled in the churches, Latin Rite, Greek Rite, Nestorian, Coptic, Maronite, and members of President Nasser's cabinet attended the Solemn Requiem Mass in St. Joseph's Italian cathedral. People crowded the streets outside the cathedral, the Egyptian press paid tribute to Kennedy's leadership and his "work for peace in this confused world." "Pray for President Johnson, too," was the banner headline in one of the newspapers.

Among the penny photographs sold in all the cigarette kiosks, a new local hero appeared, with President Nasser, Marshal Tito, Prime Minister Nehru, John Wayne and the Beatles: John F. Kennedy.

Afterward, in the days that followed, we were questioned constantly. How could it have happened in America? We said we did not know. Was it a conspiracy? We said no. But why was Oswald, guaranteed a jury trial under American law, gunned down while policemen watched? We said we did not understand. Was it not then a conspiracy? We said we didn't think so. How else could it have happened? We said we were beginning to feel we had been away from America too long to understand; we were out of touch. Perhaps things had changed more than we had thought.

Our unspoken conception of ourselves, as somewhat rare

types, competent in two cultures, was crumbling. We could no longer speak with casual confidence about America. Could we speak with confidence about Egypt? Bob was discovering that the more involved he became in local affairs, the more vulnerable he became to attacks from unfriendly elements in the local press and elsewhere. These attacks mystified and hurt him, yet there was no way in which he, as a foreigner, could respond or defend himself.

"If Omar were here, he would make fun of such nonsense," I pointed out. "Remember, the test of being truly lighthearted is to be able to laugh most loudly at one's own embarrassments and misfortunes!"

"Yes, but do you feel like laughing?" Bob returned.

To our consternation, we found we did not.

The symposium which Bob had organized to wind up the Nubian project was held in Aswan. When the papers had been read and discussed, the summary speech made and the farewell toasts presented, we walked with Karim and Mona and Dr. Laila along the Nile. New hotels were under construction on both banks and the once-quiet Corniche was filling up with traffic.

"You know, Karim," said Bob, "they say the population of Aswan has more than tripled since you and I first came here four years ago. It will be a big city one of these days."

The moon glimmered on the river. The bells on the horse-drawn carriages tinkled.

"There is new talk in London about the conspiracy that killed President Kennedy," said Karim.

"Conspiracy!" cried Bob. "There was no conspiracy. He was just a madman, sick and poor, the man who killed Kennedy."

Karim shook his head. "Have you read the English and French commentaries lately, and even the American ones?"

"Some."

"And you still think it was not a conspiracy. Why?"

"It just doesn't make sense," said Bob. "There has been no evidence of a conspiracy. Besides, that sort of thing doesn't happen in America."

Karim looked at Mona.

"Bob, Bob," said Dr. Laila, "I respect your point of view, but remember, it has been more than five years since you have lived in America. Things change. Perhaps you would not recognize your country if you went back."

Bob was silent.

Robert Lowell and his wife, Elizabeth Hardwick, were coming to Cairo at the invitation of the American University. We were delighted with the prospect, after the succession of college choirs and Ice Capades troupes which our government had sent to Egypt in the past five years as representative of American culture.

Egyptian literary figures, both in and out of official favor, turned up to hear Mrs. Lowell's graceful lecture, and Mr. Lowell's thoughtful presentation of his views. In front of the carved screens in the university's Oriental Hall, under the old gilded palace ceilings, Mr. Lowell read his poetry. Our Egyptian friends admitted they were impressed by the couple's quiet manner, their wit and obvious erudition, but they were surprised and excited by the power of Lowell's poems.

"He writes of despair and sorrow in the heroic style, like all the great Arab poets," a young Egyptian told me, amazed. "I did not know that materialistic America had poets like this man!"

During the days of the Lowells' visit, a feeling of discovery seemed to be in the air, a common passion sensed across alien boundaries. I looked forward to seeing this defined and developed in conversation at the large official dinner which followed the lectures.

The beautiful old house offered for the occasion belonged to the parents of Dr. Loutfi, a young professor of English, who had come home after studies at Oxford to marry his distant cousin, daughter of an Egyptian cabinet minister. In the main salon, filled with fine Empire furniture and Persian carpets, both sets of parents stood to receive their children's guests of honor.

But as the evening wore on in pleasantries and chatter, some of my earlier excitement faded. I remembered, sadly, that to be truly sophisticated, in the lighthearted Egyptian way, meant one did not discuss serious subjects on occasions such as this, for fear of being boring. And I began to notice the faintly astonished looks on the older people's faces as they, pleasant, cultivated wealthy people who had been pleasant, cultivated and wealthy for generations, noted in the crowd several controversial people: an embattled literary critic, a playwright who had been in and out of jail for political activities, a painter who held a government scholarship (his father had been a gardener on the Princess Fawzia's estate). How could such people possibly have been invited to this house, the polite astonished looks tinged with condescension seemed to say. When Loutfi was a child, such people did not even exist.

Mr. and Mrs. Lowell, apparently unaware of the social currents, listened. They did not say much, but then, no one gave them a chance.

"Sir," said the playwright toward the end of the long, dull evening, "maybe you do not understand our problems. America is rich and established. But we have a new society here, we need a new art."

"You do?" Mr. Lowell questioned mildly. "Why?"

The playwright took that up with a vengeance. "Why? Fifteen years ago we had in Egypt a Europeanized culture where Arabic, our beautiful native language" (his voice rose perceptibly) "was a bad word. Now what do we have? Nothing! We have had to start fresh! Fresh!"

"Nothing?" returned Mr. Lowell. "What about the Pharaonic past . . . Islam . . . surely . . ."

"Nothing!" insisted the playwright, smoking fiercely. He was perspiring through a bad complexion, for his suit was too warm for the spring evening.

Mr. Lowell said nothing; seemingly he had found the outburst less than original. Although I sympathized with the playwright, I had to agree that his ideas sounded rather commonplace. Until now, I had thought of this young man as rather interesting. Was I, too, becoming parochial?

"How great a role does politics play in the arts here?" asked Mr. Lowell after a pause.

"They tell us to write in colloquial Arabic, but it is not rich enough!" thundered the young man. "We need a—a genius like—like DANTE to forge a magnificent new language for us."

"Dante?" queried Mr. Lowell gently. He glanced at his wife, and I winced inwardly for the young playwright.

Loutfi came and sat down, uncomfortably. I could see he had been prodded to do so by his parents, hovering, vaguely troubled, in the background. The playwright's voice was rather loud; probably by now they feared this young man was preaching revolution in their beautiful drawing room.

"Mr. Lowell might be interested in the recent poetic controversy over language and form," said Loutfi smoothly, introducing into the conversation gracefully, as he had learned to do at Oxford, a neutral subject of interest to both parties, presumably. "What do you think?"

"What do I think? Of language? Form? Politics?" The playwright was off again. "Here we still have a problem of communication between classes of people."

"The alienated poet, you mean?" suggested Loutfi, with a smiling glance at Lowell.

"*Not* the alienated poet," said the playwright unpleasantly. "It is much simpler. How would you," he demanded of the Lowells, "make lower class people, objects of ridicule and pity here for generations, into real characters an audience can believe in? The garlic seller is not even alive for young Egyptian men of a certain class. *They* never buy garlic, they don't even see it, the women servants take care of that."

Loutfi looked upset, the Lowells were silent, and the playwright mopped his sweating brow with a none-too-clean handkerchief.

"We are broken, torn apart," he said in a lower tone, "we have no community with each other, we cannot see the agony and terror of the other person."

"Yes," said Mrs. Lowell kindly, "but there are different sorts of agony, you know."

By now, I felt, and I thought Loutfi felt, too, that any earlier sense of cultural recognition had disappeared. The boundaries were up again. There was no longer any communication at all taking place in the beautiful drawing room.

The playwright must have felt it, also, for he stood up suddenly, knocking over his glass. The whiskey and water were quickly absorbed in the thick opaque masses of the linen tablecloth. He stared, fascinated. There would not even be a stain. Abruptly he bade us good night, wrung Mr. Lowell's hand, and was gone.

"Who was that?" asked Mr. Lowell, only mildly curious. He did not seem to have been really stirred by anything the young man had said.

"He writes political satire, mostly," answered Loutfi, "plays, short stories, some quite good."

"Yes, one play in particular," I added, feeling compelled, though I could not have said why, to defend this bristly young man's artistic worth. He was good, I told myself, even if he was parochial.

Loutfi nodded. "I know the one you mean, B.J., the police officer who writes the novel." He turned to the Lowells. "A young Egyptian wins a lottery and spends his money to help his people and build a model state. Quite moving, that play!"

The Lowells glanced at each other. Cliché, cliché, cried that glance, but Loutfi was rushing ahead, summarizing the play. Even such virtues as it had on stage disappeared in his rather self-conscious narration.

"I think we really must go," said Mrs. Lowell and smiled. "Thank you so much."

"You're off to Luxor?" Loutfi's parents were pleasant, gracious.

"Yes, tomorrow," answered Mrs. Lowell. "We are so looking forward to the trip, the first time we've been away together for many years."

Why, I asked myself later, had I felt so embarrassed for the young playwright? He was a figure of some stature in modern Egyptian letters. He believed himself to be an authentic, honest voice of the new Egypt, and he would have said he cared nothing for any Western literary judgments, certainly not mine, nor even that of the Lowells. He did not perceive that his work lacked originality, because it was so derivative, borrowing from the same Europeanized culture which he so loudly decried. The Lowells clearly preferred the unassailable authenticity of Pharaonic art. And so they should, I thought. But had I begun to pretend, as the playwright had, that such work as his was unique because of its Egyptian setting, that Egypt itself was a somewhat special literary center, not subject to the same international artistic standards as Paris, London, New York?

I remembered a discussion with Nick about a mutual friend, a young sculptor of great promise whose most recent exhibition had been decidedly inferior to those of previous years.

"He can't see his work in any sort of perspective here," Nick had pointed out.

"What you're saying, Nicholas," answered Bob, "is that he needs to get out of Egypt for a while."

Perhaps I did, too.

On the *mulid,* or saints' day, celebration of Sayidna Hussain, the Shi'a martyr whose head is supposed to lie in Cairo, we waited on the edge of the square to catch a glimpse of President Nasser when he came to pray. He waved as he walked within the crowds to the mosque, but he looked tired and much older since that triumphal day he had come through Liberation Square on his way back from New York. His diabetes was rumored worse. The Aswan Dam was proceeding according to plan, but the birth control clinics were going slowly, and Yemen was presenting increasingly difficult dilemmas.

During the recent visit of Prime Minister Khrushchev, many political prisoners had been granted amnesties; the press of the left was operating again. This belied the gaiety of the joke which circulated after Khrushchev's departure.

"President Nasser, sir. It is said that when Prime Minister Khrushchev was here, you presented him with the keys to all of our Egyptian cities. How can you have done that, sir?"

To which Nasser replied, "After he left, dear fellow, I changed all the locks!"

Bob went to Iraq on a consulting job. It was not the first time. He was lecturing once a week at the University of Alexandria, and he had tenure at the American University now. We could stay on in Egypt indefinitely, it appeared, and he was already talking of future research.

I finished a book. We began to collect furniture. We discussed moving to larger quarters. The Port Suez School sent us a form. Did we want to reserve a place for two-year-old Laila?

"What do you think, Bob? Shall I say yes on the chance we'll be here in 1968?"

"Why not?" he answered. "Well, I don't know."

"Shouldn't we think about going home for a while?"

"B.J.," said Bob, "you know I have a sabbatical coming

up. I presume I'm supposed to spend part of my time in America. Let's see how we feel then."

The news came two months later. Bob had been awarded a postdoctoral fellowship to the Harvard Center for Middle Eastern Studies. We would spend the sabbatical year in Cambridge while he finished a book.

"But we'll be back after the year," said Bob.

"You're sure?" Dr. Laila asked.

"I'm sure," he replied. "We'll leave all our things here and sublet the apartment. All I need is a change and I know I'll be anxious to come back."

"Well, you've seen Nubia now and Upper Egypt," went on Dr. Laila, "and you've lived in Cairo; you have enough experience of Egypt to judge whether you want to return, I should think."

"Oh," said Mona, "but they haven't seen Egypt yet at all. Egypt is the Delta. You must come to my family's estate for a long weekend before you go."

"We've been to the Delta."

Laila looked at Mona. "Yes, Bob, but you should go to Mona's family estate and spend a few days. You know, before 1952, the country *ezbas* were major seats of power in Egypt, like the old feudal estates in France. They're still interesting, like all points of origin."

"Laila," teased Bob, "I didn't know you were nostalgic for the past."

"I am not nostalgic, I am just pointing out that the *ezbas* were once an important focus of life here. You should experience them briefly, at least."

"Dr. Laila, they are still important," insisted Mona.

"Yes, but not in the same way," said Laila.

"Mona," I broke in, "we would be delighted to come anytime."

CHAPTER 15

THE DELTA

We reached the estate in darkness, guided by lanterns, flickering in the sand, to the boundaries of the El Za'aty family *ezba*. At the sound of our car navigating the gravel and dust driveway, the heavy wrought-iron gate swung open, and a man's square figure came forward, a turbaned servant behind him with a lantern held high. Hassan, Mona's cousin who managed and lived on the *ezba*, welcomed us.

"So sorry about the generators," he said. "We'll have no electricity tonight, I'm afraid. Oh," he whispered, "do not wake the children." The disciplined full mouth in his proud face softened and he gently shouldered Davy to carry him into the house.

Vera, Hassan's half-Austrian, half-Egyptian wife, waited at the door with a candelabra to light us up through dim circles and corridors to a suite of two rooms with bath between. Mona helped me undress the children and tuck them into bed. The sheets smelled of lavender; the comforters were quilted in pink cotton; the tile floors were cool. Long green shutters stood open to the quiet country night, filled with the throbbing of crickets, the sweet and rank scents of farm and garden.

"I put the little one's bed here, out of the draft," said Vera timidly.

A crib of palm wood, vaguely reminiscent of Davy's Nubian crib, stood waiting for Laila.

"I had it made for her specially," said Vera. "We've had

no small child at the *ezba* for many years, and there were no proper beds in the attics. Is it all right?"

"Oh, yes, thank you."

"Not too rustic?" she persisted anxiously.

"No, it's lovely."

Mona went downstairs, but Vera stayed while I drew the sheets over sleeping Laura Ann and Davy.

Vera reached out a thin hand to touch Laila, but withdrew it quickly.

"She is a beautiful baby," she brought out, and the sadness in her voice was overpowering.

What could I say? Mona had told me how Vera and Hassan, married nine years, had longed for a child.

We started down the stairs. "It's a lovely house," I said, trying to break her tight silence.

"Yes," she answered. "It was built by Hassan's grandfather, you know. He said he was making it in the shape of a star."

She tried a small, light laugh. "It is not very precisely in the shape of a star, some arms are longer than others, and so on, it's never been really finished. The family thinks it's much too old-fashioned, but I like it. I used to come here occasionally when I was a child. I didn't live in Egypt really until I was married, you see."

We had reached the dining room, one of the short "arms" of the star, and Mona was waiting for us at the table, set with plates and cutlery, cheese and bread and honey, a pot of tea. Clusters of candles in heavy silver candlesticks illuminated the table, and lanterns stood in the corners, casting rounds of light on the floor.

"Isn't it true, Mona," said Vera, "that your father and mother think the *ezba* is much too old-fashioned?"

"They do, they do," answered Mona, whose own home in Cairo was a luxury apartment in a new building overlooking the Nile, with lucite and leather furniture, and welded sculpture by a promising Egyptian artist.

"But the *ezba* is *something*, you'll have to admit," said Vera earnestly. "It has a past, like the countryside."

"My goodness," said Mona, covering her bread with the thick golden honey, "you are so philosophical, Vera!"

Vera looked flustered.

"Yes, but I think I see," I put in. "It's rather like the flowers in that bowl. Did you do them?" The bowl was low and of copper, handworked in nineteenth-century Cairo style, an unusual piece to find on the table of an upper-class Egyptian home.

Vera glanced at Mona. "In the attics and basements I have found many things," she said, "old pots and urns that I like. I know people laugh at me, but Hassan is happy that I use the things of his grandmothers and I think one should please oneself in a few matters."

"Oh, Vera, no one laughs at you," said Mona gently.

"They do," insisted Vera. "You know they do. They think silver bowls are prettier, but they are not prettier, they are just more expensive. Why, in Europe . . ." Vera's father had been in the Egyptian diplomatic service, had married her mother in Vienna, and the family had lived abroad.

"Yes, yes, Vera," said Mona impatiently. "But we're in Egypt now, not Europe."

We all munched silently for a moment.

"Excellent jam," I interposed.

"It's *naring*, the bitter orange marmalade," said Vera. "There's a tree in the back garden, near the duck pond."

"The children will love the ducks," I said warmly. "They've looked forward to the weekend so."

"Oh, and," Vera's eyes lighted up, "we have a new baby water buffalo, and that will be fun for them, too. The water buffaloes are so small and sweet when they are newborn."

"Where are the men?" asked Mona, pouring tea. "And where's Aunt Gulnar?"

"Gulnar went to bed; she had a headache," said Vera. "You'll see her in the morning."

Bob's and Hassan's voices came to us from outside the half-drawn shutters.

"They're not as close as they sound," said Vera. "The nights are so quiet one can hear for miles. It's nice to hear men's voices like that," she smiled, "instead of just the crickets and the donkeys."

Crickets and donkeys make sounds very different from the hum of nights in European cities, I thought.

"Do you have pleasant neighbors?"

Vera was quick to pick it up. "Oh, I'm not lonely," she insisted. "Hassan's aunt and uncle live in the next *ezba;* you'll meet them tomorrow."

"What about the people who live around you?"

Vera wrinkled her brow. Mona laughed.

"She means the fellaheen."

"Oh, the fellaheen." Vera laughed too. "Americans," she teased. She had found her ground. "You always give importance to those who don't have it, and ignore those who do."

"Now, Vera . . ." Mona looked at me warily over the rim of her rose-colored teacup.

"It's not always a mistake, is it?" I said quickly, without thinking.

The candlelight jumped and settled on the dark carved chair backs, the ivory tablecloth, touched the elaborate Gothic sideboard, its arched niches holding treasures of porcelain, Georgian silver, Fabergé Easter eggs.

"Oh!" cried Vera. She leaned across the table and touched my arm. "Forgive me. I did not mean to offend."

I was sorry I had spoken. She was very defenseless and sad, the European features in the olive-skinned narrow face brought together in dismay.

"You didn't, Vera, really. I was only kidding," I said.

"But I mean," she was trying harder, "people are different from each other, and there is value in their differences."

The maid came in with a plate of bananas and dates. She was young and broad-shouldered in a long loose cotton dress, a white head scarf hiding her hair.

"B.J. understands that," Mona was intervening, trying to help Vera. She watched me, unsure of my reaction. In Nubia, Mona and I had been so close, I thought. She must have felt something, for she began, "For instance, in Nubia . . ."

"Vienna," interrupted Vera, "is different from New York, I am different from Towsa here" (at the sound of her name the maid looked expectantly at her mistress). "Mona is different from you, a fellah is different from Hassan. His value is not less, but he is different. He wants different things."

"Does he?" I asked.

"The fellaheen are like children," said Vera earnestly, "we must help them."

Yes, before they help themselves, I thought to myself, but I did not say it.

"You must be tired," said Vera, taking my silence for fatigue. "Go on to bed, you and Mona, I'll wait up for the men."

A bowl of guavas had been placed in the center of the dining-room table, but the morning meal was not yet ready. Bob had gone out early with Hassan, and I could see them across the back garden, by the duck pond, shaded by mimosas and by the bitter orange trees, sitting on the porch of the *diwan*, when Hassan received, as his father had done, the estate manager, salesmen, plaintiffs, official visitors.

A cow had calved during the night and something was wrong with the water wheel, Mona had said.

Laura Ann and Davy circled the table, their eyes on the

guavas. Laila, who had decided to play, trotted slowly after me as I tried to steer the three children out of the room, its massive Gothic chairs set against the wall to allow the freshly washed tile floors to dry. The morning sun streamed through the open windows, dappling the floor, whitening the fresh tablecloth, touching the yellow and brown guavas, bringing to blazing life a large oil painting of the *ezba* garden, which I had not noticed last night, so withdrawn was it into shadow. The faint scent of home-made yellow soap lingered in the room, mixing with the maddening ripe sweetness of the guavas and the smell of fresh bread baking in the kitchen. I was starved.

I knew that if I were to say a word to Mona or Vera, they would say, "Please let the children have a guava while they are waiting. Do!"

Someone would be brought from the kitchen to sit the children down, cover them with bibs, slice their guavas on their plates, and afterward take them to wash their hands and faces from the juices of the soft, pulpy white fruit. But I didn't want to do this.

I knew that all hands had been mobilized to prepare some kind of special breakfast for Mona's professor and his family, and that calling one of the maids out to feed the children would only delay things longer.

"Kitchen," said Laura Ann, her hand on the door. "Let's go back and see the turtles."

"No." That wouldn't do either. We had stopped general proceedings when Mona had shown us through the new modern kitchen, and taken us down a short flight of steps to the old earth-floor scullery.

"A turtle!" Laura Ann cried. A large box turtle ambled among a turkey and some noisy chickens. From the beams of the flat roof hung long braided garlands of onions and garlic and dried okra.

The three maids had shown Laura Ann how to pick up the turtle by its back, had let Davy scatter a little corn for the chickens. I could see Vera bobbing uncertainly in the background. She didn't want to shout unpleasantly at the servants in our presence, but obviously the men would soon want their breakfast.

"Let's play follow the leader! Come on. By the fountain!"

Anything to get them out of the dining room, although I was beginning to share their anxiety. How much longer till breakfast?

Not plashing, but dripping languidly into its basin of old blue and salmon-rose Turkish tiles, the fountain stood in the circular covered court, the very center of the star which formed the core of the great house. The children began to play tag around the fountain and I sank down on an old carved bench and let them run, Laila wandering to and fro in a private game of her own. From my fountainside bench I could see through the back door, across a screened porch to the driveway we had entered last night. Beehives had been built in neat gray rows under the ancient eucalyptus and acacia trees which lined the drive to the iron gate, standing open to a street of the village.

"Mama! Watch!"

Around and around the fountain raced Laura Ann and Davy. They never seemed to get dizzy, not even from lack of food.

"Ma-MA!"

Their voices sounded shrill and unnecessary in the heavy, sleepy morning of the countryside, unpleasantly high-pitched above the subdued clacking of chickens, the whirring of the pigeons, a ruminating moo from a distant cow, the zing of the bees nosing in the yellow acacia blossoms, which dropped their petals gently and continually onto the sunlit gravel of the road.

"I'm hungry." Davy sat down and flung his head into my lap.

"Breakfast will be ready soon," announced Mona brightly, coming from the general direction of the kitchen. "Why

don't we look at the house while we're waiting? You haven't
even seen the Nile. We have a lovely vista—it's one of the
most marvelous things about the *ezba*."

"Can't we eat first," asked Laura Ann. "Please?" and put
her hand in Mona's.

"Yes, darling, but first I'm going to show you and Davy
something wonderful!"

"Where? What?"

The children skipped along with Mona, followed by slow
Mama with Laila in tow, into, one after the other, the
shady corridors which led away from the tiled dripping
fountain into the recesses and wings of the house, into a
long, rectangular, beamed library and Aunt Gulnar's sitting
room.

"No," said Mona to Laura Ann, "not here, dear. Aunt
Gulnar does not like little children to touch her things."

A formal drawing room with aging blue velvet Louis
Quinze furniture, another salon in Empire style, a tiny
study with a stone fireplace and brown corduroy-covered
chairs, bedroom wings with bathrooms attached.

"No, not here, either," said Mona, "but we are getting
close," smiling at the children's growing excitement.

Paintings and engravings, tapestries and framed rare
manuscripts covered every wall of the corridors and the
rooms. Even that modern Egyptian village tapestry, which
so many of my American friends had collected, was represented. But here it was only a minor link in the chain; it
had been put in its place in this great house, interesting
but not masterful beside carefully chosen examples of European and Oriental art of many centuries.

"Where? Where, Mona?"

"Close your eyes! Quick!"

"Here!" said Mona. "Open your eyes."

"A zoo!" cried Laura Ann.

"Zoo!" repeated Davy, smiling and peering.

We were in a round tall cul-de-sac surrounding the en-

trance to the back stairway, a cul-de-sac filled with ancient
Egyptian sculpture on high pedestals, a collection of small
animals, gaily and marvelously made. A vase in the shape
of a monkey mother, cuddling her baby. An ivory gazelle
with delicate legs. The sacred ibis with his white body,
black head and tail. A crocodile of wood, with jaws that
actually moved. A bronze pig. A box in the form of a grass-
hopper. A hedgehog with iron "twigs," Davy pointed out.

"And a blue hippo," said Laura Ann, "a beautiful blue
hippo."

"Hippo!" echoed Davy.

Decorated with black-outlined flowers and birds, the
blue-glazed hippo wore a jolly painted smile.

"My grandfather collected them," said Mona. "He said the
ancient Egyptians were lighthearted, *dem khefeef*, just like
modern Egyptians, and they didn't spend all their time
thinking about death and tombs."

Outside, on the pillared veranda, the children rushed
forward into the dazzling garden, among violet and pink
petunias, tall orange day lilies beside the stone wall. Their
blond heads were dappled with the shade of the shiny-
leaved castor shrubs, the pale leaves of the nodding cottonwoods.

"See the river?" called Mona.

I paused at the gate, overgrown with scarlet bougainvillea, to look at the view, a view that a king might covet—
a majestic view of the Nile, widening here from its inland
canals and dotted with the flaring white sails of feluccas.
Date palms grew thickly on the opposite shore, and only the
thin curls of smoke rising into the blue sky indicated the
presence of brick factories behind the screen of trees. A
little spit of land ran forward into the river like a bridge or
a sluice gate where the *ezba* garden ended; beyond the
spit the river turned, and thus the *ezba* was shielded, enclosed, presented, as a natural gift, with this private view
of the river.

"Isn't it beautiful, B.J.?" Mona was at my side. "Almost as beautiful as the view we had in Nubia of the mountains, don't you think?"

Three men on donkeys clop-clopped past the gate.

"Good morning, Mona!" called the riders, two men in *gullabiyas* and a bright-eyed boy, scarcely bigger than Davy.

"Could I ride a donkey, Mona?" asked Davy, his eye on that small boy proudly handling his own steed, who turned back to smile at us.

"After breakfast, Davy, okay?"

Where *was* breakfast? My stomach was beginning to rumble in an embarrassing way.

"I want to ride, too!"

"Yes, Laura Ann, you can both ride."

"Breakfast! Come to breakfast!"

It was Vera calling, and I had to hold tightly to the children's hands to keep them from bolting rudely into the dining room.

But the specialty so long in preparation was worth waiting for, it turned out—*fateer*, layers of thin bread dough alternating with layers of cheese and baked together into a thick crisp wheel-shaped pastry. Instead of butter, there was home-gathered honey to spread on the *fateer*, and heavy *ghaymar*, the thick cream skimmed from the buffalo milk. Fried fresh eggs. Boiled buffalo milk for the children, guavas (at last) and tea.

"How do you like the house?" asked Hassan.

"You should ask Vera how she likes it, for a change," said Aunt Gulnar pointedly. "We all grew up here, but Vera came to it as a stranger."

"Gulnar, not as a *complete* stranger," Vera demurred gently.

Gulnar sniffed, and cradled her teacup in both hands while she looked us over.

Egyptian, with a Turkish mother, Gulnar had spent most

of her life in France. She must have been sixty, but with her slim erect figure in the English country clothes, her deftly made-up, still firm profile, her neat chignon held in place with silver combs, she looked a distinguished, even a beautiful fifteen years younger. Gulnar was Hassan's dead mother's sister, and had returned to her birthplace when her French artist husband died. The *ezba* was big enough for the whole family, Mona had explained to me, and Gulnar preferred to live in the country, though she kept a pied-à-terre apartment in Cairo.

"Gulnar," smiled Vera, a bit defensively, "you know I love it, wherever Hassan is."

Looking at the two women, one young, one old, both of mixed Western and Eastern temperaments, I wondered. Gulnar and Vera were both childless; Hassan was their child.

"We can ride the donkeys out to the fields if you like," Hassan said to Bob. "I have to go to the end of the south line today."

"Show him the canaria field," suggested Gulnar. "I think he'll be interested."

"Oh, Hassan, must you?" said Mona. "I promised the children they could ride the donkeys."

Hassan looked annoyed. "Here, my dear, we have work to do," he said. "You come from town and think I have nothing to occupy myself but pleasure riding?"

"I could take Davy on the donkey with me," offered Bob.

Hassan flashed a smile. "Perhaps the ladies can take a stroll and meet us by the water wheel before lunch."

"And I can ride the donkey then?" persisted Laura Ann.

"Yes, dear, but now come with me," Vera took Laura Ann's hand, "and while Mama is gone, I will keep your baby sister, if I may?" She turned shyly to me.

"Oh, yes, Vera, thank you."

Aunt Gulnar declined the pleasure of a walk in the fields

but she invited Mona and me into her private sitting room for a cup of Turkish coffee.

Gulnar's retreat was long and cool. Throughout the star-shaped house books and pictures were interposed with furniture, but here they took precedence. Books and magazines were crowded so densely one could hardly find an empty cushion to sit upon. Behind the glass doors of mahogany bookcases, in piles in the deep nooks beneath the vine-covered windows, on makeshift shelves of bricks and board, books lay, books waiting for their pages to be cut, books lying open in the middle of chapters, books under-lined, marked, books tied up ready to be mailed, presum-ably, to friends. Thumbed and piled and folded around them were newspapers and magazines, *Paris-Match, La Nouvelle Observateur, The Times Literary Supplement, Elle, Figaro, The New Yorker, Vogue.*

Gulnar sat in an old leather chair behind her surprisingly uncluttered desk, its polished walnut surface holding a pair of blue and white Limoges candlesticks. A pencil box of the same porcelain had been used as a paperweight for a pile of manila business folders; the only other ornament was a Luristan bronze on a lacquered stand.

"Are you interested in literature?" asked Aunt Gulnar, lighting a Gauloise. Amid the rich confusion of her books and papers and *objets d'art,* she alone had line and neatness. She was the central figure around which the room's chaos turned and revolved, as an abstract painting turns and revolves in light and shadow about a key shape. "American literature, let us say."

"Yes," I answered, "yes, I am."

"What do you think of Malcolm Lowry?"

"*Under the Volcano,* you mean?" I brought out.

"*Under the Volcano,* I mean," returned Gulnar. "Person-ally, *I* believe it is one of the most remarkable novels of the century; it is certainly the most interesting American novel *I* have read, and I have read a great many. Lowry had a marvelous sense of the power of land, of place, of terrain, I think."

"What other American novelists have you read?" I asked curiously.

"Hemingway, Faulkner, Nathanael West . . . oh, Towsa, what *is* it?" she said in an irritated voice to the maid. "All right, I'll come."

She drained her coffee cup. "Excuse me," she said. "The new breeding hens have begun to lay. Very exciting. Please finish your coffee. I shall see you at luncheon and we can continue our discussion. And Mona," she said, turning back as she pulled on an old pair of gloves, "be sure to show her the canaria field, dear. I shall be curious about your reaction to it."

She nodded at me. Her face had changed, the considering look replaced by eager, girlish interest. I began to understand why Mona had described her Paris-educated aunt as a force behind many of the new agricultural techniques the family was trying out on the farm.

The midmorning sun was hot. Along the banks of the canal which divided one sweep of field from another, eucalyptus trees grew, shading the path where a girl in a red dress and a black *milaya* drove forward a herd of water buffalo, mooing irritatedly and clambering along the muddy banks.

"Zainab!" called Mona.

"Ha! Mona! You're back from Cairo!" called back the girl in the red dress. "And I bet you're not married yet, O city girl!" she chided.

"Don't brag! Neither are you," answered Mona, nettled.

I knew the subject of marriage was one upon which she and her family disagreed violently. Though the El Za'atys were modern parents in wanting Mona to have a good education, and even tolerant enough to have allowed her to come to Nubia and do field work, on the question of marriage they reverted to tradition. Mona's mother and father believed that only with a solid young man chosen and approved by the family could their daughter settle down comfortably in her particular section of Egyptian society. Two young men had already indicated their desire to marry Mona, but she had refused, furiously, and was now campaigning to go abroad to graduate school.

We walked along with Zainab, who had a pretty face under her black veil, and the easy carriage that comes from balancing heavy loads on one's head from childhood.

"No, Laura Ann, that is not a *hod-hod*."

Zainab took care to answer Laura Ann's questions about the birds twittering across the moving water of the canal. She bent low to hear my small daughter speak and occasionally would straighten up to direct a remark in the general direction of the opposite bank where a young man in a blue *gullabiya* walked along, nearly even with us. He carried a hoe on his shoulder and he raised it up and down in farewell before turning off in a different direction.

"Good-by, you city folk, I have work to do," called Zainab, and prodded the protesting buffalo forward. She appeared not to notice the young man's departure.

"Who was the handsome young man in the sky-blue *gullabiya*?" I said.

Mona smiled. "He's handsome, all right."

"Who was he?"

"Zainab is a clever girl," Mona answered obliquely. "I think she and Hamid are lovers."

"What?"

"Perhaps not, but I suspect it. That's a very common way to manage to be with one's beloved without attracting attention—walking along on opposite sides of the canal."

"Can't they marry?"

"No. He is poor, and her father wants her to marry someone else."

Like your father, I thought. On basic subjects like marriage and the family, Mona and Zainab were not really as far apart as one might think.

"Well, remember what the old fortuneteller said in Nubia," I joked. "You'll marry for love."

"Aunt Gulnar says the same thing," Mona turned to me. "She has promised to try to persuade my father to let me go abroad."

"An interesting woman, your aunt."

"She's old," said Mona bitterly. "She solved all her problems by leaving and marrying a foreigner and living abroad."

"But she's come back!" I said, surprised.

"*Now* she comes back," repeated Mona. "Now, since she has some land and some money, she can do whatever she likes. It amuses her to breed chickens and teach the fellaheen to weave rope and run Hassan and so on. Her life is over. Mine hasn't even begun, B.J.!"

"Mona, Mona!" Laura Ann skipped back to us, and pointed down the road which divided the fields, fields stretching away on all sides and bounded by low walls of earth to mark plots and hold the irrigation water. "There's Baba and Davy and Hassan on the donkeys!"

Mona shaded her eyes with her hand and gazed across the fields, mostly empty now, for the cotton had been harvested. A few acres of beans and tomatoes showed bright green in the late morning sunlight, a rim of shadow edged the furrows which ran on in straight lines to a clump of palms on the far horizon.

"I don't see anybody, dear."

"There by the little house."

"Oh, yes, see B.J., those little dots? We shall soon be there, Laura Ann, but your mama wants to see the canaria first."

"What's so special about canaria?" I asked.

Mona said, "You'll see. It's one of Aunt Gulnar's ideas.

She read about it in a farm journal." Mona shook her head. "My aunt reads *everything*."

"Listen!" Laura Ann stopped and pulled on my skirt, an anxious look on her small face.

I stopped too, for I had heard a strange new sound, very faint, as of someone humming. But we were alone in the stretch of fields except for the receding blob of Zainab's red dress in the distance, the little white dots of the donkeys nearing the water-wheel house.

"It's the canaria," said Mona. The distant humming rose in volume, it became a strident whistling, rising and fading, like a wave of locusts approaching and departing, yet deeper and more resonant.

Laura Ann took my hand. "Mama, what *is* it?" she asked fearfully.

"Turn around and you will see," Mona said.

A field of tall thin golden grain stretched behind us. Yet it was not ordinary grain. The slender stems seemed top-heavy, and when a breath of wind touched them, they bent and swayed and shimmered, moving toward each other and away, whistling and murmuring in waves of singing, undulating, humming gold.

"What is it, Mama? What makes the noise?"

"It's the seeds, dear." Mona was her helpful, kind self. "They make the sound when they touch each other. Isn't it odd? See, this is what canaries like to eat. The fellaheen say it is these seeds which make the birds sing so sweetly."

Close by, the stalk showed its dark golden top to be heavy, not with kernels of grain, but with tiny individual seeds.

"Uncanny! It really is," I said. "The sound *is* almost like music and the field ripples as though it would break in half."

"Yes," agreed Mona, smiling. "You can imagine what Hassan said when Gulnar first suggested putting it in, but she insisted, and it's proved to be an excellent cash crop.

Now they have several acres in canaria. But I think Gulnar likes it just because it sings and moves like that. Ask her at lunch!"

We had nearly reached the mechanical water wheel where two irrigation canals intersected. Children in dusty *gullabiyas* came running out to look over Laura Ann. A man had risen to greet Hassan and Bob and Davy approaching on the donkeys and women had gathered on a mat around a smoking fire where the teakettle steamed. They wore mixtures of prints and white head scarves and dark *milayas* and they called to us.

"Mona! Mona! Welcome!"

"Who's the little girl?"

"Mona, aren't you married *yet?*"

We sat down on the mat, in the courtyard of the water-wheel tender's house, and heard, above the conversation, the whish, whish of Nile water pushed through the metal teeth of the wheel and into the canals.

"The first thing I did when I took over the farm was to get mechanical wheels," said Hassan, stirring his tea. "I used to have nightmares about the blind donkey that walked the water wheel around here in this spot when I was a child."

We sipped tea from glasses, tea with a faint flavor of the dung fuel upon which the kettle had been boiled.

"How has land reform affected you?" Bob is never less than direct.

Hassan considered. "If you mean, has my land been taken away from me, not much. We did not have so much you know. Oh, my grandfather did, yes, but that was long ago divided up between the cousins and the sons."

"So you have only two hundred acres, the minimum?"

"About," temporized Hassan. "And Vera owns some, and Gulnar too."

"Don't the men in the village own land, then?"

"Some," said Hassan. "Some do."

"They're sharecroppers?" Bob pushed on.

"No," said Hassan. "I will explain to you. Some own a little land, some choose to work for me still. But I pay them salaries now, not just a part of the crop. They are free to do what they want. But they don't have cash to buy seed, you see, so it's not always profitable to farm a little piece of land."

"What about the government cooperatives?"

Hassan shrugged. "They help. They are better in some places than in others."

I looked at the circle of men around him, men in *gullabiyas* and turbans and shoes; they did not seem overly prosperous to me, but they did not seem oppressed or particularly deferential to Hassan, either.

"Let us go look at the tomatoes. Abdulla wants me to see the people who have bought the crop."

We walked between the furrows where the tomatoes were ripening on their green stems, shining red against the sandy soil. The sun was hotter and I was glad to reach the shade of the field shelter, a square of matting stretched on high wooden poles where two women and a middle-aged man waited.

Hassan took off his hat and wiped the sweat from his face. "*Salaam alaykum,* peace upon you," he said.

"*Salaam alaykum,*" repeated the estate manager, Abdulla.

"And peace to you," replied the seated trio. The women offered Laura Ann and David tomatoes from a fresh-picked basket on a mat, beside a clay water jar, damp and dark with moisture.

A long conversation followed.

Hassan shook his head and stood up. "No," he said. "They are yours. You have already paid me half, the other half I get when they are sold in the market."

"What was all that about?" asked Bob, when we had reached the dirt road again.

"Some of the people who do not farm land will invest in a

crop; these people banded together to buy my tomatoes.
They were telling me now that they can't find people to pick
the tomatoes. So they want me to do it and take back part
of the money. I refused. They have to learn to manage for
themselves. That arrangement was what they said they
wanted, and they have to take the risks, too."

"How do the fellaheen feel about you?" asked Bob.

"The fellaheen?" asked Hassan. "I don't know. It is not
as it used to be maybe, but then I still have my house and
some land. And we are always busy. There were weevils
on the cotton bolls this year; the tomatoes looked bad in the
beginning. I have no time to think about the fellaheen,
frankly."

"They have more pride and self-respect now, I think,"
put in Mona quickly. "They don't bow down like they used
to before Grandfather."

"Just as well," said Hassan. "I never liked that kind of
thing, though Grandfather did, I guess."

Over a lunch so lavish and delicious that Vera and all
the maids must have toiled since breakfast, we met Sayid
Kamal Hassan El Za'aty and his wife, Sitt Fatima, who had
come over from the neighboring *ezba*. Elderly and completely bald, with liver spots speckling his hands and
face, Uncle Sayid Kamal had propped in the arm of his
dining chair a splendid fly whisk, its ivory handle yellowed
with age. He had the long nose, the full mouth disciplined
into line, the family's strong features and square build that
were visible in Hassan, that sat more lightly upon Mona.
But the other three women were obviously not of the El
Za'aty strain; Vera with her small European features in the
incongruous olive-skinned setting; Gulnar's classic Turkish
profile; and Sitt Fatima. Sitt Fatima was not old, but she
was old-fashioned, in a mid-calf ensemble of black crepe, a
diamond pin, a gold bracelet, a decorous black *milaya* covering dyed black hair, which seemed even blacker against her
startlingly white smooth skin.

"You are Mona's professor," she announced to Bob in a deep, pleasant voice. "Have you told them, Gulnar, what this crazy girl did at the cotton harvest?"

Mona, helping herself to more pigeons and rice, blushed angrily.

"Now, *Amitii,*" said Gulnar. "It is not important."

"Not important?" Aunt Fatima masticated, swallowed, and laid down her knife and fork to draw extra attention to her words. "Not important? I never heard of such behavior in my day.

"Let me tell you, madame," she went on, nodding at me, who sat opposite her, helping Laura Ann and David taste the pigeons and rice, the vegetables cooked with meat, the spinachy *molokhiya* which Hassan, over Bob's protests, had piled on the children's plates. Laila, in a cane-seated bentwood high chair Vera had retrieved from an attic, was eagerly stuffing rice into her mouth with a tablespoon.

"She insisted, madame," repeated Sitt Fatima, "this girl, Mona, my great-niece, an El Za'aty like the rest of us, I *believe,* this girl insisted on going into the fields and picking cotton with the fellaheen in the hot sun!"

"And I couldn't stand it for even one hour! I was sick and had to come in the house and lie down. That's how *weak* I am and how strong the fellaheen are!" burst out Mona.

"Bread," announced Davy shortly.

"Bread, *please,*" I corrected, but I need not have bothered. No one was listening.

"Crazy, that's what she is, these young people today are crazy," pronounced Aunt Fatima.

I waited for a diatribe against coeducation and women's rights, but it did not come.

"Some more pigeons, dear niece Vera," said Aunt Fatima, "and a little *molokhiya* in the bowl, not on my plate, all right, some vegetables, too, the pigeons are delicious. Is it the cinnamon, oh, I thought so," and she subsided to give her full energies to the generous plateful before her.

"How many bales to the feddan did you get?" Hassan was asking Uncle Kamal. "Yes, we did, too. It was a good year for cotton."

"They say the price of tomatoes is going up," returned Uncle Kamal. "You sold your crop too cheap, my boy. I told you so at the time."

"But there is still some blight, Uncle," went on Hassan, eating steadily between words.

"Ah, you have tomato blight, too." Sitt Fatima wedged herself back into the conversation. "You must try this new spray, you hose the tomatoes, first, like this." She pushed up her bracelets and rolled her sleeve back slightly to demonstrate the motion. One might have said she had done it herself, recently. But with those plump, white ringed hands?

"How do you like the house?" Uncle Kamal turned to us politely.

"It's a wonderful house," said Bob.

"Mmm," agreed Uncle Kamal, "but a bit too dark, I feel. I told your grandfather so, Hassan, when he was building it, but he said it was cooler this way."

"The dining room, though, is very light," I offered.

"Yes," said Sayid Kamal, flicking his ivory whisk at a stubborn fly that buzzed close to his half-finished plate. "It's light enough to please anyone."

The sunlight fell full upon the white wall, upon the impressionistic painting of the *ezba* garden, a glowing representation of that blossoming strip between the star-shaped house and the banks of the Nile.

"My husband painted it," Gulnar told me, "in the last years of his life."

"I don't like modern painting," put in Aunt Fatima, who was cleaning her plate carefully by dipping bread in the last rivulets of rich pigeon gravy. "I like portraits." She wiped her mouth with the linen napkin. "Family portraits. But this one Etienne did, it's all right, Gulnar."

Gulnar smiled slightly.

"Doesn't look like the garden, Gulnar, but it makes me think of the garden."

The maid set an enormous cake, Sayid Kamal's and Sitt Fatima's contribution, in the center of the cleared table.

"It's from Groppi," said Sitt Fatima, proudly.

"Groppi?" asked Bob. "How did you get it here?"

"Kamal's agent brought it from Cairo this morning," said Sitt Fatima. "It's nothing, really," but she smiled with pleasure at her own munificence and cleverness.

"Oh, Mama, look at the chocolate roses!" cried Laura Ann, and Sitt Fatima glanced across the table at her husband. The cake was obviously a success, that glance said clearly, worth all the trouble it had caused the agent, the village stationmaster and Uncle Kamal himself.

Chocolate roses bordered the cake, roses with white cream stems, rolled leaves of shaved chocolate; in the center an island of glazed apricots dusted with powdered sugar suggested a winter fantasy. Roses in winter: a true Groppi masterpiece!

Vera, flushed, brought in a baked Alaska, perfectly done to pale butterscotch brown.

"You made it yourself, Vera!" exclaimed Gulnar. "How gorgeous!"

"Why do you bother!" sniffed Aunt Fatima, "when Groppi is so good," but she had two slices, I noticed.

We devoured the rich desserts and trotted off to rest. While I lay on the pink-covered bed in the green-shuttered room, I reflected that the fellaheen were probably strong because they did not indulge in chocolate roses on top of pigeons cooked in rice and butter, and fell sound asleep, Laila beside me peacefully snoring.

We drove back to Cairo in the late afternoon of the following day. Bales of cotton were piled along the roadsides, and the highway was clogged with carts and trucks, bearing the new harvested cotton to the nearest town, for eventual transfer onto the Alexandria train. In front of us, a wagon filled with black-garbed women stopped dead and Bob, cursing, slammed on his brakes. The women sat in straight rows, like dark idols carefully stacked, in the bed of the wagon, which had been cheerfully, if rather haphazardly, decorated with orange and blue and yellow geometric designs; the hand of Fatima was etched in the tail gate to ward off the Evil Eye and *"Allah! Hua el Akbar!"* (God! He is great) had been lettered in all remaining spaces by a freewheeling, if uncertain, hand.

Bob honked; the wagon did not move. He honked again; the driver brandished his whip gaily in our direction to show us he had heard, but could obviously do nothing. A whole row of wagons had stopped in front of *him*.

"Why? Why? Why?" asked Bob in an irritated voice. "Do they have a traffic jam like this every time the harvest is finished?" He honked again and again, but nothing happened.

The wagon driver turned around and shouted something, but the women did not indicate they had noticed us. They were far too interested in their own affairs, the joys of a bumpy ride and a good gossip on the way to town.

"You think this is a crowd, Bob?" said Mona. "You should have come with B.J. and me to Tanta last fall, when we went to the Sayed el Badawi *mulid*. You could hardly breathe in the crush."

That festival, honoring the most popular local saint of Islam, had drawn thousands of people from the Delta, come to rejoice that the harvest had been good and to pay their respects to the memory of Sayed Ahmed el Badawi, a strange saint who reportedly gave up a libertine youth for a middle age of mystic trances and glaring into the sun. His celebration is said by scholars to contain elements of old Pharaonic harvest festivals, far more related in their earthiness to the earlier revels of Sayed Ahmed than to his later more ascetic life. His insignia, however, the red turban and the red banner, suited the joyousness of a harvest *mulid*.

Representatives of the different mystic Sufic orders had marched in procession through the streets, bearing red banners in honor of Sayed el Badawi, and in the open square outside the sacred mosque, a red-turbaned gypsy in spangles had stationed himself like a self-appointed herald of the day. Mounted on an elderly camel caparisoned splendidly in red, with Indian mirror-work trappings which blinked in the sunlight, the laughing gypsy beat steadily upon a great war drum. The boom of that drum could be heard in the bustling bazaars full of goods and worldly entertainments, calling the faithful to their religious duties.

Past the red-draped camel and the laughing gypsy beating his nail-studded drum, the pilgrim fellaheen had crowded forward to file past the tomb of the saint, encased in gold and protected by a fence of gold filigree, worn smooth from ritual kisses of the penitent, like the *Pietà* in the Roman basilica of St. Peter's.

"Remember the shrine?" I turned to Mona.

"Yes, oh, yes!"

We had been ushered, by a friend of Karim's, to a window niche inside the shrine room itself, and the old and the young who could not face the crowds massed by the tomb had whispered their prayers to the venerable saint through the open ironwork grill behind us.

"I wanted to go to the *mulid* very much," said Bob, honking once more at the line of stalled wagons in front of us. "But I had to work that day, if you recall."

"At last!" The wagon moved, the bells on the donkey jingled, we were off again.

In the damp soil near the water, feathery tails of papyrus moved in the wind, with the lotus and the canes of bamboo—*bambooza*, Gulnar had called it—"the belt of Osiris."

"You mean you don't know the legend?" she had said, that neat face displaying mischief. "Well, it seems Osiris

stole out of the river to make love to Isis on the bank.
When he was discovered, he jumped into the water to
escape the wrath of the gods but he forgot his belt. So
the gods, to punish him, tied it to the soil to grow forever
beside the Nile."

The afternoon light was turning the river golden, lighting
bits of white marble in a brown field, pieces of Pharaonic
and Roman antiquities uncovered by the plow during the
past season. Some of the pieces had been used to mark
new graves in a nearby cemetery. We zoomed past a camel
loaded with cotton, padding slowly along, between the
papyrus and the stones, beside the river.

"I feel a bit sad," said Mona. "I always feel sad when I
leave the *ezba*. We came here for summers when we were
small, and when we drove home, we knew we wouldn't be
back for another year. My sister was married from the *ezba*.
She asked my grandfather if she could, she loved it so
much."

"She's in Cairo?"

"No, in Berkeley. She wants to come back, but I don't
think they will. Her husband is in some kind of experi-
mental physics research; he says the equipment isn't available in Egypt yet."

"What will happen to the farm when Hassan leaves?"
asked Bob.

"Oh, he won't leave," said Mona positively, too positively.
"He loves the land, he and Aunt Gulnar both."

"But what about Vera?"

"Vera is his wife."

But who would farm it, I wondered, when the El Za'atys
had died out. Hassan and Vera had no children, nor did
Gulnar. One of Mona's brothers was an engineer in Aswan;
another brother had gone to Kuwait. Sayid Kamal was
aging; his son, a doctor in the provincial capital, had no
interest in the land. Sayid Kamal himself had said it.

"Maybe the fellaheen will take over the land," suggested

Bob, "eventually, I mean," he added at the stricken look on Mona's face.

"Hassan will have a child, I think," said Mona.

"You mean Vera—?" I stopped. I remembered something, hearing that it had been pronounced impossible for Vera to bear children.

"They will adopt a child if necessary," said Mona, softly.

"Adopt a child in Egypt? That's difficult, isn't it?" asked Bob.

Mona was blushing.

"Yes, you're right," she said hurriedly, "unless he has a child by another woman. It's happened before, you know."

We said nothing.

"But he loves Vera," brought out Mona. "He doesn't want to divorce her, ever."

In the short, awkward silence which followed, I remembered a seemingly unrelated conversation I had had with Gulnar when I asked her why she had come back to Egypt.

"I often wonder," she said, "and when I first came back, I was not sure I had done the right thing. I sat at lunch, a lunch like today's—heavy, lots of food, and I listened to Fatima and Hassan and Vera, and Uncle Kamal flicked his fly whisk around, and I thought to myself, here is the weight of Egypt falling on me again, and I could have screamed. I felt suffocated. But after a while I realized that this was why I had come back, to assume my part of the weight, to share in it, to revel in it. Egypt has engulfed me again, and I am not happy, but I am home. The problems are difficult and impossible to resolve, but they are mine."

Laura Ann said to Mona, "Aren't those sheep, there, on the boat?"

"Yes, dear, yes," said Mona, jumping at the change in conversation.

"Lotsa sheep, Baba," said Davy.

The animals were crowded on the deck of a freight

felucca navigating the narrow canal beside us. Their terrified cries drowned out for a moment the noises of the small
town we were passing.

Town or village? Or was it even a village, this collection
of half-open stalls, where dresses and sweaters swung on
hangers on the doors, cloth was draped across barrels, blue
tins of lard and yellow bars of soap were stacked on narrow ill-lit shelves. The high-wheeled carts, so out of place
in urban, cosmopolitan Cairo, belonged here, clattering
over the uneven streets, a stone's throw from the canals,
from the billowing sails of the felucca crowded with sheep,
moving toward the bridge across the canal, which was
slowly opening on middle-aged machinery to let the high
mast pass through.

Hundreds of towns like this were strewn along the net-
work of canals built to control and distribute the flood-
waters of the Nile, here proliferating into tiny tributaries
flowing at last into the sea. The towns were crowded
with people, most of them young, most of them tired, but
they were not starving, for no one starved in the rich
Delta. Yet they were not in the prime of health, either.
The parasite of bilharzia, that dreaded, enervating snail
fever, lurked in the calm waters of the irrigation canals.

Only the water was still. Everything else moved and
sounded—the donkey carts, the walking roadside signs, the
cigarette kiosks, the soft-drink sellers clinking their brass
cups against the brassbound barrels of tamarind juice
strapped to their waists. They swelled, as we in our automobile swelled, the slow dense traffic of nightfall along the
Lower Nile. Upon the water, only a car length from us,
the feluccas inched along, their hulls passing close to the
sides of the banks. They moved ahead, sails unfurled, masts
high, like giant fluttering prehistoric birds in the fading
light.

"Well," said Mona, "now you can say you have seen the
real Egypt, B.J."

The real Egypt. What was the real Egypt? Where was the real Egypt? In the *ganeena* outside our apartment house in Cairo? In Loutfi's beautiful drawing room where he had entertained the Lowells? In the spacious mud-brick houses of Nubia? In the Ramadan-lit streets of the bazaars of Khan el Khalili? In the tombs of the Pharaohs in Luxor, the tomb of the Agha Khan in Aswan? Or here, in the Delta, upon the lush green earth watered by the Nile?

No, the real Egypt was none of these things, and yet it was all these things. And Egypt was slowly engulfing us, too, like Gulnar, but it was not ours. Bob and I and the children had grown to feel at home in our pleasant apartment overlooking the Nile. We had been comfortable with our friends in Nubia, with their wild, splendid view of the river. We had felt at ease in the *ezba* with the box turtles in the scullery, the water buffalo in the barn, the whispering twittering life of the land around us. Aziza, Omar, Mona, Karim, Abbas, Saleh, Hanim Ali, Mohammed with his tambura, old Shemessa, the despairing playwright, Sitt Fatima, Gulnar, Hassan, Dr. Laila, among all of these people there were great differences, but they had one thing in common. They were all tied to Egypt in a way we were no longer tied—anywhere.

Like Gulnar, we would have to go home, I saw now. We would find problems that seemed suffocating, as she had done, and solutions that were unacceptable, but we would have to cope somehow, as she was doing. We could no longer be merely spectators. For our view of the Nile had been a pleasant one, an interesting one, but it was an outsider's view. It would always be that.

Once in Nubia I had sat with Khadija and said, "Let me watch you make the reed plate, maybe I can learn how."

She had smiled and we had agreed on a time. But when I came to the court where she sat on the mat, the purple and orange strips of dyed palm fiber in piles beside her, the center was already finished and covered, as is the custom, with a neat round of leather.

"But how does it begin, Khadija?"

"That I do not think you could learn to do," she said calmly.

She was right, I believe. I could watch and appreciate and even try to help with the weaving of the rounds, as both Bob and I could watch and appreciate the circles of Egypt's many selves, separate, yet tied together by that hidden center, of which we could never be a part.

"Egypt is changing," said Mona, interrupting my reverie. The children had fallen asleep while we drove on, toward home.

"Is it?" returned Bob. "Is it really?"

"Oh, yes," answered Mona. "Of course it is changing. It changes all the time, but at least the river is the same, and the land, we can always be sure of that."

Always? Already the Nile had been diverted to allow the final stage of the Aswan Dam construction to begin. And as we approached Cairo, we could see in the sunset light, shadows that were patches of desert in the middle of green fields, bits of the coarse yellowish graveled sands which lie beneath all the cultivated land, reminders that the land depends on the river and can also disappear. The fishes which lived on the primeval plain of Lower Egypt have been found fossilized in the petrified forest near Cairo. Some of the Pharaohs were embalmed nearby. Farouk had been brought home from Europe only recently to be buried in the Rifai Mosque.

Was Egypt changing? Had we changed? Or were we, like Egypt, ending one cycle of life, before beginning another, like our Nubian friends preparing to leave their ancient homeland.

"We must get home," I said.

"It'll only be another half hour," said Bob. "The traffic is thinning."

In centuries to come, the star-shaped *ezba* would fall, too, to lie in the graveled sand with the fossils of the fishes, the bones of the Pharaohs, the tomb of the last king. And what would be sifted out a millennium hence? Some seeds of canaria and wheat and millet, a fragment of a blue Limoges candlestick, a shred of Zainab's red scarf, the bones of the patient water buffalo, a bent brass bowl in which Vera had once arranged flowers and leaves.

"I shall be buried in Egypt," said Mona. "I will always come back, even if I go away." She stared out the window, her chin in her hand, the El Za'aty family profile showing stronger in her weariness.

"But we won't," I said. "We're going home soon."

"We'll be back, though," answered Bob with certainty, "at the end of next year."

Would we be back? Perhaps. At least we would not be able to shed the weight of the last six years immediately. We would carry with us always some burden, some patina of Egypt, the birthplace of our children.

"Do you remember that old, old woman at the Sayed el Badawi shrine, B.J.?" Mona said quietly. "The one who stayed the longest?"

I remembered.

"I came," that old, whispery voice had prayed. "I came, Sayed el Badawi. And I'm telling you now, so you'll know I was here. I didn't get all the way in, Sayed el Badawi, but I came. I was here."

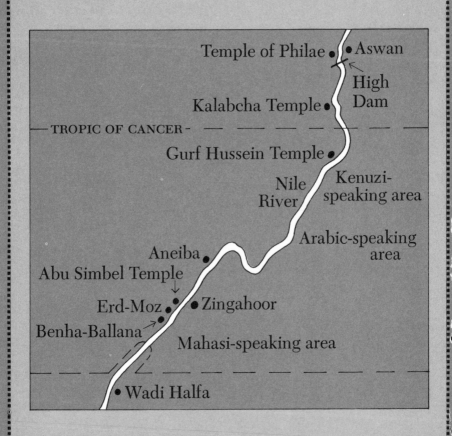

Temple of Philae • •Aswan

←High
Dam

Kalabcha Temple •

—TROPIC OF CANCER- — — — — — —

Gurf Hussein Temple •

Nile
River

Kenuzi-
speaking area

Arabic-speaking
area

Aneiba •

Abu Simbel Temple
↓

Erd-Moz •• •Zingahoor

Benha-Ballana →

Mahasi-speaking area

• Wadi Halfa

EGYPTIAN NUBIA